ACE NOTES

of related interest

Being Asexual
Eris Young
ISBN 978 1 78775 698 4
eISBN 978 1 78775 699 1

Asexual Relationships
Sarah Costello and Kayla Kaszyca
ISBN 978 1 83997 001 6
eISBN 978 1 83997 002 3

How to be Ace
A Memoir of Growing Up Asexual
Rebecca Burgess
ISBN 978 1 78775 215 3
eISBN 978 1 78775 216 0

How to Understand Your Sexuality
A Practical Guide for Exploring Who You Are
Meg-John Barker and Alex Iantaffi
ISBN 978 1 78775 618 2
eISBN 978 1 78775 619 9

Ace Notes

Tips and Tricks on Existing in an Allo World

Michele Kirichanskaya

Foreword by David Jay
Illustrated by Ashley Masog

Jessica Kingsley Publishers
London and Philadelphia

First published in Great Britain in 2023 by Jessica Kingsley Publishers
An imprint of Hodder & Stoughton Ltd
An Hachette UK Company

1

A CIP catalogue record for this title is available from the
British Library and the Library of Congress

ISBN 978 1 83997 522 6
eISBN 978 1 83997 523 3

Printed and bound in the United States
by Integrated Books International

Jessica Kingsley Publishers' policy is to use papers that are natural,
renewable and recyclable products and made from wood grown in
sustainable forests. The logging and manufacturing processes are
expected to conform to the environmental regulations
of the country of origin.

Jessica Kingsley Publishers
Carmelite House
50 Victoria Embankment
London EC4Y 0DZ

www.jkp.com

Contents

PART I

BEGINNING

Foreword

Why do we need ace stories?

For some of us, myself included, they are a survival tactic. When I first began coming out as someone who does not experience sexual attraction, the best response I got was people telling me that I would be alone forever. It was normal to be told that there was something wrong with me, to be told that I should wait to be "fixed," or to be flat-out not believed. In a world where sexuality and intimacy were bound together, people who saw my asexuality saw me as less than capable of full human connection and therefore less than fully human. When I came out as asexual, people imagined my life story without much humanity in it: a story without loving or being loved, a story without desire or passion or loss, a story without the care and sacrifice that come with family, chosen or otherwise. When I tried to imagine my own story, when I tried to imagine the humanity in it, all I could see was the gaping void that the world reflected back at me.

The first ace stories I read were like little pinpricks of light in that void, constellations that let me imagine a future worth reaching for. I read stories about queer aces finding chosen family, about romantic aces getting crushes, and about aromantic aces inventing words for their feelings. I read stories about disabled aces pushing back against stories of brokenness, about aces with histories of trauma redefining intimacy on their own terms.

Instead of falling into that void of isolation and brokenness, I began being able to imagine a life of very human muddling through. Of unrequited squishes that became mutual after an unexpected and deep conversation. Of family members learning to see the relationships I have rather than the relationships that they want me to have. Of allosexual partners who confide that, secretly, they've never found the script of sexual dating that compelling either and are down to try some new paths toward intimacy. Ace stories shine a flashlight into the void and show that, like most places, it is teeming with life.

Whether or not we identify as ace, we probably have experienced that void. It's the place you go if you're not conventionally attractive enough or not successful enough or just plain not normal enough to date. It's the place that you go if you fail to find a life partner before a certain age, or if you don't have as much sex as your friends are having, or if you meet your soulmate and then lose them. The void is a place without access to sexuality where real human connection and value as a human being are supposed to be categorically impossible.

We need ace stories because they show us, regardless of whether we identify as ace, that the void is not what we have been led to believe. It's less of a muted existential hellscape and more of a pool party with board games and cake. Fall off the edge of sexuality and you will still be loved. You will still have fun, you will still know passion and heartbreak, you will still feel a sense of worth deep in your chest and find others who will feel it along with you. We need stories that remind us of this truth.

And although I'm not personally allosexual (a person who experiences normative levels of sexual attraction), I'm pretty sure that allos need these stories, too. I imagine that it's difficult for a person who is attracted to sexuality to navigate the sexual world without feeling that void behind their back. I imagine that, for many allo folks, sex is simultaneously a thing that they genuinely want and a thing that they are terrified to be without. As long as failing to have sex is tantamount to death in the void, then all sex, even really good sex, is tinged by abject terror.

Imagine how liberated sexuality could be without that terror. Imagine how freeing it would be for all of us, ace and allo, to view sex not as a sole lifeline to human connection but as one of a cornucopia of options for building life-changing human connection. Imagine how freeing it would be for all of us, ace and allo, to view sex not as the implied definition of physical intimacy but as one of many ways to be physically intimate. We need ace stories because they give us a hint of just how much under-explored territory is out there.

There is a phrase that comes up in some discussions about ace consent: "holding the flashlight." Imagine that you are walking down a path in a dark wood with an allosexual partner. You met recently and are both excited about one another; you both have a feeling that you want to go *somewhere* together, even if you're not entirely certain where that somewhere is. But you come across a tree that has fallen in the path, and it becomes clear that you won't be able to go any further. Your partner is disappointed, or you're scared that they're disappointed, but you don't try to hack your way through the tree and you don't turn back. Instead, you walk to the side of the path and shine a flashlight into the darkness. You say, "I want to go somewhere with you, and I was curious if you'd be open to joining me in stepping off this path into something that fits the two of us better."

The thing about holding the flashlight is that, in my experience, it works surprisingly well. Describe a queerplatonic partnership, and people will be curious to try. Talk about co-parenting, about living in intentional community, or about the many, many kinds of attraction that one can feel that are not about sex, and many people will be intrigued. The path is appealing, but it is also confining. The unknown is scary, but it is also where we go to find the possibility of liberation. Holding the flashlight does not mean that we have all the answers or that we are done being scared. It means that we are comfortable enough in our struggle, wherever that struggle is, to invite others to join us.

Ace Notes: Tips and Tricks on Existing in an Allo World gives us this kind of invitation. We need to share stories about how to get by, practical advice on how to navigate the sexual expectations that pervade the world around us. We need to tell stories about how to date if dating makes sense to us and how to find other forms of connection if it doesn't, how to navigate microaggressions, and how to navigate the intersection of aceness and the other identities we hold.

Why do we need ace stories? Because we've tried ace silence, and we're over it.

David Jay, American asexual activist and founder of AVEN
(Asexual Visibility and Education Network)

Prologue

I think I first started to realize I was asexual when I was around the age of fifteen or seventeen. Back in high school, surrounded by mostly straight (or seemingly straight) classmates and media, I didn't really connect to much of the hook-up culture I saw around me, whether in person or in mainstream media. (As a side note, it's very concerning how much adult-made content about teenagers revolves aggressively around sex, but that's a topic for another day.) Instead of actively looking for someone to make out or have sex with, for the most part I was content studying and geeking out with my friends over cartoons and comics.

But there was still a sense that something was "off," that I wasn't quite like everyone else.

Around the same time, some of the people around me had started coming out as queer or questioning their sexuality, which may have helped open up the idea that maybe my own assumed "straightness" wasn't so solid. And thanks to the likes of Google, I eventually stumbled across the word "asexual," which, although I didn't know it at the time, kind of changed my life.

Because as cliché as it might sound, coming across the word "asexual" and all its associated definitions and sub-labels felt like *something* just clicked. As though there suddenly was a vocabulary open to me that could help me name and define my own experiences. That helped me realize that I wasn't alone in who I was.

But as I got older, I soon started to realize how much of an anomaly this was. Talking to other aces and reading accounts from aces online, I began to realize how many people didn't come into any knowledge of asexuality until later in life, and how many grew up feeling alone, feeling "wrong" or "broken" for who they were. And it breaks my heart every time I hear about it.

No one should have to feel "broken" for being who they are.

I wish for so many of us that we could have vocabulary at an early age. That we understand there are multiple ways to exist in this world, including ways that aren't defined by sexual attraction. That we have the visibility and awareness that makes knowing and understanding asexuality that much more accessible. I want so much better for other aces. And I wanted better for myself, too.

While the early 2010s were obviously not the darkest age for queer visibility, ace visibility was still pretty absent. When I first started getting into the realization that I was ace, *BoJack Horseman* and Todd Chavez (who, frustratingly, is still one of the only visibly, canonically asexual characters on television at the time of writing) wasn't yet a thing, nor were there any characters on the big screen that I could relate to. As a teen, I scrolled through books, trying to find some literary mirrors for who I was, to see myself reflected in the pages I loved. In high school, there was no mention of asexuality in the already rudimentary sex education we received, nor did I find any mention of it in the few Gender and Sexuality or Psychology courses I took in college. There was no specific guide to being asexual. No book on how to navigate coming out as ace, or what to do after encountering an acephobe. No mainstream article that went beyond the Asexual 101s of how asexuality means "little or no sexual attraction to others."

Since realizing I was ace, I've felt I had to dig like an archaeologist, scouring through lists and documents and archives to learn what I now know today.

I hope this book saves you some of that time, energy, and effort, and instead frees up space to learn more about yourself, including figuring out how to exist more comfortably as an ace in this strange, allonormative world.

Before moving forward, I should note a few things.

One, I want to make something clear. I am not a queer educator or a professor. I am simply an ace person who has some years of lived experience under their belt and wants to offer whatever insight they have that might make it easier for other aces who read this book.

Two, my perspective on aceness, just like my perspective of the world in general, is a limited one. While I may experience some forms of marginalization, because of the skin and body I occupy, I do not have to face some of the same prejudices or barriers to access and protection that other aces, such as BIPOC* aces, do. That is why I have invited other aces who have generously donated their time to speak about their perspectives on the diversity and intersectionality found within the ace community, including speaking on subjects of gender, disability, race, faith, and more.

While not everyone who reads this book will find their specific experiences reflected in it or resonate with every word written, I hope that what you might find in these pages will provide some sound advice and comfort. And I hope that this book will become one of many titles in the larger canon of ace literature, and that it will be joined by many other amazing ace voices in the very near future. And who knows, maybe you'll even be one of them.

* BIPOC: Black, Indigenous, and People of Color.

PART II

ACE BASICS

What Is the Ace Lens?

Ever been to a silent disco?

If you've ever seen a group of people wearing headphones standing together, moving their limbs (well or badly depending on the individual) in a noiseless space, then you've probably encountered the likes of a silent disco.

Once upon a time, this would have been something that you would have only imagined in a science fiction novel, the seemingly ridiculous idea of people dancing to silence, to a music no one else but them could hear. As philosopher Friedrich Nietzsche would say, "Those who were seen *dancing* were thought to be insane* by those who could *not* hear the *music*."

Yet to the people looking in, the ones without the headphones, gazing at a seemingly vibrant space with smiling, apparently happy people looking as though they're having the time of their lives, there can sometimes be an unsettling fear of missing out. Or, on the flip side, the people inside the silent disco—those with the headphones—maybe point to those without and think *them* "insane" for not hearing the music.

For me, that's what it feels like to be asexual.

* Note that the author is aware that the word "insane" carries ableist connotations and is often used negatively in reference to those with mental illnesses. See Neda Ulaby, "Why People Are Rethinking the Words 'Crazy' and 'Insane.'" NPR, July 8, 2019, www.npr.org/2019/07/08/739643765/why-people-are-arguing-to-stop-using-the-words-crazy-and-insane.

For someone who doesn't experience sexual attraction in a mostly allosexual (meaning not asexual) world where most people do, I sometimes feel like I'm on the outside of a silent disco, facing a group of people dancing to music I can't hear.

When the majority of people around you operate on the basis of sharing the same lived experiences, it creates a situation of presumption, judging those who don't share those experiences as "abnormal" and holding them up to unrealistic expectations of how they should act and operate in the world.

According to allonormativity, a term that refers to the "assumption that all human beings are allosexual, i.e. that they experience sexual attraction to other people,"[1] it would seem that anyone who doesn't identify as allosexual doesn't qualify as human. And let me tell you, that is a pretty shitty thing to feel.

And yet this lens is so pervasive that it is written into our pop culture, our social system—hell, even our legal legislature (i.e. marriage consummation laws).

And trying to explain this to someone who's not ace and who lives in a world that's built for them (as it would be trying to explain ableist architecture to someone who's non-disabled, or trying to explain how a racist institution operates to someone who's white) can sometimes be tricky without the shared bridge of experience.

Which is where more metaphors come in.

In their research, American academic Dr. Melissa Harris-Perry coined the "Crooked Room" theory, analyzing psychological studies that compared the experiences of women of color living at the intersection of racism and sexism to standing in a tilted, or "crooked," room with "crooked" images relating to misogynoir stereotypes, such as "Mammy" and "Jezebel," and perceiving themselves to be looking "straight," while in reality existing on an "unlevel plane."[2]

As queer artist Sharon Lee De La Cruz called it, "Imagine living in a society where you had to align yourself with the crooked images around you. What does that perpetuate?"[3]

It can perpetuate the idea that being allo is "right" and "normal," while being ace is "wrong" and "broken."

And what an awful idea that is, to believe that you are fundamentally "broken" because of who you are.

But just as male isn't the norm, cis isn't the norm, white isn't the norm, non-disabled isn't the norm, middle-class isn't the norm, neither is allosexual.

As the line from ZooNation's production of *The Mad Hatter's Tea Party* goes, "There's no such thing as normal!"

So rather than beating yourself up for not fitting into a "crooked room" that wasn't made with you in mind in the first place, let's acknowledge it for the nonsense that it is, and then let's tear it down to build something better. A space that's more open-minded, more inclusive, and more accepting.

And remember, just because we're not dancing in the silent disco, it doesn't mean we can't also have a party. Even if we don't wear the headphones, maybe we're already tuned in to a different frequency, moving to a beat of our own.

Coming Out as Ace

When it comes to coming out, it's almost never an easy or simple thing.

In contrast to how daytime television portrays it, coming out isn't always a grand, one-off occasion, in which everyone in your immediate and non-immediate vicinity knows instantly that you have come out. Given the combined and pervasive natures of heteronormativity, allonormativity, amanormativity, cisnormativity, etc., most societies operate under the assumption that all, or almost all, individuals are straight, allosexual, alloromantic, cisgender, with anything else being an unspoken deviation.

Which means, in the most likely case, that unless you're wearing a big Pride pin proclaiming whatever identity you align with, almost every person you encounter in your life will have their own assumptions about who or what you are.

Yay. (They say sarcastically.)

In the case of coming out as ace, there is also an added element to consider. As opposed to coming out as gay (in most Western societies, there is usually some general cultural framework for explaining what same-sex attraction is), coming out as ace may be a bit trickier. (Note: I didn't say *easier*. Just *trickier*.)

Because of asexuality's status as the "invisible orientation," the most likely context in which the average person will likely hear the word "asexual" is within the realm of biology. (*Rolls eyes*, thank you, jokes about asexuals being plants or reproducing through mitosis (i.e. asexual reproduction). If only it were that easy.)

This means that, in most cases, upon coming out as ace, one usually follows up with a Ted-Ed length lecture to the person they're coming out to, explaining the nuances of asexuality, what it is and what is isn't. Which can be exhausting. Especially when, after all that effort, some people might still go ahead and dismiss you and your asexuality anyway.

Which, frankly, hurts.

In that case, here are a few things to keep in mind when considering if and when you're ready to come out to someone as ace.

Note that I am not a professional LGBTQ+ educator, and coming out can be a precarious, stressful, and even compromising process, so please take these tips with a grain of salt. If you're looking for more specialized resources on how to come out, I'd suggest checking out your local LGBTQ+ community center (if one is nearby), or looking up the following organizations: GLSEN, The Trevor Project, Scarleteen, Human Rights Campaign (HRC), Matthew Shepard Foundation, PFLAG.

Who Do You Want to Know?

When you already know you're ace (or are seriously considering that you are ace), ask yourself: Who do you *want* to know and who do you *need* to know? If you have friends around you constantly inquiring about your sex life, asking who your next "hook-up" will be, or saying you just need to "get laid," then perhaps coming out as ace might provide something to counter their invasive comments. If you're in a romantic relationship and you're discussing the possibility of sex with your partner/s, perhaps them learning about asexuality will help provide important information on what physical boundaries you need to establish in order to find a mutually comfortable compromise.

In the case of being *out* in other places, such as the office, it might be okay to ask yourself if this is a place you want to be fully out to, or if you would consider this part of your personal information that's on a "need to know" basis. A lot of aces—and other queer folks, for that matter—have a pick-your-battles mentality when it comes to disclosure, only coming out to the people who matter to them or have a significant presence in their lives.

And remember that you don't need to be out to everyone in order to be "out and proud," or even validated as asexual.

Personally, I feel as long as you know and feel comfortable with yourself, then that might be enough.

Assess the Situation

Before you jump in the water of "coming out," dip a toe in the pool and check to see whether it's warm and welcoming or icy and judgmental. Coming out to an open-minded LGBTQ+ support group might be an entirely different experience than, say, coming out to a straight-cis parent who's never had to question the pink-and-blue gender binary or boy-meets-girl romantic narrative.

One thing you can do before diving in is to test the waters.

When hanging out with the person you want to come out to, maybe consider bringing up certain LGBTQIA+ issues or topics in casual conversation, and see what their general stance on that may be (note: if this person is known to be homophobic or queerphobic in general, then the likelihood of them being ace-friendly is pretty low). You can try watching BoJack Horseman together and see what their thoughts are on Todd Chavez. Or you can pull up the Instagram of a famous ace, such as model/advocate Yasmin Benoit (note that some of their photos might be NSFW*), and see if their reaction is positive/encouraging or the opposite.

Although this won't provide a guarantee of acceptance, since most of us aren't psychic and can't predict people's reactions, it does at least help provide some build-up to the potential disclosure so that the other party won't be caught entirely off guard.

* NSFW: Not safe for work.

Be Prepared

As I mentioned earlier, the majority of non-aces will be unfamiliar with what asexuality is, so you might have to be prepared to be their instructor. While the idea of unpaid teaching/emotional labor might seem exhausting (especially when you have to do it *over and over and over again*), nevertheless it might be necessary if you want the other person to understand where you're coming from.

In that case, it might help to prep a bit beforehand.

Look up the definitions and terms (bring note cards if you want to). Explain the basics of what asexuality is and what it means to you. If there's still a look of confusion on the other person's face, maybe you can sit down together and pull up videos on the subject, such as other aces vlogging about their own experiences (it can help non-aces to recognize that your asexuality isn't an individual eccentricity and that there is an entire asexual community out there). Or you could direct them to AVEN (Asexual Visibility and Education Network) and other similar resources.

If they express an interest in learning more, you can even introduce them to some ace literature such as *The Invisible Orientation: An Introduction to Asexuality* by Julie Sondra Decker or *Ace: What Asexuality Reveals About Desire, Society, and the Meaning of Sex* by Angela Chen for more in-depth research on the subject.

Another point I would mention is being prepared to be patient. Sometimes explaining asexuality will be a thing you have to do over and over and over again. A lot of people are set in their ways when it comes to their perception of the world and others, so if new subjects are introduced to their environment, it can take time for things to shift and for mindsets to change. Sure, it might be annoying to have to continually explain to people this part of yourself. But think of it this way: if you told your parent you were vegan and they still kept offering meat-based dishes after you told them the first time, it would definitely be frustrating. But then you could just roll your eyes mentally and remind them to be more mindful of your needs the next time.

Also, it's good to remember that when it comes to the people you love, it's valid to hope that they would be respectful and interested (even if the actual reality says otherwise).

For me, even if I was uninterested in a subject a friend or family member was passionate about—say, monster trunks or fashion brands—I'd still take the time and effort to listen to them, and even study a bit on the subject, if it was something that mattered to them. If something is important to you, whether it be asexuality or veganism or anything else, then it should be important to the people who are important to you or consider you important to them.

If possible, I would also advise you to consider having another person by your side if and when you decide to come out. Having a supportive sibling, friend, or mentor may give you the emotional co-chair necessary in the presentation (and possibly defense) of your sexuality. And sometimes simply having moral support by your side might provide the security or comfort you need in this emotionally vulnerable situation. Which leads me to...

Safety

Content Warning: This section discusses acephobia.

While some people may not think of coming out as ace as a particularly precarious situation—compared with coming out as gay, for example—coming out as ace has its own risks and complications.

Some aces I've spoken to and read about have reported receiving hostile reactions upon coming out, be it religious parents arguing that their orientation goes against their interpretation of whatever faith they practice or scripture they follow (i.e. the doctrine of "be fruitful and multiply") or romantic partners becoming indignant at the idea of their ace partners not desiring sex with them. Acephobia, defined as the discriminatory attitude that "encompasses a range of negative attitudes, behaviors, and feelings toward asexuality or people who identify as part of the asexual spectrum,"* like homophobia, is a real thing. In worst-case scenarios, acephobia can manifest as forms of verbal, mental, and/or physical abuse.

If you feel you would be unsafe were you to come out, or suspect even the slightest bit of danger, I would strongly advise you *not* to come out. Your safety should, above all else, come first. But please understand this: other people's ignorance or negative reactions are not your fault.

No *one* is entitled to your identity, your body, or your sense of self. If you feel you or someone else you know might be in danger from your immediate environment, I would recommend looking up the following organizations for help/guidance:

* ★ RAINN (Rape, Abuse & Incest National Network)
  www.rainn.org
  1-800-656-HOPE (1-800-656-4673)

* ★ National Domestic Violence Hotline
  www.thehotline.org
  1-800-799-SAFE (1-800-799-7233)
  If you or someone you know is in need of help in an unhealthy or abusive situation, call 1-800-799-7233 or visit www.thehotline.org for resources and chat services.

* ★ Crisis Text Line
  www.crisistextline.org
  Text HOME to 741741
  Crisis Text Line is free, 24/7 support for those in crisis. Text

* "Discrimination Against Asexual People." Wikipedia, https://en.wikipedia.org/wiki/Discrimination_against_asexual_people.

from anywhere in the USA to text with a trained Crisis Counselor.

★ The Trevor Project
www.thetrevorproject.org
1-866-488-7386
The Trevor Project is the leading national organization providing crisis intervention and suicide prevention services to lesbian, gay, bisexual, transgender, and questioning (LGBTQ) young people aged 13–24.

And remember, no matter how they identify, no one deserves to experience abuse for who they are.

Alternatives to "Coming Out"

It's okay if you're not ready yet.
I can't stress this enough.

Back in 2019, some new art made the rounds on Twitter for Pride Month. The world was introduced to Hue the Pride Turtle who hid in their gray-colored shell, with the words, "It's OK if you're not ready yet." In their original tweet, the artist captioned the picture with the essential message, "You are valid, whether you are out or not."[1]

During his lifetime, amid the (even more) rampant homophobia that existed in the 1970s, political activist and gay icon Harvey Milk urged his queer constituents to come out.[2] He argued that by doing so the people surrounding them—the ones who voted for homophobic laws, such as the Briggs Initiative, which would ban openly queer teachers from working in California's public schools, into effect—would suddenly be able to actually see the people they were affecting, to understand the impact of their actions on their friends, their family, and loved ones.

For Milk, coming out was one of the most political things a person could do. It was seen as a demonstration of bravery, an act of advocacy against the enforced invisibility of a heteronormative society that shoved people into the closet. He even made the slogan of his campaign "Come Out, Come Out, Wherever You Are," establishing coming out as a cornerstone of his fight for gay liberation.

Coming out is a brave and radical act.

To be open about who you are in a world that demands conformity, silence, and invisibility is noteworthy and even honorable.

But it isn't the only thing.

In their book *Sissy: A Coming-of-Gender Story*,[3] non-binary author and activist Jacob Tobia called for a more compassionate metaphor for being in "The Closet," finding the term judgmental of those who weren't ready to come out. Instead, they advocated for adopting the metaphor of "coming out of our shell." In their writing, they state:

> When a person hides in The Closet, we act as if it is their responsibility to come out. But when a snail hides in its shell, we don't delegate responsibility the same way. A snail only hides in its shell because the world outside feels hostile. If a snail recoils at the sight of you, it's not because you are cowardly or lying or deviant or withholding, it's because the world and people around us felt predatory; because someone scared us—intentionally or unintentionally—and we were trying to protect ourselves.[4]

Later in the book, they go on to say, "I do not blame myself for retreating into my shell, snail-like, when I felt threatened."[5]

The world can be a pretty damn threatening place if you stray outside cis/straight/allo/amanormative lines. Between politicians failing to enforce (or forcefully taking away) protective legislature for queer rights and schools banning LGBTQIA+ books, there's a reason why coming out today is still a political act. Even those as fabulously out as Tobia have had compassion for themselves, negotiating when and where would be the right place to come out, navigating the space between comfort and discomfort, between visibility and safety.

And one has to remember that not everyone has the same set of circumstances or privileges to come out. Depending on one's geographic region, political environment, social/religious contexts, etc., one's emotional comfort and physical safety can be severely compromised upon coming out.

Hell, even I have people I'm not fully "out" to, because it's safer that way for me personally and less emotionally draining.

In my own personal opinion, no one has to be fully "out" in order to qualify as being "ace" or "queer" or feel connected to the ace/queer community. Anyone who demands full visibility (without compromise or empathy) is not someone doing that community any favors.

The term "coming out" was said to have derived from a ritual in early queer underground subculture, in which members of the queer community mimicked a débutante's coming-of-age party, marking her "coming out" or introduction to high society, with the remix of hosting drag balls, celebrating "the coming out of new debutantes into homosexual society."[6]

As non-binary poet and performance artist Alok Vaid-Menon has said, "It was linked to being witnessed by other people, and it was about actually joining a collective."[7]

While coming out today seems like a terrifying and vulnerable process (and it often is!), it is also about community, about joining people in solidarity and joy, being recognized and affirmed by people who share your identities, who are your people. It is about realizing you aren't alone.

When I was first coming out to myself, acknowledging the fact I was ace, it was a bit disorienting. At that time, it meant feeling alone, knowing I was "different" from most people around me. But at the same time, reading about other aces' experiences online or finding representation in books and comics made coming out to myself easier, recognizing that my feelings were shared by others, that I wasn't alone in my experiences.

Like Tobia, *Queer Eye* expert Karamo Brown advocated the use of another term in place of coming out, suggesting instead that every time we share this part of ourselves with new people we are "letting people in."[8] Rather than disclosing something shameful, or allocating people power over us by denying or accepting who we are, we are instead granting people the privilege of knowing us, all of us.

So to review...

Coming out was seen as a rite of passage, a demonstration of activism against the idea that one needed to hide, that visibility can be powerful.

And all of that is still true today.

But it also helps to remember that not everyone has the means to "come out."

That "coming out" means opening the door of a political/social "closet" that is not of your own making.

That even without "coming out," you already exist in the world just as you are, and that you do not need other people's validation in order to be qualify as being ace. Even if you just say, sign, or think the words to yourself, "I am ace," that is enough. *Period.*

"Coming out" can be as grand as a celebration or simply as quiet as sitting down with a loved one for a cup of tea while you share your truth.

And whether you "come out" online or IRL, to a hundred people or just one (even if that one is yourself), you are still valid. You are whole. You exist.

Just remember, if and whenever you decide to "come out," you can do it in your own time and at your own pace.

And when you do, the ace community will be waiting with open arms and plenty of cake.

Analogies to Explain Asexuality

Because we live in a society where asexuality is not (yet) in our mainstream vocabulary, often we have to explain it ourselves. Over and over and over again.

Now for those who are not asexual, perhaps it might be hard to fully comprehend what asexuality is. After all, how do you explain what is essentially a lack or an absence?

As a writer, I've often drawn upon descriptive language, particularly metaphors and similes, to help describe to others what is incomprehensible to them.

Below is a compilation of analogies I (and other aces) have used to help explain asexuality to other allos out there.

Hunger

Remember that scene in *Sex Education* when drama enthusiast Florence (the one with the yellow beret) explains what sex means to her:

> I don't feel anything. I have no connection to it. It's sort of like I'm surrounded by a huge feast with everything I could want to eat, but I'm not hungry.[1]

Often, the best metaphor aces can use to describe sexual attraction is hunger. Hunger is a pretty decent metaphor in that it's a visceral sensation which most people (allo or otherwise) have an instinctive understanding of. Allos may not get what lack of sexual attraction means, but they know about intense physical feelings, and they know what hunger and not being hungry feel like.

For aces, hunger might be our closest parallel to how allos feel when they *do* experience sexual attraction. One of my favorite asexual headcanons in fiction is demisexual Yuri Katsuki from the anime *Yuri on Ice* (stay with me here). In the episode "I Am Eros, and Eros Is Me?! Face-Off! Hot Springs on Ice," Yuri has trouble relating to the theme of his program routine "Eros" (i.e. sexual love).[2] The closest thing he can use (at that time) to conceptualize "eros" is pork cutlet bowls, something he actively drools over and craves. In this instance, pork cutlet bowls (or hunger) take the place of "eros"— that is, until he associates "eros" with *himself* as a person and *with* someone else, the source of his attraction, his love interest, Victor.

And sex is often compared to food, anyway. Our cultural vocabulary describes sexual desire or attraction as something you consume, something you "hunger" or "thirst" for (cue jokes about being "thirsty"), and in many ways sells sex like food on a menu (there's a reason why there's so much sexual subtext in food advertising).

Make no mistake, though: while actual hunger (the one found in your stomach) is related to a drive that keeps us human beings alive, sexual hunger (the one found in your nether regions) doesn't really exist as a drive.

Sure, plenty of people talk about sex as a drive. For a long time, individuals such as sex therapist Helen Singer Kaplan viewed sexual desire like thirst or hunger, as one of the "drives or appetites that subserve individual and species survival."[3] Something that marked us as "human."

But here's the thing: unlike other parts of the human motivational system that push us to find warmth, shelter, or water (you know, the actual things that keeps us *alive*), sex acts as an "incentive motivation system." Much like the "high" someone gets when they gamble, when they are in chase or pursuit of a "prize," "incentive motivation systems are all about being pulled by an attractive external stimulus," rather than an "uncomfortable internal experience, like hunger."[4] Think of sexual attraction as "hunger" for "pleasure," rather than survival.

In other words, as animal behaviorist Frank Beach said, "No one has ever suffered tissue damage for lack of sex."[5]

So while "sexual hunger" may be something hit or miss for asexuals, with the exception of those like demisexuals who may "hunger" (i.e. experience sexual attraction) for a "meal" (sex) if it's made by someone they have an emotional connection with, many asexuals may also "eat" out of boredom or simply "share a meal" as a way to spend affectionate time with a partner.

The Fridge (Related to Hunger)

Another common analogy I've found useful is the "fridge metaphor." As previously discussed, an asexual can see a "stocked fridge" and find nothing appetizing, "food" being the relative word for "people" and "eat" being the relative word for "*wanting* to have sex with."

In this case, hunger can also stand for libido. Libido can be defined as the body's desire for sexual activity or release. Just as you can be hungry for food, despite not wanting to be hungry or finding the timing inconvenient, the body can "hunger" for other "things" without "you" actually "wanting" that "thing" or person.

If that's still confusing, think of it this way: sexual attraction can be defined as a directed hunger—looking at a specific person and wanting to have sex with them: "I want to eat *that*"—versus libido being an undirected "hunger"—"I want to eat."[6]

In this case, libido can be "hunger" without a target. Which, frankly, can be *extremely* annoying. Much like an itch you want to scratch or just want to go away. Luckily, unlike hunger for literal food—where if we don't satisfy our hunger, we'll starve—the other kind of "hunger" most times usually passes if you don't wish to engage with it. Or, if anything, you can go for a "self-made" meal (i.e. masturbation).

Coffee

Bear with me while we continue to roll on the topic of consumption.

Think of sex as coffee. We see people drinking coffee everywhere. We see coffee advertised on billboards and in commercials. People drink coffee in the movies and on TV. Coffee is so ubiquitous that it's considered to be a part of a person's essential routine, something with a constant presence (walk to your nearest grocery store or pass a few urban streets and you'll likely find a coffee shop), as well as something very marketable. Essentially, we see a world that caters to coffee drinkers.

Now, lots of people like drinking coffee. They might drink it once or three times a day, and several times a week. Sure, maybe not all of them enjoy drinking it in the same way. Some prefer different blends and flavors. But generally they enjoy drinking it. They love the smell of it, the taste of it, etc.

Now imagine you're someone who's not that into coffee.

While some asexuals can be the type who may sit down for a "cup of coffee" if it's available or if it's lovingly made by someone you care about, or they may enjoy one type of "coffee" but not another, maybe you're the type of asexual who prefers a different beverage to get through the day. Like tea or water or fresh-made kompot.

While there's nothing weird about not liking "coffee," certain people can get a bit hypercritical if you don't "drink coffee" or don't drink it in the way in the way *they* think people should drink it (if you've ever met someone who judges others for not drinking their coffee black, then this attitude should be familiar).

Roller Coaster of Attraction

Before I switched to humanities, I was essentially a science scholar in undergrad, which meant taking chemistry classes. So while I eventually did not graduate with a degree in chemistry, I did take one interesting thing away from the class.

For anyone not familiar with Chem 101, according to the First Law of Thermodynamics (i.e. the branch of physical science that deals with the relations between heat and other forms of energy), energy cannot be created or destroyed, but is simply converted from one form to another. Which means there's always the same amount of energy, in one way or another. And that energy can be defined as kinetic and potential.

Kinetic energy is the energy of an object in motion—it's motion-relative—while potential energy is the energy of an object at rest—position-relative. Potential energy is "not actively doing work or applying any force on any other objects."[7] A catalyst, the substance that increases the rate of a reaction, can speed up the process of transforming potential energy into kinetic energy.

Think of it as a car going up a roller coaster. On the way up to the crest, you have potential energy, energy stored, but energy that's not yet activated. When that car reaches that crest and goes downhill, though, the potential energy converts into kinetic energy once the object is active in motion.

Now apply that to asexuality, more specifically demisexuality.

The way I see it, libido is potential energy, and sexual attraction is kinetic energy. The first energy exists, but it feels as if it's just sitting there. It feels like undirected energy. But when a catalyst enters the equation (i.e. someone with whom you have an emotional connection), the energy changes. Suddenly, that libido feels directed, and now you might be experiencing sexual attraction.

Now, I'm not entirely sure this analogy is completely accurate, and it might be a little too technical for some people, but it is in tune with some of my own experiences and may appeal to those who are a bit scientifically nerdy.

Marbles in a Jar

Back when I was first navigating asexuality, I stumbled across this beautiful article by a demisexual writer, in which they describe how they conceptualize their demisexuality:

> Imagine that your (sexual) friends have a jar filled with tiny clear marbles. You, a demi person, have a jar filled with only a few marbles, but your marbles are large and multi-colored with swirling fantastic designs inside them. Your friends play with their marbles daily, throw them around, clank them together, and misplace them. They shrug it off, no big deal. If the marbles break, they'll get more from inside the jar. It's like their jar is constantly refilling with marbles. For you, each marble is like a treasure. You only play with them using the utmost care and diligence. Your number of marbles is limited, and you don't know when you'll be down to your last marble or if you'll ever get another marble again. Sometimes, you feel like your jar is empty, but it might not be so. There's always the possibility that there's one more marble waiting for you in the depths of the jar. When you reach in to pull a marble out, it might be a small, clear marble. You look at this marble, hold it in your hand, and feel nothing. It lacks the same enthusiasm you would experience with one of the larger, intricately designed marbles. So you drop the clear marble back in the jar. It wasn't meant for you to play with.[8]

To other people, the world may seem like a giant toy store or a jar of marbles, filled with things to play with. But maybe you're not like that. Maybe you seem a little "pickier" when it comes to people; when it comes to what you're attracted to, to what you feel comfortable and safe with. Maybe you can't be casual. Maybe the "fun" that comes with hook-ups and "lust at first site" doesn't feel like a game you can play. Just maybe you have to wait until the right factors are in place, until the right "marble" comes along. As the author of this lovely essay said, "We just need to do it in our own way, on our own time."

Sensory Parallel

If your allo friend has trouble understanding what it's like to exist as asexual in an allonormative world, there's this quote from Tumblr user thestarlesswanderer that pretty much seems it up:

> Being asexual is like being born without a sense of smell but every-where you go people are spraying perfume in your face and when you ask them to stop and tell them it's irritating and you can't smell the perfume anyway they get huffy and respond with "Don't lie to me; I can clearly see you have a nose. Everybody has a nose therefore everybody smells things and besides maybe you just haven't found the right scent yet." and then you want to scream.[9]

And if the smell parallel doesn't appeal to you, you can describe it as being around people wearing headphones all tuned to the same frequency, listening to a sound you can't hear.

Ice-Cream Shop

Imagine you're in an ice-cream shop filled with an infinite number of flavors. Vanilla, chocolate, orange sherbet... And while everyone else is drooling over these options, you're the one who's lactose intolerant. No need to fear, though: there are still plenty of other desserts to enjoy. For instance, cake is always an option...

Blunt

There are times when it is best to cut to the chase.

> A person can be as beautiful as a painting. Doesn't mean I want to make out with the painting. I can like looking at the car, but that doesn't mean I want to ride it. I can appreciate a good-looking face, I just have no inclination to sit on it.

Courtesy of Yasmin Benoit[10]

If none of these help, try doing a little research and seeing what situations or parallels click for you.

How to Identify an Asexual

Hey there!

Looking to spot other aces out in the wild?

Here's how.

First, look for a hat. All the famous aces have one. Think Jughead's iconic gray crown beanie from the *Archie Comics*. Or Todd Chavez from *BoJack Horseman* and his bright yellow beanie. Or Florence (that one ace character from *Sex Education*) and her mustard beret. Or, even more recently, Esperanza "Spooner" Cruz from *Legends of Tomorrow* and her dashing vintage cap.

Next, find a plain white T-shirt with the words "I'M ASEXUAL!!!" ironed on to it.

Then, if you're still not sure whether or not I'm joking...I am.

Listen, I get it. Having an easy shorthand visual language (if you rely on visual cues, that is) for identifying other asexuals would make it so much easier to find other people like you, or to signal to the world who you are. And to be honest, it's not the first time someone in the LGBTQIA+ community would have tried something like that.

When you're not "allowed" to vocalize something directly, such as being openly queer in certain times or places, queer coding or queer signaling through aesthetics might have been a safer alternative to indicate to other like-minded folks that you were both a place of safety and part of a fellowship. Other times, it could be a proverbial "wink" of queerness, the inside joke that escapes the notice of the straight population.

Take, for instance, the "hanky system." In the cruising era of the 1970s, queer men used an elaborate system known as flagging, or the hanky code, to signal to other queer men their sexual preferences and kinks by placing specific colors in certain pockets to signal the sexual position they were interested in.

Queer women (and many gender-nonconforming AFAB* individuals) post-WWII relied on a butch–femme dichotomy and variations in between, playing with masculine and feminine presentation to demonstrate "visual resistance" to patriarchal heteronormativity through challenging "normative conceptions of gender" and compulsory heterosexual partnership.[2]

Unsurprisingly, there's a long history of queer symbolism through the language of flowers.[3] From Oscar Wilde's signature green carnation, worn in the lapels of the queer men who followed him, to violets, which became known as a symbol of affection among Sapphic women after their reference in the poems of legendary Greek lesbian poet Sapphos. (Sapphos, Sapphic...get it?)

Today we make jokes about lesbian flannels and bisexuals rocking jean jackets and cuffed pants, which, although clichés, seem to have some truth to them in how often they appear.

So it doesn't seem much of a stretch to say that fashion as a cultural signifier is as old as queer history itself.

But then we come to the question of what could be defined as the asexual aesthetic.

In an article featured on the culture and entertainment site Vulture, the writer described Elliot Page's looks in the 2010 sci-fi film *Inception* as "asexual chic," and not in a good way. Basically, they referred to Page's character's style as the "asexual sidekick" as "a cross between a boy scout and the Swedish Chef."[4] Looking like a

* AFAB: Assigned Female at Birth.

little boy and a Muppet doesn't sound like much of a compliment (no offense, Ms. Piggy).

Unfortunately, to the rest of the allosexual world, the word "asexual" conjures up images of *sexlessness*, of neutered individuals with no sense of style or appeal (sexual, romantic, or otherwise).

Because of negative assumptions and stereotypes about asexuals, including the assumption that we only identify as being ace because we're too unappealing to attract anyone (yes, this a thing people say, and I hate it) or how we don't experience attraction and therefore dress to repel attention, neglecting aesthetic value in favor of our asexuality.

Which is honestly so inaccurate, not least because some of the aces I know have the most amazing style!

Take, for instance, aromantic and asexual advocate and model Yasmin Benoit. Currently one of the most visible faces of the asexual community, Benoit is known for their eye-catching looks as a goth/alternative fashion and lingerie model, disrupting the notions that asexuals can't look sexy. In previous interviews regarding the apparent disconnect between their work as a model in a hypersexualized field and their asexual identity, Benoit stated, "It's just fabric to me—clothes are clothes, really. I don't really place different meanings on different clothing. Some have more fabric than others. That's the only difference."[5]

And that's the kicker. We, as humans, place meaning on appearances. Not the other way around.

We assign meaning to the clothes we wear, whether individually or as a culture/subculture. A ring of keys may not have been originally seen as a queer symbol, but it became such after being noticed in the circles of working-class blue-color butch lesbians, later becoming a beckoning signal in the language of queer semiotics.[6] As the song "Ring of Keys" from the musical *Fun Home* goes, "It's probably conceited to say / But I think we're alike in a certain way."[7]

Whether or not aesthetics are a sure-fire way to guarantee sexuality or the type of attention we wish to receive is a whole other story.

Many aces feel conflicted about the way society places or (I should say) presses meaning on to appearances, oversexualizing or objectifying based on the way one dresses.

In their book *Ace: What Asexuality Reveals About Desire, Society, and the Meaning of Sex*, author Angela Chen interviewed a trans ace woman to get her thoughts on the nature of perception:

[A] lot of people now assume I'm a hypersexual person because I present myself like I want to be desired... People frequently assume I want and will have sex with them, and my "nos" are extremely difficult for people to deal with. Now it's like, "If you're ace, why do you dress like that...?"[8]

But let's just get one thing straight (excuse the pun).

A person in a revealing outfit does not consent to inappropriate touch or behavior any more than a person covering up almost every inch of their skin. And guess what, both can still get harassed!

And also guess what, you can't tell what someone is just by looking at them.

Despite society's attempts to box everyone in definite, limited categories, such as "male" or "female," or "masculine" and "feminine," the natural gender diversity (and accompanying gender presentations) of our world is wide and varied. There are femme lesbians, who, despite society assuming there's one way to look "gay" (i.e. butch), would rather fight you to the ground than give up their pretty dresses (or their pretty ladies). There are futch bisexuals, who can rock lipstick and a three-piece suit, and would flip you the middle finger if you suggested they're only allowed to look one way (or be attracted to one gender). There are trans and/or non-binary people who, despite society's vigorous gender policing, can and will choose to dress in whatever clothes they feel are the most gender-affirming to them.

The point is (in my own opinion at least) that unless a person feels comfortable signaling or vocalizing directly who they are or what they want from other people, assumptions made on appearance alone should be made on a limited basis.

So what then, returning to our original question, *does* an asexual look like?

Easy.

Asexuals look like anything and everything!

A few years back, Yasmin Benoit coined the #ThisIsWhatAsexualLooksLike hashtag, inviting asexuals to post pictures of themselves online in order to showcase the diversity of the asexual community, ranging from skin color to body types to style choices.

Perhaps the best way to end this section is by sharing the thoughts of fashion writer and designer José Criales-Unzueta from their article, "What is Queer Fashion, Anyway?":

The bottom line is that queer fashion exists both in intention and aesthetic, both provided by designer or wearer, or both. This queerness, however, goes deeper than trends or archetypes; it is intersectional to other identities and, above all, carries the same multiplicity that makes fashion such an essential tool for expression. There is no single identifiable queer code or aesthetic for fashion because it, like queerness, contains a myriad of meanings and offers different readings to whoever carries or observes it.[9]

So whether you dress like Mister Rogers or Jessica Rabbit (ace in many people's headcanon!),[10] there's no one way to look asexual. Just dress in whatever way feels best for you!

Low-Key Ways to Show Ace Pride

While I did just spend an entire section saying there's no way to "look asexual" (which there isn't), if you are interested in showcasing some ace pride in ways other than draping an ace flag across your shoulders and wearing it like a superhero cape (although that does sound amazing!), here are a few things you can try. (Extra bonus if you decide to shop from local and independent queer/ace artists and businesses. Personally, I'd advise putting your money toward the community, rather than the corporation.)

Wear a Black Ace Ring on the Middle Finger of the Right Hand

Now, I'm not quite sure what the origin of this symbol is, but nevertheless it is a subtle (and fashionable!) way of showing ace pride. If you're not quite ready to come out to those around you (or are not in a situation where it would be safe or comfortable), then I feel like the ace ring provides some subtle under-the-radar pride for when you're looking for some validation. Plus, if you ever find yourself going to an ace event or meet-up group, you're likely to spot a few other hands wearing black rings too, which really gives that warm sense of connection. Plus, it's a nice accessory to have when you need to flip the middle finger to any acephobes!

Dress in Ace Pride Colors

If you can't or don't want to wear a
literal ace flag, be a walking ace flag
yourself! Bonus is that purple,
black, white, and gray look
great with most skin tones!

Purple/Black
Nail Polish

This goes back to wear-
ing ace colors. Plus, this
combined with the
ring makes for very
elegant hand fashion.

Pins

If you feel comfortable, try wearing a small ace pride pin. Pins are
pretty convenient in the way they're generally accessible fashion
statements, being both affordable and adaptable to most cloth
surfaces (be it a T-shirt or a backpack). They're also a subtle way
of signaling to other aces that you're near. Or if you're more extro-
verted, it can even help facilitate conversation when others see the
pin and ask what it means, perhaps leading to an educational and
friendly dialogue. Plus, if need be, you can take it off at a moment's
notice, and put it back on again when you're in a safer space. Also
recommended in addition to ace flag pins: cake pins, playing card
pins, etc. (see Ace Symbols guide toward the back of the book).
Ditto for key chains.

Try Ace-Themed Shirts (the Punnier, the Better)

If there's anything aces love, it's a good pun. If you look up ace shirts online, you'll probably come across some clever word play, such as: "Space Ace," "Ace and Anxious," "Asexual Error 404: Sexual Attraction Not Found," and, one of my personal favorites, "I've Got An Ace Up My Sleeve (It's Me, I'm Ace And I'm In These Sleeves)."

Surprise Me

Have fun with your look. Fashion can be a powerful tool for self-expression, so use it in whatever way feels most comfortable and authentic for you. Whether that means decking yourself out to the nines in ace gear or quietly wearing your pride on your sleeve (or middle finger), you do you.

Ode to a Black Ring*

Over the years I've collected quite a bit of jewelry. Some noteworthy pieces include an imitation pearl necklace from my maternal grandmother that I wore as a kid due to my obsession with Audrey Hepburn, and the crystal prism earrings I lifted from my mom's collection that remind me of her every time I wear them. Yet there is one small item that remains very personal and is an intrinsic part of my identity.

One day during an Asexual and Aromantic Conference during WorldPride 2019, there was a small white table on which a collection of small black rings in an array of sizes stood waiting to be picked up. On that day I selected a simple black band, hematite in color, androgynous in form, neither too feminine nor too masculine, a little loose yet sturdy and solid around the middle finger on my right hand.

Within the queer community, there is a long and complex history of coding, from flagging—the handkerchief system used to indicate sexual preferences and kinks—to the subtle subtextual portrayal of LGBTQ+ characters in film, restricted to subtext due to Hollywood's homophobic censorship policies.[1] In a sense, coding has evolved in reaction to hostility and as a form of queer solidarity, a nod from one queer person to another, saying that even if you do not

* An earlier version of this section was published in *The Gay & Lesbian Review*, November 24, 2020, https://glreview.org/ode-to-a-black-ring. Reproduced with permission.

or cannot say who you are out loud, we recognize and acknowledge you anyway.

For some, this language of coding is found in fashion, as seen in joking remarks about flannel being an iconic staple of lesbian style or cuffed jeans and jean jackets for bisexual culture. For the asexual or ace community, whose status as a community is relatively young in comparison to other parts of queer communities and whose visibility may be a little more subtle, one of the small signs we have adopted is a black ring on the middle finger of the right hand.

While the history of the origins of the ace ring is a little murky, one theory about this particular placement includes the decision to wear it on the right hand so as not to clash with the engagement ring typically worn on the left hand within most Western countries, while other possible reasons include a way of declaring self-partnership with oneself rather than with another person (although many aces can and do experience romantic attraction and have romantic partnerships).

For me, the black ring stands as a way for me to affirm my asexuality, whether in solidarity with other aces who also wear and recognize the symbol, or as a safe way of rebelling in a household or world that does not recognize this part of my identity. As a woman of Slavic descent, I come from a culture where the ticking clock for marriage generally starts at twenty-five and the pressures for heterosexual partnership are reinforced from day one. As a person who experiences attraction to people of various gender identities, even if rarely, homophobia dictates that I keep my romantic attractions to myself in order to protect my own sense of personal comfort within my home, while acephobia dictates that I do not exist at all.

The law of compulsory allonormativity (not unlike Adrienne Rich's coined term "compulsory heterosexuality"[2]) states that all people must experience sexual attraction or else be considered something "foreign" or "strange." In various moments when I have come out as ace, I have been called a baby, a prude, a "snowflake," and, in one particularly hurtful and intense interaction with a family member I came out to, a "f-cking weirdo." Online, the language directed if not personally at me, then at my asexual community, is usually "frigid," "cold," and "inhuman." To all the straight and queer individuals who have questioned me on my sexuality, saying that I just need to have sex (as if that would change my sexuality), let me ask you: Who would want to go through all that for an identity that is not valid or real?

Some days it feels hard to say I am asexual out loud, because the invisibility surrounding my community is a vicious net that slices us every time a canonically asexual character is erased on screen or someone implies we are not "queer enough" to be part of the LGBTQ+ community. And on those hard days, when my family starts talking around me about needing to find a boyfriend/husband, or society says I need to fundamentally change my nature in order to be "normal," I hold on to my black ace ring like an engagement ring, a quiet commitment to myself, saying that I am valid and enough on my own.

Asexuality and "Snowflake" Syndrome

When we think of the word "snowflake"—outside the context of snow, that is—it's usually referring to something unpleasant.

We think of a crybaby with easily hurt feelings A self-inflated, delicate ego with paper skin and a glass heart. Someone who dares to call themselves "special" in a mundane world. As the line in the American film *Fight Club* goes, "You are not special. You are not a beautiful and unique snowflake. You are the same organic and decaying matter as everyone else."[1]

In Western slang, what was once a symbol of winter has become shorthand for someone who thinks themselves as "special as a snowflake", individualized on a molecular level, completely separate and unique. And although the word itself as slang has carried several meanings throughout history for different types of people,[2] as it currently stands today, it often refers to someone liberal, someone whose identity falls outside the cis-hetero-allo mainstream. Otherwise, someone who is seen as niche and irrelevant.

As someone who is part of the asexual community, I've heard this term mockingly used a number of times to refer to someone like me, with asexuality being referred to as a "snowflake orientation," something we only call ourselves to feel "special."

First of all, there are plenty of things that are special about me besides my orientation, thank you very much.

Second, I don't identify as asexual just to feel "special."

I identify as ace because it's who I am.

When you're ace, you exist in the world differently from how you would if you were allo. There's a distinct sense of feeling "off" in a world that constantly prioritizes sex and sexual attraction; that considers you only human if you experience it, and a "weirdo" if you don't. In this way, you can start to feel alone in the world, a small piece of ice in a blizzard.

I don't identify as ace to seek attention. If I did, that would mean intentionally inviting the attention of trolls who would call me "snowflake" in the first place.

I identify as ace because it feels right, because it feels authentic to who I am and to my experiences.

If someone calls you a "special snowflake" because you're ace, suggesting you're only doing it as a way to grab attention, then that says more about the other person than it does about you.

It says that this person is being rude and ignorant, refusing to even take one step toward understanding an experience they're not personally familiar with.

It says that they're taking the cheapest shot to feel superior in an argument, like some alt-right conservative who calls you a snowflake for expressing a "liberal" opinion, suggesting trigger warnings for media content for those who might have PTSD or anxiety issues, or advocating for universal health care (which, in my opinion, should *definitely* be a thing already!).

Can some people be over-sensitive? Some, sure. Are some people attention-seeking? Absolutely!

But being asexual doesn't mean you're either of those things.

Politicians love to call younger generations (i.e. millennials and Generation Z) the "snowflake generation,"[3] rolling their eyes at our use of terms like "political correctness," "safe space," and "identity politics." But is it really so self-righteous to ask for a world that's a little kinder, a little more thoughtful? A world that doesn't always demand a thick skin when it comes to barbed insults meant to make us bleed.

There are millions of snowflakes in the world, just as there are millions of people. While there are ways we (and snowflakes) may be similar to each other and not so "special"—as Dash from the Pixar film *The Incredibles* (2004) dubbed it, "if everyone is special, no one is"[4]—that doesn't mean we can't also be different. Each snowflake has a unique signature, like DNA, its ice crystals forming in a pattern that, as it falls and moves through the world, is unique. As one comic book character beautifully said:

> You know, it's such a cliché, but the metaphor of people and snowflake? It's completely true. Exquisitely, utterly true. Every human being is a snowflake, perfectly and gorgeously unique. They exist for a brief, inimitable moment, and then they melt away. Their heartaches and failures, occurring only once in the vastness of space and time.[5]

So rest assured, you're not being a "special snowflake" just because you're asexual.

And if someone does call you a snowflake, then just be a blizzard and give them frostbite.

On Neuroticism and Labels

The word "neurotic" is a loaded term for many people. Me included.

As a Jewish woman who has dealt with anxiety on and off throughout my life, I've been hit with this label various times, whether jokingly (though not a joke to me) by family members or culturally through stereotyped and often one-dimensional portrayals of Jewish women (the latter dyed with a certain brand of antisemitic sexism that I could go into a whole other essay about).

While the concept of neuroticism, as it is recognized in psychology, is defined more as a personality type than an actual mental disorder,[1] many people continue to throw the word around with a certain pathologizing air at anyone who appears a little anxious or introspective about life.

And as an asexual, the word continues to pop in and out of my life, with asexuality being an orientation that many people continue to associate with excessive navel-gazing. A sort of (a)sexual neuroticism, if you will.

While I can't speak for everyone within the LGBTQIA+ community, there is a certain level of contemplation one enters into when they realize they don't fit into the cis-het binary system society assumes we're automatically born into. And I find that is especially true for asexuals.

When you're ace and realize that your life doesn't fit into the given scripts around sex and romance (i.e. that love can exist without sex or that sex can exist without love, particularly if you're also aromantic), then there can be an overwhelming sense of panic, wondering where the hell you *do* fit in.

As such, many aces begin to question...well, everything. Their romantic orientations, their sexual orientations, etc.

And that's not necessarily a bad thing.

By questioning the status quo, you begin to challenge all the "should bes" (as in you "should be" allo, or this or that) and start to realize and acknowledge how things *actually are*, which basically comes down to being a lot more complicated than a simplified "check one box" identity category system likes to believe.

And, in turn, by questioning and analyzing certain things that most people take for granted, such as different types of attraction, it can help bring a level of emotional and social intelligence that will allow you to have a better understanding of the relationships in your life and a more intimate understanding of yourself.

However...

There is sometimes a point where one maybe can question *too much*.

While it can be useful to find so much nuance within the ace community, what with the number of sub- and micro-labels to describe specific identities and experiences, it can also be pretty overwhelming, especially when you're first introduced to all this terminology.

Personally speaking, it can make your head spin trying to dissect every facet of your identity and every nuance of the ways you experience (and don't experience) attraction. Especially when there can be certain pressures to figure everything out right away, as though taking the time to figure yourself out will compromise the legitimacy of who you are.

All of which can be *a lot*.

Neuroticism itself is said to be associated with various negative effects, including "anger, anxiety, self-consciousness, irritability, emotional instability, and depression,"[2] which, unfortunately, are things that are not uncommon within the asexual community.

Often, it can feel like the chicken-and-egg scenario, asking which comes first: neuroticism from being ace or neuroticism from existing in a world that erases and pathologizes asexuality while also demanding instantaneous and easy categorization of who and what you are.

What I'm essentially trying to say here (or at least what I'm hoping to say) is that it can be stressful figuring out what kind of ace (or what kind of person) you are, and that it's okay if you don't know right away (or even ever).

Identity is a lot more fluid and ambiguous than we give it credit for.

Before I identified as ace, I had identified as "straight" (turns out being heterosexual was the "phase"), and since then I have identified as a number of other things, including demisexual, grayromantic, and more. And I may probably find other labels later on as I gain a better understanding of myself and who I am.

The answer to the question of who we are can change depending on the information and resources we have available at the time, as well as the experiences we accumulate throughout our lives.

While it can be easy to fall into the panic spiral of over-analyzing and worrying about our identities, sometimes there are moments when we simply need to step back and accept that we may not know all the answers, and that that can be okay.

As the famous poet Rainer Maria Rilke once wrote, "Live the questions now. Perhaps then, someday far in the future, you will gradually, without even noticing it, live your way into the answer."[3]

And if you never know the specific answer, that's okay, too.

The answers might keep changing anyway.

Asexuals Are Here, and They're Organizing*

Since the time of Stonewall, the LGBTQIA+ community has changed in ways that our queer ancestors could not have imagined. We now have multiple resources at our fingertips for figuring out our identities at earlier ages and for connecting instantaneously with a wide network of individuals, or even a community, with whom we share similar experiences. One group that has especially come out and come together in the digital age is the asexual community.

Some of the best-known resources for the ace community have been created online, including AVEN (Asexual Visibility and Education Network), the largest online community and archive on asexuality. The organization was originally founded in 2001 by American asexual activist David Jay when he was a college student seeking resources about asexuality, at a time when this orientation was barely acknowledged. Since then, the platform has received thousands, if not millions, of visitors from around the world seeking information and/or interaction with other asexuals.

As an asexual person, I have benefited tremendously from the sociological resources the internet has provided. Back when I was

---

* An earlier version of this chapter was published in *The Gay & Lesbian Review*, September–October 2021, https://glreview.org/article/asexuals-are-here-and-theyre-organizing. Reproduced with permission.

first coming into my own as a queer youth, most of what I initially learned about the LGBTQIA+ community came from online. It was actually on YouTube that I discovered other vloggers and online journalists who identified as asexual covering the topic and discussing their experiences, many of which resembled my own. From a video, I discovered a meet-up group in New York where I could both digitally and physically converse with other asexuals, and that was possibly the first time that I didn't feel like the only asexual fish in a rainbow pond.

However, since identifying as asexual, I have come across a number of microaggressions directed at our community, including trolls calling asexuality an "internet orientation." The idea here is that asexuality is merely a creation of the internet, a recent fad that emerged only in the last few years, whereas the fact is that asexuality has a longer history. For example, as far back as 1972, the Asexual Caucus of the New York Radical Feminists published a paper titled "The Asexual Manifesto."[1]

Granted, the asexual community is relatively young compared to other parts of the LGBTQ+ community, as it has only started entering into mainstream discourse over the past twenty years. But as queer history shows, just because the word for something hadn't been invented yet doesn't mean it didn't exist.

The words people used in the past to describe LGBTQIA+ identities were not the same words people use today. Yet the absence of modern language does not predicate the absence of queer individuals. Despite colonialism's attempts to erase it, indigenous histories reveal an extensive record of non-binary and trans identities that have long resisted a violent gender-binary system. Poetry and letters have preserved like amber the tenderness of same-sex affections, even when those romances had to be hidden behind closed doors.

The reality of asexuality doesn't have to depend on there being a word for it, as asexual people have undoubtedly existed throughout history. While research and literature on it are still limited, asexuality has begun to be taken seriously as a sexual orientation in its own right, thanks in part to the efforts of asexual writers and scholars (and allosexual allies) using the internet to build an asexual canon and archive online.

Something else to consider is the extent to which bars and clubs have served as meeting places for LGBTQ+ people historically and still today. Such venues served and continue to serve some parts of the community quite well. But they don't work as well for other groups. For those whose religious practices do not mesh well with alcoholic spaces, neurodivergent types for whom the loud music, flashing lights, and crowds of people can create a chaotic sea of sensory overload, or recovering addicts, the bar represents a space that, rather than "safe" and welcoming, feels hostile and uncomfortable.

Jeremy Lin, author of the book *Gay Bar*, pointed out how, despite their historical significance, gay bars are limited in the kind of patrons they can serve:

It's hard for me to think of gay bars as safe spaces at all—in that they rely on the consumption of booze, usually neglect to provide adequate wheelchair access, are lookist and ageist and have been blatantly racist and sexist, too.[2]

And not only that, but bars often contain an element of "hook-up" culture, something not exactly inviting for asexuals. As Lin stated:

Bars, after all, are commercial spaces, and sexuality of course has been repurposed as a weapon of commerce. Bars and other institutions of gay culture were selling sex even at the height of AIDS infections—they just sold an idea of sex, of its promise, and not just a promise of getting laid but of power and status.[3]

While asexual bar nights,[4] focused on not hooking up or drinking, sound perfect in theory for other aces, the reality is time and money have always factored into physical spaces, and as the last few years of the pandemic have shown, that's not always possible or available.

The reality is that the rise of the internet as a public domain for meeting and organizing has allowed people on the edges of the queer community—among them asexuals—to find spaces to connect that simply didn't exist before. So while asexuality is not an "internet orientation," the internet is a large part of the ace community, and a large part of why it exists the way it does today.

Moving forward, the internet will continue to play a huge role in the lives of asexuals. Rather than scoff at those who use it to validate themselves, let us honor the innovative ways in which the asexual community and other marginalized communities have come together, and the ways they will continue to grow and evolve as time goes on.

Interview with Maia Kobabe

This is a transcript of an audio interview. This interview has been condensed and edited for clarity.

Michele: Okay, to start with, how would you describe yourself and your space on the ace spectrum?

Maia: My name is Maia Kobabe. I describe myself as a non-binary person, a queer person, an author, an illustrator. Someone who is very happy and comfortable in the queer community and identifies as asexual and aromantic.

Michele: Thank you for sharing that. So do you want to talk a little about how you got to learn more about being on the aspec spectrum?

Maia: Yeah, it was definitely a long and slow journey. I think of all the various queer identities I have, asexuality is the one that's still very mysterious to me, and I still feel like that even into my thirties. I'm still very much figuring it out...not questioning in the sense that I don't believe it, but questioning in the sense of "more to discover."

So I think I first heard the term "asexuality" when I was maybe in eighth grade or early in high school, so maybe thirteen or fourteen. And I remember just think-ing, "That's really cool, I'm glad that exists," and kind of thinking, "Oh, I sort of wish I was that, but I don't think I am." [Laughs.] Which is so classic of a queer person's experience, like you hear about something and you're like, "That would be cool if that was me, but it probably isn't." And I just remember being glad there was a word to define that experience.

I remember seeing a Pride march in San Francisco in 2010 or so and an ace group showed up. I cheered for them so loudly that several people in the march turned to look at me, like, "Who is cheering so loud for the ace group?" and it was me. [Points to self.] The ace group had these really cool signs, some classic ones that I thought were very funny, like, "Why have sex when you could have cake?" But I just remember thinking, "Oh, this is so great!" Like, look at these cool people! And then, I think, it was only when I was into my late twenties, when I was still finding that I wasn't interested in pursuing the type of sexual and romantic relationship everyone else seemed to want and be interested in, and I was like, "Maybe these terms really do fit me." But it seemed like I had to wait until later in life for that lack of interest in sex and romance to be proven by many years of lived experience before I started to understand, "Oh, I think maybe this is where I am in this queer spectrum."

Michele: I think it's definitely relatable. I also think it has a lot to do with language, which you've talked a little bit about in your book and through other interviews. How, when certain language isn't accessible at the time, you just try to go for the language that fits best.

So to talk about your book, one of the things I loved

about it is that often when people talk about asexuality, they talk about it as an absence of something, which it partially is. But then they also talk about it as if it's devoid of joy, devoid of passion. Meanwhile, your book is literally full of color. Like it's showing this very nerdy, very colorful way of existing in the world as an asexual that I really love.

Maia: I mean, I am very happy to be the way that I am. I definitely wouldn't change things even if it were possible to—being ace and being aro, I mean. Both of them are braided in so tightly with my experience of gender that it is also very hard for me to know where one ends and another begins. It's hard to know if I was more romantically inclined, would I be more interested in having sex be a small part of a relationship I had with someone? Or if I didn't have gender dysphoria, would I have more interest in sex than I have now?

It's really hard for me to answer any of those questions. But I also think that being asexual can be quite cool. And it can also open up things that might not otherwise be there. I don't think it's just a lack. I think it's a different path. And I think that partly because I have a very deep experience of friendship. And I have many friends and many friendships in my life that have felt very intimate and very close. Both in physical touch, like cuddling, and also in a lot of sharing of deep emotions and thoughts. There are a lot of people who I feel really, really close with. So that is something that I consider a positive and a joy.

Michele: I definitely agree with that in the sense of platonic relationships, they just become that much richer. Or maybe not that much richer, but it's just you recognize how rich they are when you're an ace or aro person.

Maia: Yeah, and you have the time to invest in them and the motivation to invest in them.

Michele: Definitely. And I actually want to touch on that point of what you said about your gender intersecting with your sexuality. From what I can tell from other non-binary and trans people's accounts, asexuality can go in either one of two ways. One in which before they start to transition, they feel asexual because they don't access their libido or their sexuality in a way until the dysphoria fog clears up.

Maia: Yeah, exactly.

Michele: But then the other way, other trans people who have already transitioned still identify as asexual because it's not like their sexuality is tied to their body parts. It's just tied to another part of themselves.

Maia: I think you described that really well. And I relate to both sides of that, which just goes along with being a person who never wants to choose one of two options. [Laughs.] Before realizing I was non-binary and realizing I was trans, part of my asexuality was a very deep discomfort with my body or the idea that someone might look at my body and desire it, seeing it through a feminine lens. That was really uncomfortable to me. But then coming out as non-binary, I was like, "Oh, I am now a little bit more interested in understanding where some of the hesitation and doubts and fears of the past come from." But it doesn't mean that I'm not still asexual, even when I understand one of the facets of it. And I'm very much in the camp of "people who are asexual can obviously still have sex if they want to, or if they make a choice to based on various factors."

           But yeah, dysphoria is a piece of my asexuality, but it is not the entirety of it. It is definitely its own thing outside of gender stuff, too. But tied together. Mixed and hard to separate. But also two separate things. I don't know. [Laughs.]

Michele: Yeah. I say when people want these little really "neat" labels, it's just so hard because life isn't neat, you know? Everything intersects together.

Maia: Literally nothing is black and white. It's shades of grays and colors forever.

Michele: At times, walking through the world with the body I have, I am very uncomfortable with the way my body's received, and how sexualized my body is. How can I reconcile that with a sexuality I'm uncomfortable with?

Maia: It's hard. Because you can't really even imagine how you would feel about your body without the lens of society's take on it. Or you can try to imagine yourself in that space. Or you can step into a really supportive community that's tried to lift all of those expectations and pressures off. And I do know people who are specifically ambiguous about something like breasts. Some people can like having them in one context, and not in another, or like them on some days, and not other days. And it's so rarely clear-cut.

Michele: Just talking about the future, what do you want to see for the ace community in the future?

Maia: I want to see the ace community thriving. I just want everybody to be really happy. And out there living our best lives. And I think a lot of ace people are already doing that. But I think that some people do encounter barriers. There are a lot of barriers for people who are outside of queer and ace communities not fully understanding it or not accepting it, who are seeing it as a "bad" thing. And again, there are these expectations society laid on you that you need certain things to achieve happiness. When, in fact, what you need is to achieve your own goals, even if they're different from the people around you. So, yeah, I just hope all ace people can find that comfortable place of knowing what they want, and knowing what makes them happy and not worrying if it's not the same as what their peers are aiming for.

Michele: Definitely. And touching on another question that I want to ask you... In discussions that we've had before, when we talked about the different identities that we occupy, whether it relates to gender queerness, aceness, or aromanticism. We talked about how when you don't align with certain binaries in one way, then sometimes you're more likely to not align with other binaries.

Maia: Yeah, if you don't fit in in one regard, it opens your eyes to question other aspects. So if I'm already questioning my gender, it's a smaller step to also question my sexuality or vice versa. I do love that. And I do love how existing outside of certain structures like the gender binary or heterosexuality can give you a real freedom of perspective. It can lead to some really interesting and creative insights on problem solving on the way you want to live your life or the way you want to structure your relationships or your career. And it can give you a really beautiful wide view on what life can be outside of a standard set path.

Michele: I think that was one of the privileges coming into aceness has given me. When you first start coming out as ace, it's kind of terrifying, knowing that you're not performing to a cultural script that's been shoved down your throat since you were really young. But not following that script, you get to see the other paths that are available. You get to learn, "Maybe I can just make my own path of existing."

Maia: Absolutely. I agree.

Michele: It actually reminds me of one of my favorite pages in your
            book *Gender Queer*. It's on page 179. You said, "I remember
            when I first realized I never had to have children, it was
            like walking out of a narrow valley into a wide-open path.
            I never have to get married. I never have to date anyone. I
            don't even have to care about sex. These realizations were
            like gifts that I gave to myself." I would love to hear you
            expand on that.

Maia: I also love that page. And I'm glad that it resonates with
            people. I think specifically the one realizing I didn't have
            to have kids, I think it was a realization I had pretty early
            in high school, like fourteen or so. And it felt like sud-
            denly a huge amount of time had been given back to me.
            And I was like, oh, having a child...it's a very worthy and
            wonderful thing to do if you want to, but if you don't
            want to, it can look like a huge time commitment. And
            just being like, "Man, there goes probably two decades
            of my life, where I'll have much less time to pursue my
            own creative hobbies." And when I was like, "Oh, I don't
            have to do that if I don't want to," I was just like, "Wow!"
            Think about how many more books I'm going be able to
            read, how many more drawings I'm going to be able to
            draw. How many more stories I'm going to tell, and how
            much more time I'll be able to spend hanging out with
            friends or just doing literally anything else. Traveling,
            baking, sleeping, etc. Time that would be taken out by
            the project of child care.

            But if I'm not interested in the project of child care,
            I can have all of this time for myself. So that was the
            beginning of it. That was the beginning of a cascade of
            realizations. Like, "Oh, you know, a lot of people around

me seem really stressed about the fact that they want to date and are finding it hard or time-consuming or demoralizing. I can just not do that. I can just choose not to and do something else with my time." And I still find it very valuable to really examine anything that you feel like you have to do, but are feeling in your gut that you don't want to. Check in with yourself. Like, "Is this something I actually have to do?" Or is this genuinely something that I can set aside and that I do not need to do in my life? I can do something else. That brings me joy.

Michele: Yeah, definitely. And for the record, for aro and ace people, maybe we just need to do it a little differently from other people.

Maia: Famously, David Jay, who we both know, the founder of Asexuality.org, always wanted to be a parent and has been very open about his experience and journey of being an asexual parent and a third parent, going through the process of a third-parent adoption, and how amazing that's been, and how much he always wanted that, and how wonderful it is that he made this family. And I love hearing about that! I'm just like, "Wow, that's amazing." Not for me, but amazing.

Michele: Definitely. And actually, a friend of mine told me recently that they found it really cool that I was on the aspec spectrum, because they said they would feel they would get a lot more done in their life if they weren't non-ace.

Maia: Yeah, exactly. If I surprise myself, if I do fall in love with someone, I'm imagining it would be in my fifties or sixties. Then I'm like, "Well, if it happens, then it will happen when the time is right." But I am completely uninterested in putting time into pursuing it, because it's not a thing that I want to pursue. It's sort of like only something I want if it just stumbles into my lap at the perfect moment. If it comes, it comes. If it doesn't, both are good. Like both options are equally good. And equally interesting, and equally full of possibility. But instead, I'm pursuing the things that I really want—to write and draw queer narratives, and publish queer books, and be very active in a community of queer writers and authors and illustrators and readers.

Michele: I want to talk about your art for a second. Because your book is actually one of the first graphic novels in which I've seen someone talk about asexuality. So I would love to hear why you decided to include that in your book?

Maia: I mean, I definitely wanted to include it because it is a big piece of who I am. It was one of the major things I was thinking about in my teenage years, and then into my early twenties. I'm trying to remember if I set out with a really conscious goal of including this alongside other things. When I was outlining my book *Gender Queer*, I went through all of my high school diaries, and I reread all of them. And I wrote down a bullet point list of anything that happened to me that seemed relevant to the topic of gender and sexuality. And a lot of them were about asexuality, or questions about asexuality, or thoughts, such as actually wondering, "Do I need to come out as not cis if I don't plan to pursue a relationship?" Like wondering whether my gender only mattered in relation to a romantic or sexual partner? And then eventually realizing, "No, I actually think it really does matter that I come out as non-binary, and that my community sees me as non-binary. Because I think it's really affecting all of my relationships, including my relationships with my parents, and teachers, and co-workers, and all of that.

It's not just something that would affect a relationship with a potential romantic partner." So, in that sense, I do think that the threads of asexuality and aromanticism were very important to include. And I wanted to talk about them in the same way as everything else, which is to the best of my memory, but with a touch of warmth, and humor, because I wanted everything in the book to have kind of a warm perspective. And I also feel like I've had a very warm and loving life. So it's accurate.

Michele: I'm glad. On both counts—that you've had a warm life and that you wanted to translate that into your work. I think that's something that I wanted to do with this book. I just remember being in high school, and I'd just stumbled across asexuality. And so I didn't realize at the time, but I think it saved me a lot of grief that older ace folks tell me about feeling "broken," because it gave me a language, a kind of shield against that.

Maia: I feel really lucky that in my teenage years I was very resistant to peer pressure. Partly it was out of stubbornness and a slightly contrarian nature. I was like, I'm not into anything that "everybody" is into. Whatever the fad was, I was not into it. I was like, "I'm not joining MySpace or getting a cell phone. I'm not dating. I'm over here reading my fantasy novels, my comic books, I'm into something else. Y'all have fun with whatever you're into, but it's not for me." And I had a couple of close friends who respected my quirkiness. And I really never felt pressured into anything that I didn't want to do. Like, to me, dating seemed very uncool.

I went to a very, very small high school, so my class had twenty-eight people. So whenever anyone would start dating someone else, I'd think, "You know, you're probably going to break up within a month, and our class is so small that you will have to see that person every single day until the end of the school year. So in my humble opinion, dating is a very bad idea. Just putting that out there. Maybe try dating someone from a different school, if you must, but like, come on now."

Michele: Oh, my G-d! I remember friends and family members talking to me about feeling horny, and wanting to have sex, and I'm like, "I'm sorry. I can sympathize. But I don't get it."

Maia: You can say, "I'm sorry you're going through that. I don't really know what it's like, but you make it sound like you're suffering. So I hope you feel better soon."

Michele: Talking about the books and media part. Was there ever any moment in your life that you ever saw pop culture reflecting on asexuality? Because I think pop culture is a big deal to both of us, honestly.

Maia: Yeah, I'm trying to think when would have been the first time I saw an asexual character in literally any media. The only examples I'm thinking of are really recent ones, from the last five years. I don't know that I have a specific memory of a first ace character that I read. Unfortunately, I think a lot of my experiences were of reading a character who I would relate to up to a point. And then often that character would at some point become interested in sex and romance. And I'd have to be like, "Well, here's where my story and their story diverge." When I look back on my childhood, there were many characters that I loved, but very few that I related to.

Michele: And is that what partially motivates you as an artist today, to reflect those experiences?

Maia: Yeah, that's definitely part of it. Wanting there to be more different stories that didn't exist when I was young. That's a huge part. I think my very first motivation for wanting to be an author was wanting to be friends with other authors. And I thought, "Well, it seems like authors are friends with each other. So I think maybe the fastest way to befriend my favorite authors would be to become an author." My first instinct to become published came from wanting to be included in this community of authors.

Michele: Community is really important. What you said about seeing the Pride Parade, seeing other asexuals out there. Like even if you're not directly part of the community, just knowing the community exists out there can just make you feel more hopeful.

Maia: Yeah, I'm thinking now about the first person I met who identified as asexual when I was in college, and it's someone I'm still friends with to this day. And like, that was really cool. Meeting someone my age who had already happily settled into identifying as ace. I thought, "Whoa, you already know that about yourself. Oh, that's so cool that you already figured that out." Because I still felt like I was in the middle of figuring it out. And it was also interesting that it was somebody who had a much higher libido than mine and somebody who would talk way more openly about things, like sex toys and masturbation. And I asked, "Wait, you're into all this, and you're really comfortable talking about it, and you're ace, both at the same time?" And they said, "Yeah." And I was like, "Wow! Cool."

Michele: I think that's something a lot of people who are not inside the ace community don't really realize: that asexuals can have a complicated relationship with sex and desire, too.

Okay, now that we've talked about pop culture, something else I want to ask is: What's something you would want someone to take away from this conversation?

Maia: I really think everyone, asexual or allosexual, queer or straight or cis or trans, should deeply question their identity, and their sexuality, and their gender, and their desires. I think everyone could stand to examine these really closely. And I honestly wish that everyone in the world thought about it as deeply as asexual people do. In the serious light and the frivolous light, thought about it really deeply and then made silly jokes about it, too. But really I wish everyone deeply considered what they want, and what they think would make them happy, and what things they need and want in their life, and what things they maybe don't need and don't want in their life, and align their life around these clearly and deeply considered goals. That's what I hope. Because I think it's valuable for everyone. And I worry about people who don't examine these things so deeply and end up sort of just falling into the "standard path" and end up pursuing things that are maybe not the thing that would make them the most happy just because they think they have to. I wish everyone would be able to pursue their truest self, their truest goals, their deepest desires or lack of desires.

Maia Kobabe (e, em, eir) is an author and illustrator from the Bay Area, California. Eir first full-length book, *Gender Queer: A Memoir*, won a Stonewall Honor and an Alex Award from the American Library Association in 2020. It was also the number-one most challenged book in the U.S. in 2021. Maia's short comics have been published by *The New Yorker*, *The Nib*, and *The Washington Post*, and in many print anthologies. Before setting out to work freelance full-time, e worked for over ten years in libraries.

Interview with Shari B. Ellis

This is a transcript of an audio interview. This interview has been condensed and edited for clarity.

Michele: So let me start off with the question, how would you describe yourself in terms of who you are, what you do, and as a person in the ace community?

Shari: So I am a Black woman and my pronouns are she/her. And as an ace, I describe myself as panromantic, possibly demiromantic because I've never experienced a romantic attraction outside of a friendship. In terms of what I do, I'm an animation production manager/aspiring producer. In fact, I've written a script with an ace main character.

Michele: Awesome! I can't wait to see that one day. So I guess another question that I would want to ask is, how did you come to be aware of this part of your identity? The ace identity.

Shari: It took a lifetime because I grew up in the 1970s and 1980s when we didn't have the term—at least, we weren't applying the term "asexual" to humans.

Michele: Plants and asexual reproduction, right?

Shari: Yes. [Laughs.] But I must have heard it in biology class because I have journal entries where I basically asked myself whether or not I'm asexual. And my senior year, I got really into philosophy thanks to a religion teacher, and I think I had this idea that, well, if I'm really serious about philosophy, then it makes sense if I'm asexual. So I was definitely using it on an individual level, and then I put that aside because it just didn't occur to me that that might actually really be the case. And especially the message all around was "Oh, you just haven't found the right person." Or "Maybe you're just not into men," or whatever. And it certainly wasn't "Maybe you're just not into sex," period. And it wasn't until I would say maybe the mid-to-early 2000s, on LiveJournal, I joined in an asexual community, and I started using the term "gray-asexual." And then I was doing some cleaning, like a major overhaul of my apartment, and came across one of my old journals again, and in it I read a description of a concert that was like the height of puberty. And I talked about this in Angela Chen's book *Ace*, but basically I went to a Duran Duran concert and it was my first Duran Duran concert. And the lead singer, like, I don't know why, but he just got really inspired and he threw off his shirt and started rolling around on the stage. And it was one of those things where all the women around me were like, "Oh my gosh!" They would have thrown bras if they had them, you know? Bras and panties and all that. Just hormones out of control. And I remember having a sort of distance. Like I was excited, I was like, "This is cool!" but that was the extent of my excitement. And reading that journal entry, I realized that I've known all along that I was asexual. I just let other people talk me out of it, you know? So then I started to embrace the term. And then I started looking into asexual groups in Los Angeles and I found one. There were actually a couple at one point, and one of the organizers, one of them just sort of died off and the organizer of the other one got burned out. And so I took it over on the condition that I could find a co-coordinator, which I have, and so now I'm co-executive director of Ace L.A. And we've maintained that structure because really I'm old enough to have been a part of several movements, and burnout is always at the top of my mind, and I always teach the others to make sure that if you need help to ask for it. And so I always make sure that I always have help.

Michele: That's great. About discovering that early in life, and also the activism thing. And I really hope you don't get burnout, by the way!

Shari: Thank you.

Michele: We do need to take care of our activists because as important as activism is, we also need to remember that within the fight, we need room for joy and relaxation.

Shari: Mhm. Absolutely.

Michele: It's also funny what you mentioned about the whole concert thing because I remember kind of a similar experience when I was at an Angel Haze concert.

Shari: Oh, yeah?

Michele: Yeah. It was in a tight-packed club venue and the singer was on stage, and they were performing and they had this like magnetic energy that you could see in a very queer crowd. And I also identify with the label "queer," but at that time here were these people going wild for Angel Haze and I felt like I was in my own little bubble of "not getting it" or not being in that same energy.

Shari: Right. [Nods.]

Michele: So it's always an interesting experience of bringing asex-
           uality to different venues and just comparing yourself to
           other people's reactions.

Shari: Oh, that's so interesting that you had a similar experience.
           I wonder if there are others.

Michele: I assume so. I don't think we're alone in that.

           You're also actually the second person I've talked to for
           this book to mention Angela Chen's book. I recently inter-
           viewed Maia Kobabe, whom you might remember from
           the Flame Con panel "Out of the Deck: A Conversation on
           Aro Ace Identity and Representation"[1] that you had both
           spoken at. I remember the panel getting into a discussion
           about how when you identify as on the margins in one
           aspect of your life, you are more likely to identify on the
           margins of other aspects. So for Maia, it was identifying
           as non-binary and relating to that in terms of asexuality,
           and I think I remember you mentioning relating to that
           in terms of neurodivergence, correct?

Shari: Right. I'm autistic and that was another thing that
           I found out late in life. I'm autistic and I have ADHD
           [attention deficit hyperactivity disorder]. Both of which
           were diagnosed pretty late in life, both as an adult.
           The ADHD thing I was diagnosed with mid-2000s, so
           definitely earlier, but autism I wasn't diagnosed with
           until 2019.

Michele: Mmm. I think that's actually pretty common for a lot of
           people who are assigned female at birth to discover it
           later in life. Because, as you might know, science is part
           of an institution and it can be a very sexist and racist
           institution. So a lot of the diagnostic criteria were based
           on young white boys.

Shari: Yes. Exactly.

Michele: It's interesting because both autism and asexuality are defined as a spectrum. Different people having different experiences. So I was wondering if you maybe you could talk possibly about some of the commonalities between those spectrums or those identities.

Shari: That's an interesting question, because to be honest I kind of go out of my way to not tie the two together because so many people assume that autistic people must be asexual. They de-sexualize autistic people. And, in fact, someone asked me that not too long ago. Because I did mention that I'm autistic, and they asked me if I thought there was a correlation between the two, and I said no. I just think it's a happy accident. And it may be a matter of because we're already willing to look outside of hetero norms, and in order to discover our asexuality, maybe there's a level of self-awareness there that makes us more likely to discover if we're neurodivergent. But it's definitely a matter of correlation doesn't mean causation.

Michele: Exactly. And oftentimes when people within the autistic community or within the asexual community come out, they both describe being perhaps infantilized.

Shari: Yes, for sure. So I definitely can relate to that. When I consulted on BoJack Horseman and I was asked what I didn't want to see in the representations of aces, I said I'd really like for us to not be seen as childlike. Which was funny because, of course, Todd Chavez is very child-like, and apparently later there was a talk with Raphael Bob-Waksberg where he was relaying what I said and apparently at the time he was thinking, "Oh no!"

Michele: [Laughs.] Okay, we can also argue that Todd Chavez is childlike, but he's also very emotionally mature compared to the rest of the cast.

Shari: Exactly. I certainly wasn't upset that he was the asexual character.

Michele: I think there's room for aces to be childlike and goofy versus being infantilized.

Shari: Right, right.

Michele: Which is another thing I wanted to mention because how cool it is that you worked as a consultant for BoJack Horseman! Because Todd Chavez is one of the most visible ace characters...and honestly one of the only asexual characters who is canonically ace right now on mainstream television. Can I ask you, how did you get involved with BoJack Horseman?

Shari: It was a combination of David Jay from AVEN and GLAAD. They had reached out to GLAAD who reached out to David Jay, and David Jay and I already knew each other. So he mentioned Ace Los Angeles to them, and as I'm the one who works in animation, it was just a natural selection for me to be the representative who went and spoke with them. Definitely the animation connection made it a natural fit.

Michele: That's awesome. And I love the part about aces looking out for other aces.

Shari: Yes. We're such a small community, and I say that we're a very tight community in many ways.

Michele: You kind of have to be. It's like a survival mechanism, you know?

And actually that brings me to another point about animation because I believe you and I are both very big pop culture fans. And what I want to ask is, what has it been like for you seeing or not seeing this part of yourself reflected in the media you consume, and what the implications of that might be?

Shari: Well, it gets back to me being told most of my teen and adult life that I just needed to "find someone." When I started to come out to people, one of the first things someone asked me was whether I was scared of sex, and I was like, "No, not scared at all. I'm just not interested." And someone else said to me, "Well, you're boy crazy." And I was like, "I can be boy crazy and still be asexual." I call it "boy happy" now because I want to avoid that ableist term. [Laughs.]

Michele: I love it!

Shari: But without representation, it means that every time we come out, we have to engage in educating people and it becomes a lesson. And sometimes that's a little exhausting because when you're trying to explain the absence of something, it's not quite the same as just saying, "Well, I'm gay" or "I'm attracted to people of the same sex." Like the way I explain it, the simplest definition of asexuality is experiencing little to no sexual attraction. And underneath that, there's this whole umbrella of behaviors and attitudes. So people end up being really surprised because they're not exposed to asexuality in media, or barely know anyone who is asexual, so they end up being surprised to hear that some of us have sex, that some of us are sex-positive. There's that stereotype that we're all sex-negative, that we're all virgins, that we don't date, that we're robotic.

Michele: Uggh, I hate that.

Shari: Yeah. And especially that robotic thing. That's something that I've experienced being an autistic person. So that's another way that there are some similarities that I've had to fight. So we definitely need to see any kind of representation. But we definitely need to see more diverse representation that encompasses people of color. That encompasses intersectional identities like disability. Actually, just gender would be nice, because most people think that asexuality is a white male thing or a "white person's thing." And it's just because they don't know any better.

Michele: I definitely think there needs to be a greater conversation on intersectionality with the ace community, because being a person you don't exist in a vacuum where being ace is the only thing that affects your day-to-day life. You know, I walk through the world as a woman, as a white person, as a Jewish person. So each of those things intersects with my ace identity and vice versa. And we need to understand that when you're ace, it's a major part of you, but it's also not the *only* thing about you. So you need someone to see *all* of you.

So another question I wanted to ask you is, what is something you would like to see in media regarding aspec characters?

Shari: Let's see. Well, it gets back to what I want to see within the community, which is more diversity. Particularly with regard to people of color. I'd like to see diversity across lifestyles. I'd like to see the media tackling asexuals who have sex, I'd like for that to be normalized. I'd like for queerplatonic relationships to be normalized—the idea that people can be in an intimate relationship without having sex, and exploring what that means.

Michele: I really would love to see that, too.

So before we end this conversation, what are some things you would want someone to take away from this conversation about asexuality?

Shari: What's the best way to put this? More open-mindedness, more compassion, less gatekeeping. And I think that goes as much for within the ace community as outside it. I think, in general, if you can approach people with that mindset, a lot of problems would be solved. But particularly with regard to aces of color.

Michele: I think if we brought mindfulness for people who are questioning their sexuality and for aces regarding other aces in the community, then we could have a less painful experience just navigating the world as we are.

Shari: I think approaching with mindfulness and also a sense of personal accountability would make this a safer space for all of us.

Michele: Wholeheartedly agree. I think that's a great answer. Thank you.

Shari: Thank you.

Shari B. Ellis (she/her), born and raised in Chicago, attended Yale University to study philosophy and psychology. Naturally, she went to work in the film industry. Since moving to Los Angeles, she's had the pleasure of working for such greats as Disney, Sony, Marvel, Netflix, and Apple in the animation and visual FX industries, and is developing her own animated television comedies for adults. As co-executive director of Ace Los Angeles, a non-profit 501(c)3 social, educational, and outreach group for asexuals in the Greater Los Angeles area, Shari consulted for the character of Todd Chavez on *BoJack Horseman*, as well as other upcoming projects in production.

PART III

GETTING INTO THE NUANCES OF SEXUAL AND ROMANTIC ATTRACTION

Explaining the Different Types of Attraction

Hypothetical situation.
Let's say you've met someone.

Being around this person makes you feel a number of things, which possibly include being giddy, dizzy, excited, etc. Beyond just a passing interest, as you would experience glancing at a stranger on the street and looking away, never to see or meet them again, part of you wants to get to *know* this person, to know more about them. You may even experience a desire to be *close* to this person, whether in a physical and/or emotional capacity.

To put it bluntly, you might be *interested* in this someone.

Now, whether that interest is in their heart, their mind, or *any other body parts* is another question.

Speaking from personal experience, when you find yourself "attracted" to someone else (whether for the first time, though technically every encounter with a new person could be considered a "first time"), you can find yourself going into a panic, especially if the experience is new to you. Especially when you're not quite sure *what* you're feeling.

As sexual wellness expert Natasha Marie states:

Attraction is profoundly personal... As the adage goes, "beauty is in the eye of the beholder," and multi-faceted. However, pop culture peddles another, flatter version of attraction: an inherent assumption that when you are "attracted" to someone, it's all-encompassing, meaning you are, all at once, romantically, emotionally, physically, spiritually, and sexually attracted to that person.[1]

When it comes to attraction, most people, as Marie suggests, tend to conflate it with a number of meanings—sexual desire, romantic appeal, etc. However, for aces who are familiar with the reality that romantic attraction does not necessarily exist in tandem with sexual attraction, as well as aromantic aces who experience neither romantic nor sexual attraction, the idea and reality of "attraction" may indeed become something more ambiguous, fluid, and multifaceted.

Quoting from French-Canadian artist Isabelle Melançon's illustration[2] and a few other terms frequently used within the ace community, we will be discussing different types of "attraction."

Sexual Attraction

"Sexual attraction is a feeling that sexual people get that causes them to desire sexual contact with a specific other person."

Note that sexual attraction can be separate from sexual desire, the "experience of sexual attraction and wanting to act on it, or the feeling of arousal and desire to find relief by masturbating"[3] (otherwise known as libido or "horniness") and sexual arousal, the feeling of sexual excitement in one's body parts or "being turned on," often motivated by physiological processes and hormones.

While the distinctions between sexual attraction, sexual desire, and sexual arousal may seem confusing, try to think of it this way: much in the same way a hungry dog can start drooling when a plate of food appears in front of them, the human body can be "aroused" by a person they might find visually "appetizing." Pavlovian conditioning dictates a physiological response in the way our body reacts to the world and outside stimuli, meaning a physical reaction that's more responsive than voluntary.

In order words, you can be "aroused" by a person (i.e. feeling that "pulse" in your nether regions) without necessarily wanting to "sleep" with them.

For instance, you could be randomly watching a movie when an attractive actor appears on screen shirtless, looking "fine" as hell, and your "interest" could peak in more ways than one. But if that actor were to suddenly manifest in your bedroom, asking if you wanted to have consensual sex with them, that would be another story.

While both asexual and allosexual people can experience arousal and/or have varying degrees of libido (high, low, etc.), the distinction is that allos may have a libido that is directed by a "target," meaning there's a desire to have sex with a specific person they're attracted to, while for aces there's little to no sexual attraction at all.

Romantic Attraction

"Romantic attraction is a feeling that causes people to desire a romantic relationship with a specific other person."

We often see portrayals of romantic attraction (at least the straight, cis-het-allo kind) in the media, usually qualified by various characteristics and actions, such as the desire to be around the other person, coupled with feelings of enchantment or devotion. There are also the expectations of

desiring physical contact with that other person, including (depending on personal comfort) hand-holding, kissing, cuddling, having sex, and more.

The main way most people (and most allos) tend to differentiate a crush from a platonic bond with a person is by describing "liking" that person as "more than a friend."

Yet this distinction in itself can be flawed.

By saying "more than a friend," one intentionally or unintentionally undermines the value of friendship by suggesting that bonds that are not romantically intimate in nature are lesser.

While traditional romantic relationships are thought to signify a "deeper" commitment—cohabitation, social and legal legitimacy (in the case of marriage, especially those traditionally granted protection under the law, i.e. monogamous and initially only heterosexual partnerships), children, etc.—the truth is you don't need to be in a romantic relationship to have any of those things. There are those who platonically co-parent, such as asexual activist David Jay, who shares custody of his child with another married couple, who he is not romantically connected to.[4] There are best friends who co-habit and enter "platonic marriages"[5] for the sake of receiving the legal benefits and protections that would befall a romantic couple wishing to get married, as well as seeking a tradition honoring the lifelong commitment they are making to another person, even if that commitment isn't romantic or sexual in nature.

Also, one can share physical affection with those they are not romantically linked to. Various non-Western cultures around the world express forms of physical intimacy that are not necessarily related to romance, such as kissing or holding hands. In fact, the idea of kissing on the lips as one of the most romantic gestures possible is also a highly Western Eurocentric idea, with many cultures finding the idea of public lip-kissing excessive or unappealing.[6] There's also the added reality that sex can exist in relationships that are not romantic, and romantic relationships can exist without sex.

So, then, what makes a romantic attraction different from any other type of attraction?

Perhaps you could compare platonic attraction to ginger ale and romantic attraction to champagne (or seltzer if you're not into alcohol). Both are bubbly liquids that look pretty alike on the surface. The difference lies in the taste and how they make you feel.

You may find yourself with a taste for one, while finding the other utterly repulsive.

Yet what's important is that you avoid dehydration.

Ultimately, we need people like we need water, socialization being a natural human instinct and survival mechanism. We nourish ourselves with our bonds with other people, regardless of whether those bonds are romantic or not.

Crush

"A crush is a romantic attraction to someone, a desire for a romantic relationship of some kind, a desire that is possibly temporary in nature, possibly never to be acted upon."

Also linked to romantic attraction, a crush is the experience of infatuation and/or adoration toward a person, and may or may not include a desire to form a romantic attraction to another person (one may choose not to act on a crush).

A crush may also be defined by a range of symptoms, including elevated heartrate, sweaty palms, shortness of breath, fluttery nerves in stomach (i.e. "butterflies"), nausea... There's a reason why people call it "love sickness."

Squish

"A squish is an aromantic crush, a desire for a strong platonic relationship with someone."

Know how straight women often talk about "girl crushes" when they find themselves admiring other women in an intense way, but in a sense they say is not sexual or romantic? Aside from the possibility they might not be as "straight" as they thought, there's also a strong possibility that a "girl crush" is actually a squish.

In many ways, a squish can be just as intense as a romantic crush. That intense pull toward another person, the desire to get to know them, can manifest in a number of different ways, including appreciation for a really cool celebrity, that young adult writer you want to emulate, the kid in your class who you really, really want to be friends with because you think they're just *so cool*. Truthfully, that amount of emotion can feel just as awkward or embarrassing as romantic feelings.

One good example I found to describe a squish comes from the short story "Girl's Best Friend" written by Lisa Jenn Bigelow, in which a young girl named Roxy experiences a squish for the first time:

> She'd watched friends moon over other kids, movie stars, teachers. They dreamed about kisses and dates, weddings and babies. This wasn't that. She simply wanted to spend every spare minute with Tess. She wanted to know what she was thinking, share opinions...to snuggle under a blanket watching a movie, leaning her head on Tess's shoulder, holding her hand... She didn't need more. She didn't want more.[7]

Again, bringing up the champagne and ginger ale metaphor, the difference between a crush and a squish is maybe just in how that attraction personally feels to *you*.

Sensual Attraction

"A desire to do sensual (but not sexual) things with certain people, especially relating to tactile sensuality such as cuddling."

While the word "sensual" may conjure up a certain sense of eroticism, in reality sensual attraction ultimately has more to do with *sensation* than *sex*. More specifically, the pleasure of engaging your physical senses, including the sense of touch.

Think of how it feels to get a good massage by a licensed massage therapist. Physically, the practice is extremely pleasant, though not sexual in nature (at least I would hope not during a professional session).

In the same way, one may desire touch from others that isn't erotic or necessarily romantic in nature.

For instance, in Korean slang, there's even a term called "skinship," combining the words "skin" and "friendship," that describes the non-sexual physical affection found between friends and family members.[8]

The merits of touch have been noted not only culturally but also scientifically.

Kangaroo care, otherwise known as the "kangaroo hold," is the practice of holding a baby that involves skin-to-skin contact. It yields a number of positive effects for the child, including stabilizing heart rate, improving breathing patterns, helping with sleep, and even reducing the mortality rate of premature babies.[9]

And babies aren't the only ones who benefit.

For years, scientists have documented the benefits of physical touch, noting how simple cases of human contact help to reduce negative health outcomes, such as anxiety, depression, and immune system disorders.[10]

"Skin hunger," the longing for touch, is a documented psychological phenomenon, in which human beings *literally* crave physical contact from others, in much the same way as we crave food. A simple warm touch can signal to the brain safety and comfort, reducing cardiovascular stress and triggering the release of the hormone oxytocin, otherwise known as "the love hormone," which regulates stress levels and positive emotions."

Based on all that, it would seem that one of the most potent forms of human intimacy is touch.

To limit touch to the confines of a sexual and/or romantic context seems to me almost unnecessarily cruel and restrictive. If some forms of affection may feel more appropriate to you within the context of certain relationships, such as kissing a romantic partner, that's fine. However, the next time you want to cuddle or hold hands with your platonic bestie, I'd say go for it (with their consent, of course).

Aesthetic Attraction

"An attraction to other people that is not connected to a desire to do anything with them, either sexually or romantically. They simply appreciate their appearance."

Out all of the attractions, this one seems the simplest to explain.

Aesthetic attraction basically describes appreciation for another person's appearance. Now, while aesthetic attraction may in part be tied to romantic or sexual attraction (or not, since plenty of people seem to have sex with people they don't find visually appealing), it can also exist on its own.

In the same way that we can appreciate a pretty painting or a beautiful landscape, but have no personal reason to touch it, we can also appreciate another person's appearance without feeling pulled to make out or have sex with them.

As aesthetic attraction is very subjective—beauty being in the eye of the beholder and all—and every person has their own individual preferences for aesthetics (personally, I tend to prefer dark-haired characters in shows to blond, but that's just my thing).

While it might be easy to confuse aesthetic attraction for

romantic or sexual attraction (or at least have other people assume that you have a "thing" for someone just because you say they look nice), it helps to remember that "beauty" is only skin-deep, and what counts most is what's beneath the surface.

Which brings me to...

The Primary vs. Secondary Attraction Model

This is a hypothetical model of sexuality that divides sexual attraction into two subcategories, primary and secondary:

★ **Primary Sexual Attraction:** A sexual attraction to people based on instantly available information (such as their appearance or smell) which may or may not lead to arousal or sexual desire.

★ **Secondary Sexual Attraction:** A sexual attraction that develops over time based on a person's relationship and emotional connection with another person.*

In other words, primary attraction can be defined as "first impression" attraction—getting to know the "primary" layer or surface layer of a person right off the bat, such as their aesthetics and charisma—while secondary attraction requires a deeper look, delving into the layer underneath—the person's core personality, ethics, etc.

Many aces, especially aces who also identify as demisexual, find this model useful for explaining why the concept of "lust at first sight" might be a bit difficult for them. For many aces who only experience sexual attraction after an emotional connection is made, secondary attraction can help to clarify the factors needed to experience a particular kind of attraction, particularly time and trust.

* "Primary vs. Secondary Sexual Attraction Model." AVENwiki, http://wiki. asexuality.org/Primary_vs._secondary_sexual_attraction_model.

Though no judgment toward those who experience either! Another good model to use is...

The Split Attraction Model

According to LGBTQIA+ Wiki, the Split Attraction Model (SAM) "separates romantic attraction or desire for romantic relationships from sexual attraction or desire, thus dividing romantic orientation and sexual orientation into different identities."*

Examples of this include:

★ **Homoromantic asexual:** A person who does not experience sexual attraction, but can experience romantic attraction to people of the same gender.

★ **Biromantic demisexual:** A person who can experience romantic attraction to more than one gender, yet only experiences sexual attraction after an emotional connection is built.

★ **Aromantic pansexual:** A person who experiences little to no romantic attraction to anyone, yet can experience sexual attraction to people, regardless of gender.

According to this model, there's a nearly infinite number of possibilities for identity combinations.

Now, while not all aces feel comfortable with this model or find it useful (many asexuals prefer referring to themselves solely as ace and do not wish to define themselves by romantic attraction), the split attraction model has proven to be pretty useful for some to explain the nuanced way they experience attraction, both romantically and sexually.

* "Split Attraction Model." LGBTQIA+ Wiki, https://lgbtqia.fandom.com/wiki/Split_Attraction_Model.

For those who identify as both asexual *and* queer, the split attraction model acknowledges their multidisciplinary position within the wider LGBTQIA+ community.

Now before anyone can excuse me of making this up or saying that the SAM is just another "modern" (therefore "uselessly millennial") invention, the idea of distinguishing orientations is actually a concept that can trace its origins further back in history. German researcher Karl Heinrich Ulrichs, considered to be among the first pioneers of sexology and an advocate for the modern queer rights movement, was one of many scholars to discuss how certain people may develop different feelings for different genders, documenting heterosexual men who expressed "tender" (i.e. romantic) feelings for men and women, yet only expressed "passionate" (i.e. sexual) feelings toward the latter.[12]

American psychologist Dorothy Tennov, author of *Love and Limerence*, used the term "limerence" to describe romantic love where physical attraction was not the main focus, stating, "the most consistent desired result of limerence is mating, not merely sexual interaction but also commitment."[13]

Many today even use the phrase "affectional orientation"* (i.e. a person's romantic preference for certain genders) as an alternative term for sexual orientation, to emphasize the emotional aspect of orientation away from sexuality.

Conclusion

What can I say?

Attraction is complicated.

Considering the various forms of attraction listed above, one can

---

* "Affectional Orientation." Dictionary.com, www.dictionary.com/browse/affectional-orientation.

gather that attraction is not always clear-cut, and, in fact, various forms of attraction may overlap with one another.

Now, the point of this isn't to give you a headache or make your head spin from over-analyzing.

The point is to expand our thinking about what "attraction" is. To turn away from the notion that all attractions to another person/other people are physical/erotic in nature, and to understand that the pull we feel to others, to form intimate social bonds or relationships with them, is not always romantic and/or sexual, and can be multifaceted.

By recognizing that we may all experience attraction in different ways to different degrees, we can increase our emotional intelligence, to understand when we may be "falling" for someone simply based on their looks, or whether the connection might be deeper, and to understand there is no universal standard for attraction.

Ultimately, when thinking about the type of "attraction" you may be currently experiencing or may experience in the future, it's up to you to trust your personal intuition to assess your own emotions.

However, talking about it with someone you trust is always recommended.

The Flip Side of the Asexuality Coin: Aromanticism

While asexuality is defined as the orientation in which one experiences little to no *sexual* attraction, aromanticism is the orientation in which someone experiences little to no *romantic* attraction.

Although many allo folks tend to conflate being asexual with being aromantic, in reality they are two completely different identities.

Still, when it comes to asexuality and aromanticism, often one does find overlap between the two.

Both orientations are identified by an "absence."

Both engage in deconstructing societal expectations around relationships.

Both face a similar type of invisibility within mainstream media, sharing a disappointing lack of authentic representation and a general lack of resources (i.e. educational, medical, etc.). *Sigh.*

And both have their misconceptions and stereotypes, which include the idea that aro and ace are "cold," "broken," and "robotic."

It is because of these similarities and the fact that ace individuals will sometimes also discover that they are aromantic or somewhere on the aro spectrum, or aro folks might realize they're also asexual or somewhere on the ace spectrum, that I feel it's worth mentioning in this book.

In reality, asexuality and aromanticism sometimes run as parallel tracks, existing alongside each other but never touching.

And other times they intersect within the same body.

As Angela Chen said, "The aromantic community is connected to the asexual community, but not everyone who is aromantic is asexual." And vice versa.

So, without further ado, let's get into some things.

Being Aro Doesn't Make You "Loveless"

I've noticed that for many of us, when we first come out as ace and are trying to explain who we are, we often immediately say, "But I can still experience romantic attraction" or "But I still want to fall in love," as a way of combating the deromanticization that is often associated with being ace. This can be a legitimate desire.

At the same time, there sometimes seems to be an undercurrent of repudiation with that "but," a hasty denial of anything aromantic, as if to say just because we're ace doesn't mean we're "heartless," as if equating being aromantic with being "loveless."

So first of all, let me get one thing "straight."

Being aromantic, experiencing little to no romantic attraction, doesn't make a person "heartless," "unloving," or "loveless."

While amanormativity[2] suggests that everyone aspires to be in a romantic relationship (while also prioritizing it above other relationships, such as platonic), the reality is that, like allonormativity, amanormativity is a made-up system designed to make people feel bad if they don't conform to expectations of being "sexual" or "romantic" in the way mainstream society expects.

The majority of fictional narratives, from literary to cinematic, feature romantic storylines, whether as the main focus or as a major subplot—especially if it's considered "women's fiction," since apparently romance is something all women are focused on (*rolls eyes*). When every fictional storyline feels like it must exist with a romantic plotline, what does it say for our stories in real life? That our lives are worth less without a love interest in the picture?

This reminds me of an anecdote from comedian Katherine Ryan's stand-up special *Glitter Room*, in which she talks about attending a friend's aunt's funeral:

> It was a beautiful day, and her aunt was such an inspiring woman. She lived to be ninety-five years old, she escaped the Nazis, and started an incredible business. And as we saw her off, a man next to us said, "Oh, so sad. Ninety-five years old and never able to find a man."
>
> I was like, "How do you think she lived so long?"[3]

Best burn ever!

It is sad to realize that if one's life—even a life as incredible as the one described above—doesn't include or isn't centered around romantic love or attraction, then that life is considered "sad."

And, honestly, aromantic folks get a really rough break as it is.

The "Villainous Aromantic Asexual"[4] is so ubiquitous as a stock character in media, being known for their depravity and antisocial tendencies in part because they can't seem to form intimate (i.e. romantic) relationships and/or they express no interest in them, that any person in real life who's not in a relationship or not seeking one is considered to have something morally wrong or reprehensible about them.

(For the record, there is no moral superiority for someone who experiences romantic attraction versus someone who doesn't. A person also isn't automatically a fuckboy/girl/enby if they're interested in sex without romantic attachment involved. Same goes if you're allosexual/alloromantic, too.)

If anything, think of it this way.

An alloromantic man who frequently cheats on his girlfriend ("cheating" defined as acting dishonestly by not giving all involved parties informed consent, i.e. hooking up with other people when in a committed relationship without their partner's awareness) is probably less ethical than an aromantic man who experiences no romantic attraction whatsoever with the women he sexually engages with, yet communicates his intentions clearly and honestly.

I also really hope it goes without saying that there is an obvious difference between someone who uses people for sex and someone who may not experience romantic attraction or desire a romantic relationship, yet still treats the people with whom they interact with respect and consent.

Honestly, many of the aromantic people I know subvert the stereotypes I've talked about, being some of the warmest, kindest, and most affectionate individuals I know.

Many aromantic individuals, even without experiencing romantic attraction (although many can and do form romantic or romantic-esque partnerships), can still form caring, loving relationships, including with friends, family, and even queerplatonic partners (which we will get into later).

Just as Leo Tolstoy said, "If it is true there are as many minds as there are heads, then there are as many kinds of love as there are hearts,"[5] and there are as many types of love one can form and experience in this world, regardless of whether you experience romantic love or sexual attraction.

The point is that in trying to validate our asexual identities and community, we cannot throw the aromantic community under the bus.

Otherwise, we would just be hurting those like us, both aro-aces who exist as part of both worlds and the general aromantic community whose unique struggles to be recognized and seen as human mirror so much of the ace community's.

On Marriage and Queerplatonic Relationships

Remember that word I mentioned earlier, "queerplatonic"? Let's circle back to that.

A queerplatonic relationship* (also known as a QPR) is considered to be a close relationship between two or more individuals that is emotionally intimate in nature, without necessarily being sexual and/or romantic. While, on the surface, a queerplatonic relationship may look like a "just friends" situation, a QPR is meant to infer a deeper level of commitment than a casual acquaintanceship. While the specific context of a QPR may vary from pair to pair (or triad, quad, etc.), the general framework may resemble that of a romantic partnership, including sharing physical actions that are traditionally thought to be reserved for couples (such as kissing, cuddling, sex, etc.), sharing the same domestic space, or raising a family together, without the element of romantic love.

The word queerplatonic may refer to "queering" (as a verb) the idea of a relationship, not in the sense that the occupants of a QPR are themselves LGBTQ+ (although many are), but in that it disrupts traditional ideas surrounding intimacy and love.

Take, for instance, queer writer Deidre Olsen who, in their essay "Why I Married My Platonic Best Friend," describes how they and

* "Queerplatonic Relationship." LGBTQIA+ Wiki, https://lgbtqia.fandom.com/wiki/Queerplatonic_relationship.

their "platonic soulmate," Chiderah, decided to get married: "As in many marriages, Chiderah and I pledged to spend our lives together in a partnership based on caregiving and emotional support. Unlike most marriages, we've also decided to not make romance the hallmark of our relationship."[1]

While the two seem to have incompatible orientations, with Olsen labeling themselves as gay and Chiderah as straight, the writer claims that they both "found in each other the unconditional love and acceptance" they've always dreamed of. And although their marriage is not defined by sex or romantic love in the way most "traditional marriages" are often considered to be, Olsen went on to say in the article that they intended on planning a life together, including one with pets, possibly children, and a domestic space shared together.

In the *New York Times* article "From Best Friends to Platonic Spouses," the author interviewed a series of married couples, none of whom claimed to be physically intimate or romantic with the other. Throughout the piece, the couples stated their various reasons for getting married, including finding emotional support, establishing an "official" familial unit, and "legally" recognizing their strong emotional connection with their respective "partners." As one of the couples stated, "Isn't the point to marry your best friend?... So why can't it be your literal best friend?"[2]

While the word "queerplatonic" may seem like a recent term (evolving out of the relatively modern coalition of the "asexual" community—although, let's face it, aces have probably existed since the beginning of time), the concept itself is not new.

"Boston marriages" (the term said to have been inspired by Henry James's 1886 novel, *The Bostonians*) was a term used in the nineteenth and early twentieth century to refer to two unmarried (as in not married to men) women who lived together, essentially sharing a domestic life together.[3] While many queer historians have theorized that some of these Boston marriages were actually lesbian or Sapphic in nature (because why not?), there is also the very real possibility that the individuals may have been ace/aro and/or simply living together platonically.

And on the subject of marriage, historically speaking, marriage was not traditionally reserved for those in "love" (referring to romantic love, that is). In early records of marriage contracts, marriage was literally just that: "a contract"—a logistical alliance or business proposition that ensured the political unification of different groups, the acquisition of land, and the legitimization of heirs (if a woman only "belonged" to one man sexually, then the chances of any stray "baby daddies" were decreased exponentially).[4]

Romantic, right?

Now, I'm not denying the cultural significance of marriage. As a ritual, marriage can hold a lot of emotional and spiritual value, as a way of observing one's familial traditions, as well as honoring a commitment in a publicly recognized manner, including through recognition by one's family, friends, and state.

However, it is the limitations within the institution of marriage that are the issue.

In their article "The Escalating Costs of Being Single in America," Anne Helen Petersen details how the expenses of living in America—rent, health care, student loans, utility bills, food, etc.—seem to be accumulating to the degree that it's no longer manageable (if it ever was) in a single-income household: "All the expenses of existing in society, on one set of shoulders."[5]

The writer goes on to say how American society is more organized to accommodate the lives of partnered and cohabitating people (i.e. married people), through the way it not only celebrates people being married more than being single, but also financially rewards them. As Petersen points out, "so many of the structural privileges of partnership still revolve around the institution of marriage. (The

US Census still conceives of the status of 'single' as anyone who is not, at present, married.)"

Married couples (because marriage is often reserved for couples) get certain legal and monetary privileges that single people do not, including (at least in the U.S.) marital tax deductions, health insurance benefits, hospital visiting privileges, etc. A social and financial safety net if you will. Which means anyone who's not married, such as non-partner-seeking folks and divorcees, are screwed.

Hell, it can be financially *hostile* to be single (though, again, I can only speak from a North American perspective). Makes you want to scream, right?

Petersen goes on to say:

> Marriage is stabilizing, then, but largely for people who are *already* stable or on the route to it. It's become a tool of class reproduction, benefiting those who've always benefited within the American class hierarchy: financially stable white men and the women married to them.

And if we're talking about those who specifically benefit from marriage, we also need to talk about the people who have historically been denied marriage. Until 2015, same-sex marriage in the U.S. was not universally legalized, and at the time of writing this book, disabled individuals continue to lack marriage equality, as "the disability marriage penalty punishes people with disabilities in the U.S. who get married by stripping them of disability benefits such as Social Security benefits and Medicaid."[6]

Which is so messed up on *so* many levels.

Beyond the need to establish full marriage equality (as in marriage equality where people with disabilities can get married without losing their income, disability benefits, or health insurance), maybe we ought to reconsider if marriage should be given so much privilege.

And on that point, why not consider building better support systems, so that those who wish to be partnered and those that don't do not have to be financially compromised or pushed between choosing their living benefits and living the life they want to live?

We need to recognize that romantic attachments, while nice for those who have them, are not the "be all and end all" for everyone.

That anyone, regardless of whether they experience romantic attraction or not, can have strong, emotionally fulfilling bonds that enrich, if not save, our lives.

And we need to recognize that romantic attachments and feelings, while nice for those who have them, are not the highest attachment we can make.

Queerplatonic bonds, or any other strong emotional connections, can be just as valid and powerful as romantic relationships and marriages, if not even more so sometimes.

Models of Love

As a history nerd, one of the things I love about ancient Greece (bypassing the misogyny and slavery for a minute) is the philosophical recognition of different types of love as follows:

★ *Eros* (sexual love, a carnal attraction defined by sexual or erotic desire, related to the Greek god of love, Eros)
★ *Philia* (love between friends, opposite of "phobia," fear)
★ *Ludus* (playful love, defined by casual flirting, light-hearted banter, and games)
★ *Agape* (unconditional, selfless love, often associated with love for a spiritual being like G-d*)
★ *Pragma* ("business-like" love, love that is convenient or pragmatic, i.e. a political marriage or "longstanding" love, a mature, realistic love built on compromise and patience)
★ *Philautia* (love of self, self-love)
★ *Storge* (familial love).[1]

As a small exercise, think for a moment of the different relationships in your life and see where they might fit into the seven Greek models.

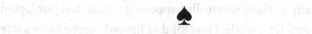

* "Why do some Jews write 'G-d' instead of 'God'?" ReformJudaism.org, https://reformjudaism.org/learning/answers-jewish-questions/why-do-some-jews-write-g-d-instead-god.

Interview with Julie Sondra Decker

This is a transcript of an audio inter-view. This interview has been condensed and edited for clarity.

Michele: Hello, and thank you for taking the time to talk with me today! So my first question is, how would you define yourself both as a person and as a person on a sexual spectrum?

Julie: Well, I guess, first and foremost, I'm a writer, activist, and educator. I am a forty-four-year-old cisgender, white, non-disabled woman of Jewish descent, and I am an aromantic, asexual person.

Michele: So how did you come into the realization of your ace identity?

Julie: Well, when I was the age that people generally are when they start figuring out who they like romantically, sexually, nothing was really happening for me. So I just "opted out" for a while; I just kind of figured maybe I was a late bloomer. But by the time I was about fifteen, I thought that had gone on too long for me to say that it was just "late blooming-ness," so I called myself non-sexual and I didn't think it was permanent. I didn't think it was going to be like that forever. I just wasn't really in any rush to change that. And I dated a little bit, but it was always someone else's idea. And my relationships were never very satisfying for me because they were always mostly defined by other people wishing that I would want things that I don't want. So by the time I got to college, I was just using the term "non-sexual" and I chose not to date anyone, and mainly just told people that I had already followed other people's ideas of what I should be doing and what I should be wanting, and never found anything from taking their advice. So, I would need a sign from myself, my body, my mind to change that, and it has never happened.

So, sometime down the road, I started to see that some people online were responding to messages I had written. Like I had a rants page on my little website in the late 1990s and I used to write rants on there about various things that annoyed me. I made a "top ten" list of the things that I hate when people say these things to me when I say I'm not interested in sex. At that time, not being interested in sex, and not being interested in dating, and not being attracted to anyone were all just this one big mishmash of things I wasn't interested in. I didn't understand that they were really different things because I had no community. I had nobody to talk to about those things. I just figured it was just a big off-switch for me. So, it took a while before I got a more nuanced understanding of the different attractions that I am collectively not experiencing, but that took a community, that took definitions, that took evolution.

Michele: Evolution. I like that term.

Julie: I received some nice messages from people, mostly comments on my essays about the things [about asexuality]
that I don't like being told, such as "you must have just
got out of a bad relationship" or "you're secretly a lesbian
and you haven't accepted it."

Michele: Of course. [Sarcastically.]

Julie: Those kinds of things. I organized them in a "top ten" list
format. At the time I was listing, "you must have just
gotten out of a bad relationship" was number one, most
common. I think number two was "you can't find a man,"
which is like almost the opposite of the first one, and
they always assume it's a man. It's annoying. Anyway, I
got some messages from other people who felt similarly;
most of them seemed like they had had a worse time than
me because I was more, I don't know, I was pretty happy
with myself. I was pretty confident. I didn't have a lot
of self-esteem issues. And even though I'd heard these
negative messages, I had not really internalized them. I
had never felt that "broken" kind of thing that so many
ace people talk about when they realize that there's a
community of people like them and think "maybe I'm
not 'broken.'" I never felt that, but I felt so sad when
other people did that I wanted to do more writing about
it. I wanted to do more education about it. But it was
also in its infancy, you know, and this is before AVEN. So
when AVEN did start to exist, I actually didn't join it for
a really long time because I kind of thought it was more
for people to reach out for support and I didn't really feel
like I needed any support personally.

Michele: You wanted to be a support system for someone else,
right?

Julie: Right. Eventually, I just decided to start a YouTube chan-
           nel based on my "top ten" list that I wrote in the 1990s
           and I made little individual videos just talking about it.
              It was very heavily focused on my experience, though.
           And I made some mistakes. I didn't really get a lot of
           call-outs for it, mostly just harassing trolls. I didn't get
           fallouts from my own side, but I later recognized a lot
           of things that I realized later were not complicated
           enough or were possibly throwing other members of my
           community under the bus. And I wrote about that and
           talked about that later in my career as an activist. But,
           you know, eventually I came to the conclusion that it was
           right around the time that I started making the YouTube
           videos that I started using the word "asexual" instead of
           "non-sexual" because it connected me to the community.

Michele: What I want to say to that is that you were kind of like
           one of the first ones. You came out in the 1990s and that's
           before even AVEN existed. So I think you can give your-
           self a little credit for the mistakes you made because
           literally you were paving the road for someone like me
           to come along and write, too. Because, like you, I didn't
           necessarily internalize the feeling I was "broken," but I
           am disheartened by how many people say they are. And
           so, and partially because of your legacy, I'm able to write
           about the stuff I do today.

Julie: Yeah, that's what I was always hoping to do with the stuff
           that I was doing. I didn't quite know that I was doing it
           at the time because I was mostly writing it just because
           I've always written about myself. I've always written what
           I was thinking. Not necessarily because I needed anyone
           to help me confirm it or conceptualize it, but more just
           because I've always felt like I just need to get stuff out

there, and it turned out to be helpful for some people that were not used to hearing the kind of things I was saying, and I was like, "Okay, that kind of galvanizes me, right?" That makes me want to make more for people to be able to find because I don't want people to feel like that in a society like ours where, if the stats are correct, ninety-nine out of a hundred people are not like us.

Michele: Which brings me to the subject of *The Invisible Orientation*.[1] What motivated you to write this book?

Julie: I felt like there needed to be a mainstream published book on the topic. And there were some that predated me. But one was academic Anthony Bogart's book on asexuality. It was not written from an ace perspective and it was very technical, and then a couple of self-published books predated me, but they don't have the distribution that mainstream published books do. And what was really frustrating for me about there being no really accessible mainstream books on the topic is that not only can the people who need to be able to find them for themselves, they're not able to find them in their libraries or their bookstores, but the people who control their lives are in that same situation. Those tend to be more "traditional" people, people who may give more credence to "traditional" publications; they may not want to take something seriously if they have to go watch a YouTube video about it or buy a self-published book from the internet. They may think, "Okay, this is fake, this is internet stuff." And even though I think all of that stuff is just as valid, and I really like that we have developed all of these alternate paths to getting information out, not being controlled entirely through mainstream channels, we still needed to be represented in those channels if some of those people who control those readers' lives are going to be able to understand and take us seriously. And, of course, it also opens doors to mainstream press doing stories on us and just having something come up when they type it into the bookstore computer. So I just wanted something to be there for them to find.

Michele: Yeah, there is a certain legitimacy that paper text can give to a subject. Like you said, internet culture is very valid, but there's also something very tangible about going to a library or going to the bookstore and then seeing something available. And it says a lot about access, too. Like how for so long asexuals didn't have access to the materials that they needed to learn about themselves, to learn that they weren't alone or weren't "broken." And so right now there's still a lot of controversy because there's an active surge in book banning and conservative parties, like you said, wanting to control the media we consume. So we need to keep pushing that, to keep all channels of information, all chance of access available, whether digital or print.

Julie: Right. And I wanted the book to be like...I called it an introduction to asexuality partly because I knew other books would have more nuance and more focus on certain things. Like, Angela Chen's book is amazing and I felt like it was a lot more personal narrative driven and that was something that people kind of said mostly they missed in my book. It was kind of by design, and that's why I included with permission several ace bloggers—I don't know, sixteen of them or so—quotes to humanize it because I really wanted to lean away from it being *my* personal narrative. I had already done that, and there was honestly enough of that out there already. So I wanted there to be a more broad tone about the whole thing. You could never cover everything because you're never going to be able to anticipate everything. And it is an internet-based movement largely, so we are seeing changes in terminology that are very rapid, but at the same time, I felt like it would pave the way for more people to be able to write about those things in mainstream markets, too.

Michele: Well, as someone who's read your book, I still find a lot of the information in the book very relevant today. Even if people say they prefer Angela Chen's book, there's still room for your text, too. There shouldn't be a monolith for asexual voices.

Julie: Right. I think that I happened to get pretty lucky with the timing. I think, even twelve months before, it might not have been as well received.

Just some of the pushback that I got in the publishing world when I was trying to find an agent for the project and trying to find a publisher for it after I got the agent. It's just...some of it was very ignorant. I got one agent saying...I mean, he had obviously never heard of asexuality and he seemed to think that I had made it up.

And even though I referenced the existence of a community, it was like he read every other line or something, and just explaining to me, well, "if" asexual people exist, you know, if they're out there, they probably do not consider themselves in any way to be queer. And I'm like, "Why don't you ask us?" We asked us. Incidentally, here's how many of us use that word, and here's how many of us consider ourselves queer allies. And, you know, this is definitely where we would look for books on ourselves. But what do I know? I'm just a community leader in the community that you think I just "made up." [Sarcastically.]

Michele: Yeah, it sucks that ignorance was like that for you. And it sucks that it's like that today, unfortunately, in some ways. I once went to a book event where this aromantic writer said that a publisher wanted her to erase her main character's aromantic orientation because they didn't think it would be "marketable."

Julie: The only thing that can make you "interesting" is if you have a romantic arc. [Laughs.]

Michele: Or a sexual one.

Julie: Right. It's just that so many of us would be relieved and excited to see aromantic main characters or even characters whose whole narrative is not motivated by romance and/or sex.

Michele: Speaking as someone who's on both the asexual and aromatic spectrums, are there any interesting ways that you find your identities intersecting in your life?

Julie: Well, being asexual and being aromantic, I feel like that is the double A there. I don't have to deal with any of those things. I don't have to deal with the expectations of romance, and that way inside of the relationships that I have, there isn't a sexual expectation because everyone that I keep in my life understands.

I'm forty-four, and a woman, never had children, never got married, and never had a sexual partner. People don't have a nice word for that. If anything, it's a sad word. It's something like, "you don't want to be like her." And for some reason they just assume I have cats, which is not true. I'm allergic to them. But it's awful that that is how they think of it, that it's synonymous with loneliness to them. And it's not synonymous with loneliness to me.

Michele: I think there's also something to be said when talking about gender with asexuality. So many times when you see media, you see people like David Jay and *BoJack Horseman*, you see these male figures of asexuality. But meanwhile, a lot of times when I go to ace meet-up groups, the majority is femme aces because not a lot of male aces in real life would identify as asexual because (a) they don't have the resources and (b) society has taught them it's shameful to be a man who is not intrinsically "horny" for sex all the time.

Julie: Yes, but with men, I think the idea that you are a successful and worthy human is tied up with being sexually successful. So a lot of them just don't want to think that there's anything wrong with them or be dehumanized.

Michele: Yeah. And I think a lot of the time it's kind of the opposite, at least in terms of romance for women, because so many of our narratives are around finding a partner, specifically finding a man. And so when you take that out of the equation, that kind of says, "What are you as a woman?" You're just incomplete.

Julie: Yeah, there's a lot of assumptions about what we must be feeling, and that anything else we say about it must be overcompensation or trying to "save face" because we're embarrassed that we're unloved or that we are not "chosen" by someone. That's just throughout history, the idea of becoming marriageable has been so tied up with womanhood. Like you're going to end up old and alone and, "Oh my G-d, you're not going to have kids!"

Michele: Well, you can definitely have kids without a man.

Julie: You certainly can. At least in my case, I'm not planning to do that either. But it's just...it's very ignorant. It just makes a lot of assumptions, and then grafts them on to me. And those things are not in my head. They're obviously in my head now because people keep putting them there, but they're certainly not the things that came from any insecurities that I have or any emptiness that exists in my life.

Michele: Speaking as someone assigned female at birth, a lot of my culture places heavy importance on marriage. I feel like there's a ticking "time bomb" for me as a person to be partnered, which is very exhausting to deal with.

Julie: Yeah. And the longer it goes on, the more people assume that you are intrinsically upset about this. I mean, if I die a happy centenarian, people will still say what a shame it was.

Michele: Yeah. Ageism, it's definitely a factor both in the ace community and in the allo community as well. Which is something we need to talk about more. But I feel like there's also...as we get older, when we see older people of the LGBTQIA+ community like Ace Dad,* who I'm not sure if you're familiar with or not?

Julie: Oh, yes, I am!

Michele: It's really lovely to see. But also there's this double-edged knife idea of queer mentors because you and Cody are relatively "not old," but within the LGBTQIA+ community you two very much stand out because we don't see a lot of elders or people who live to be older in life and could share their guidance and experience with others.

Julie: He's only a few years older than me. Which is funny because he's got the gray hair and the beard and stuff, so he kind of looks all "mature," and I've got my fuzzy sweater and my pink hair thing...but I'm forty-four. [Laughs.]

---

* Ace Dad, otherwise known as Cody Daigle-Orians is an asexual writer, educator, and creator of "Ace Dad Advice," an online project that aims to help young people and those questioning their sexuality find the courage and confidence to live their best ace life.

Michele: I love the fact that you both exist because there is contentment to be found in your lives as older aces.

Julie: Mmm. Yeah, definitely. I think it is a problem that we don't have that many people who are my age and older. Really, it was very strange to me even ten years ago that people considered me almost an "elder" because there were mostly in the ace groups, you did see people who skewed young. But that was also because of where we were doing that research. I mean, we were all standing in on online communities. And did you see the ace documentary (A)sexual?[2]

Michele: Yes, I've watched it.

Julie: I like that they interviewed an older person who was a pilot. I think her name was Barb, and she talked about identifying as a lesbian for a really long time, but just not really being interested in sex. And she tried to, she had lots of sex, and it just wasn't her thing. I thought that was really cool that they included her. It was refreshing to see an older person who was not really in the community for most of her life. She came to that identity after a long time of relating more closely to another one. And you can't say that somebody, especially that age, was following some kind of internet trend.

Michele: I find that a lot of us throughout our lives work through different labels. We're working with what's available. Like lots of people who identify as non-binary today may have identified in the past differently before they found the right label that they feel comfortable with, you know? It's all about taking the time to figure out what fits. And time, whether it relates to ageism, it's just something we also need to talk about taking the pressure off. Like if you find out you're ace at fifteen, amazing for you! If you find out you're ace at fifty-five, also amazing for you!

Okay, one last question: what would you like to see for the future of this community?

Julie: For the community? Oh my gosh! Well, I definitely would like to see more community leaders, both coming forward and being supported by others who are not white. I love what Yasmin Benoit has been doing. She's pretty amazing. I would like to see more disabled people talking about asexuality and disability intersection, how it works for them. I would like to see a diversification of the talking heads and stuff. And even though I understand that people are going to keep coming to me because I wrote a book and I did a lot of stuff that turned out to kind of be pioneering, sort of by accident, sometimes by design... But I'm a white woman and white people have a lot of options. And I tick a lot of the boxes for "unassailable" asexual. So it's easy to write off other people, but still accept me, and I don't like that. So I think that maybe other people like me and other people who are mainstream activists can do more work trying to bring in more people of less represented backgrounds of all kinds. And I would like there to be more books. I would like there to be more media representation. It's happening. And I think, other than that, I just want to see what happens.

Like I want to see the creativity of our community give rise to new concepts, high-level discussions, more conferences, and maybe more inclusivity in the LGBTQ community. It's happening more now than it was even back when my book was published. I think that some of the sections of my book that talked about the LGBTQ community sound different now because it's so much more inclusive now than it was when I wrote it. I was a lot more cautious. Like I didn't want ace people to get hurt. I didn't want them to try to go to these meetings (LGBTQ meetings) and find out, "We don't count you, we think you're straight." If you think about it, that's kind of homophobic, to be like, "Well, if you're not interested in anyone, that's straight by default." [Laughs.] Like that's not how it works.

Michele: But it is getting better.

Julia: It is getting better. And I would like to see that continue.

And I would definitely like to see just more automatic inclusion of the ace perspective, not just in special panels and specific talks at conferences, but also with how we talk about sex in general. I would love to see less assumption that sex is part of everyone's life. I would like to see less virgin shaming and less shaming on the other side for asexual people who do have sex. We can change our language pretty easily to be inclusive. I would really like to stop hearing phrasing like, "Just like everyone else, we want to find love."

Michele: There's room for aros, there's room for everyone in the conversation.

Julie: I think so.

Julie Sondra Decker (she/her) is an author from Tampa, Florida. She writes fantasy and science fiction for adults and children, and is known as a prominent voice for the asexual community. Her non-fiction title *The Invisible Orientation* (Skyhorse/Carrel) was published in September 2014. Her non-writing interests include baking, drawing, singing, cartoon fandom, drinking coffee, and engaging through social media.

PART IV

ON SEX AND INTIMACY

Let's Talk about Sex

Now, some of you may be wondering why a book on asexuality would have a section on sex.

And frankly, it's because, as aces, we need one.

One of the first things to understand is that asexuality does not equal celibacy. A lack of sexual attraction doesn't always correlate with lack of interest in sex.

The truth is, like everything else about the ace community, attitudes about sex exist on a spectrum.

Some aces may be what might be referred to as sex-repulsed or sex-averse (which sound similar, but are also slightly different in their exact definition, which I will be getting into later), in that they have little or no interest in sex and/ or do not wish to engage with sex or sexual content at all, while others are more open to the idea of sex and adjacent materials (i.e. porn, sex toys, etc.). Some may actually start out in life with one attitude and find themselves flipping or changing to another

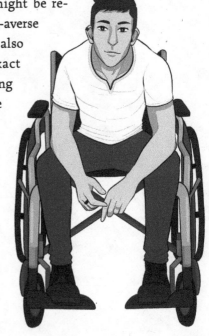

for various reasons, including hormonal flux, genuine curiosity, and more.

As such, asexuals (like everyone else) require inclusive educational resources on sexual health, including information on contraception/reproductive measures, consent, guides on finding and maintaining healthy social partnerships (sexual, romantic, and platonic), etc., in order to validate their mental and physical autonomy, as well as achieve physical experiences that are both ethical and pleasurable.

In the Beginning...

If you had anything like the sex education I did growing up, you didn't get much of it.

Sure, they taught us about standard stuff, like STIs and condoms (which is more than many students in more conservative regions can say), but overall I found the class redundant, boring, and lacking, especially when it came to education on non-cis-het identities. And this was back in 2010s Brooklyn, New York.

Yet while my education was lacking, my curiosity was not.

As an asexual person, even when the practice of sex was not something I was actively drawn to, the theory of it was (and continues) to be interesting.

As a writer, sex intrigued me as a plot device. Akin to a song in a musical, it couldn't just be placed in randomly, but had to fit into the larger narrative arc, used as an action to help move the story forward. And it fascinated me in the ways it spoke about human bodies, as well as human connection, reflecting on the elements of intimacy, care, and touch.

And if I wanted to have sex in the future, I wanted to be prepared, so that I wouldn't be caught off guard and get hurt or potentially hurt partners in the process.

Yet that wasn't really what I got out of sex ed. What I got instead was erasure.

Negligence (even if educators hadn't intended it, that was what it was) left me and other LGBTQIA+ students in the lurch. Where was the information on safe sex that went beyond P-in-V (penis in vagina) penetration? Where was the information on how to have safe sex as a person whose body may not fit the typical male/female binary? And where was the information on how to navigate sex and intimate relationships, including specifically as an asexual person?

All these blank spaces left me confused, frustrated, and hungry for actual information I could use.

Luckily, thanks to the help of libraries and online resources, such as informational web comics and even fanfiction, I soon found other means of education that were more thorough, diverse, and entertaining.

And while I am not a licensed sex educator (and would never claim to be one), I do want to touch base on some of the lessons I've learned about sex and how that might apply to the asexual community.

Sex-Positive, Sex-Neutral, Sex-Repulsed, Sex-Averse, Tomato, Tomahto, Etc.

Within the asexual community, you might casually come across these terms and have no idea what the heck any of them mean. Does sex-positive mean the willingness to engage in sex? Does not liking sex or not wanting sex make you sex-negative? What does sex-positive or sex-negative even mean?

Fortunately, we can try to break it down here.

Note that vocabulary within the ace community is often in flux, so the definitions below are generally aligned with what I know of the terms above.

Sex-Positive/Sex-Favorable

Before we proceed, I should note there are technically two definitions for this term here. Confusing, right?

The first definition of sex-positive, as it specifically applies to a sociopolitical movement addressing cultural attitudes about sex and sexuality, is "an attitude towards human sexuality that regards all consensual sexual activities as fundamentally healthy and pleasurable, encouraging sexual pleasure and experimentation."[1] Within this definition, there is the general belief that human sexuality encompasses a wide spectrum of identities and experiences, and that most sexual activities between consenting adult partners can be regarded as generally acceptable.

The second definition as it applies to a sex-positive asexual is often taken to mean an asexual who is willing to engage in and even interested in engaging in sexual activity (despite experiencing little to no attraction). The term is also used sometimes interchangeably with sex-favorable.

In my perspective, there is a slight difference. The way I see it, sex-positive can refer to attitude, while sex-favorable can refer to behavior.[2] This means an asexual person can be sex-positive, regarding other people's sexual behaviors (if done consensually, of course) with general acceptance, without necessarily being sex-favorable, meaning favorable toward engaging in sexual activity oneself. As one asexual stated, "For me, being sex-positive and ace means recognizing the importance of sex for others even if I lack a desire to have it with other people myself."[3]

It should be noted that regardless of whether you choose to engage in sex or not, neither is a moral indication of your level of "open-mindedness," or verdict on your authenticity as an asexual person.

In general, I find many asexuals fear being labeled as "sex-negative" upon disclosing their discomfort or disinterest in sex, fearing they may considered "prissy" or "prudish" or not "sexually liberated" enough in a culture that sometimes promotes competition of sexual "daring" (i.e. those who have the most partners or the most risqué adventures are often considered by many to be the most "sex-positive"). In reality, being sex-positive has nothing to do with the amount of sex you have (or don't have).

One definition of sex-positive that I personally love comes from queer sex educators and comics creators Erica Moen and Matthew Nolan, who interpret it to mean, "embracing what's **right for you** and being cool with other people doing what's **right for them** (*as* *long as it's consensual*) even if you might not understand the appeal personally."[4]

Or, as a sex-positive but non-sex-favorable character, such as Anwar from *Shades of A*, would say, "Hey I'm sex-positive! Positive I don't want it, ta very much, and I don't like it right in front of me."[5]

In my opinion, it doesn't really matter what label we give ourselves, as long as we understand that consent should always be prioritized, and that we as a society should work toward a culture that's less about "stigmatizing" and "shaming" sex and asexuality, and more about providing inclusive and comprehensive sex education that emphasizes respect and tolerance for all identities, orientations, and consensual practices (in which all individuals are able to make informed choices and decisions concerning their own bodies).

Sex-Negative

Now that we have covered sex-positive, let's try tackling its polar opposite term, sex-negative.

As opposed to the more liberal definition of sex-positivity's "anything goes as long as it's consensual" mentality, sex-negativity is a social attitude that is exactly what it sounds like—a negative attitude about sex, "a mind-set that sex is inherently dirty, dangerous, risky, pathological or deviant."[6]

Rather than simply viewing sex as a physical act like any other, sex is given an additional moral weight, as something that "stains" the person who engages in it. In a way, sex-negativity is the backbone of purity culture that says girls (and often it is only girls) are only "pure" if they manage to abstain from sex until marriage; otherwise, they are considered "unclean."[7]

Within sex-negativity, anything beyond the confines of a monogamous, married, and presumably heterosexual and procreative relationship is generally regarded as "wrong" or "immoral." Hell, even things that aren't necessarily sexual in nature, such as showing "excess" skin on a hot day or breastfeeding in public, are regarded with disgust and shame.

As social activist and sexuality educator Aida Manduley says, "Sex-negativity approaches sex and sexuality from a place of fear, oppression, and stigma."[8]

Examples of sex-negativity include:

★ abstinence-only sex education
★ slut-shaming and victim-shaming (especially in cases of sexual harassment and assault)
★ discrimination and violence against sex workers, especially against trans/non-binary femmes of color
★ double standards in dress codes (e.g. demanding stricter guidelines and punishment for female students than for male students; chastising girls for showing skin as a "distraction" to the boys' education).

If it sounds like there's a reoccurring theme here of which bodies are most penalized under sex-negativity, there is. Within cultures that are sexphobic there are underlying currents of misogyny and queer-phobia that seek to discipline and "correct" bodies that aren't cis-gender male, especially bodies that are disabled and/or non-white.

Sex for the sake of pleasure and not procreation has been something actively denied to femme and/or queer persons throughout history, as seen through the stigmatization of homosexuality and other non-straight orientations.

Now, while some asexuals can be sex-negative, asexuality itself isn't a branch of sex-negativity.

In fact, many asexuals happen to be sex workers, engage in kink, or have polyamorous or other "non-traditional" relationship structures that reject the "nuclear" coding (i.e. nuclear family dynamics) permitted within sex-negative societies.

If anything, asexuality challenges the idea of compulsory sexuality/heterosexuality that everyone should desire and have sex in only one limited way.

If someone tells you you're being sex-negative for being asexual, challenge them by asking how they would define sex-negativity and sex-positivity. If their definition of "sex-positivity" is a world that shames people for not following the same model of sexuality that they do, that punishes them for being who they are, then that says more about them than it does about you.

Sex-Averse/Sex-Repulsed

As we touched on earlier, an asexual person can be sex-positive, meaning supportive, or at least tolerant of other people's behaviors around sex, while still being personally uninterested in engaging in sex itself and/or engaging with sexual materials or content. This is where we stray into sex-aversion and sex-repulsion.

According to Ace Week, "sex-repulsed" describes a "person who is disgusted by the idea of themselves having sex or by being exposed to sexual content or situations," while "sex-averse" describes "someone who does not want to have sex."[9]

So while the two terms sound similar, the latter describes a lack of desire toward the act of sex, while the former more broadly describes discomfort or disengagement with the concept of sex as a whole, including real-life situations or media portrayals.

While sex-averse asexuals can have a sliding scale of comfort around sexual materials or language—some aces may enjoy "dirty" innuendo-based humor or entertainment with sexual content—often those who define themselves as sex-repulsed are not interested in engaging with anything to do with sex or sex-related content.

Now, before anyone allosexual reading this assumes all aces must be completely disgusted with sex and must have their pure, delicate little souls protected (*rolling eyes*) from sexual content (i.e. physically covering their eyes every time a "sexy" scene is on screen), understand this: sex is not the be all and end all. Just as some might not have the stomach or the taste for true crime fiction, someone may not be into "sexy" content, and that doesn't make aces "babyish" or immature.

Aces who are sex-averse and/or sex-repulsed can and do find pleasure (including enjoying platonic touch) and connection in other ways, and that's completely valid.

Many of us live concurrently in an over-sexualized and sex-negative world, a capitalist system that runs off the objectification and commodification of human bodies, without fully honoring human sexuality in all its multiplicity and diversity.

If you're sex-averse and/or sex-repulsed, you are in no way contributing to a sex-negative culture. You are simply acknowledging your own personal boundaries and comfort zones, and that is something everyone should respect.

Sex-Neutral/Sex-Apathetic

Sex-neutral or sex-apathetic also sounds like what it means, a neutral-ness or apathy toward sex. Unlike sex-favorable or sex-repulsed, which may imply stronger feelings about one's desire to have or not have sex, sex-neutral aces may have a "take it or leave it" kind of attitude toward sex, meaning they can be indifferent as to whether they engage in it or not.

For some sex-neutral aces, this can mean not being repulsed by sex, but not actively seeking it out either. For some, sex may be just a dish on a menu; it may not be their favorite dish, but some may choose to order it from time to time.

Now, while the idea of having sex without sexual desire or attraction might confuse some people, in reality it's something that's pretty common for a lot of aces.

In the same way that you can eat and share a meal with another person without being hungry, you can also engage in sex without experiencing desire or attraction, the other type of "hunger."

Many asexuals may engage in sex for different reasons, including procreation, curiosity, and a desire to please a romantic partner.

As for that last part, while some people might think it might be "taking advantage" of an asexual person to have sex when they do not experience sexual attraction, that's not always the case. Many sex-neutral asexuals are comfortable with the idea of having sex with their partner/s because they see it as a way of providing pleasure for someone they care about, even if they do not get the exact same "benefits" out of it.

An example of this attitude may sound like this asexual person who, on being asked why they have sex with their husband if they're ace, answered, "He needs that to feel close in a relationship, and I have no problem giving that to him."[10]

To some aces, sex can be a way of providing the care their partner/s may need or desire, as well as a way of sharing physical intimacy with them (although plenty of aces can experience intimacy with their partners in non-sexual manners as well).

Like anyone else, asexuals are also capable of giving consent (which we'll talk more about later) and may wish to engage in sex or not.

In my opinion, if an ace chooses to have mutually consensual sex based on their own informed decision (without being pressured by their partner/s), then I see no problem with that whatsoever.

Ultimately...

Whether you're sex-positive, sex-favorable, sex-averse, sex-repulsed, sex-neutral, sex-apathetic, or any other unnamed possibility, you are no less or more valid as an ace person or anyone else. Ultimately, it is up to you to figure out your own comfort levels around sex and physicality, and to practice consent (not just during sex) in a way that honors all bodies, including your own.

On Relationships and Consent

Learning about consent may be one of the most important lessons you can ever have, and one of the lessons least emphasized in sex ed and in our society.

According to the author of A *Quick & Easy Guide to Consent*:

> Consent is an explicitly communicated, reversible, mutual agreement made when all parties are capable of making that decision.
>
> Consent may or may not be verbal, but it has to be unambiguous and voluntary.
>
> In short, to consent is to communicate yes, with all your decision-making capabilities in functional order and full knowledge of what that " yes" means![1]

Now, while consent should be emphasized as an everyday practice for both sexual and non-sexual situations (i.e. asking permission before taking another person's photograph or asking for a hug), for this section we're going to focus on the former.

So, as discussed earlier, there is a spectrum of attitudes among asexuals regarding sex. Which means navigating giving (or not giving) consent for sex is something we have to talk about.

As an ace person, you may never want sex in your life. And that's perfectly valid. And as an ace person, you may also consent to having sex sometimes. And that's also perfectly valid.

Now if you're in the first camp, not being interested in sex while still interested in having a romantic relationship or currently in a romantic relationship with someone who may want sex, here's the moment where you may pause.

In our society (at least according to the part of North American society that I am familiar with), we have these spoken and unspoken expectations drilled into our heads about sex and relationships. Whether it's waiting until the third date to have sex or waiting until marriage, there's always the expectation that in a relationship sex is going to come around eventually.

While society approves some valid "excuses" for not wanting sex, such as "feeling under the weather" or "not being in the mood," often this is only conditional on the premise that one will eventually be back "in the mood." Especially if you're in a committed relationship with someone who is often "in the mood."

But here's the thing you should understand.

You are never obligated to have sex if you don't want to. EVER!

While your partner/s may have certain sexual "needs," that doesn't mean *your* needs become negated in comparison.

So many times, in cases I've heard about asexual–allosexual relationships, the ace partner is automatically expected (or possibly pressured) to have sex with their allo partner.

Now while some aces are open to having sex with their partners (some very enthusiastically so), often there seems to be a bias in society toward "accommodating" an allo partner, suggesting that it would be "selfish" on the ace partner's part to deny their allo partner's desire for sex.

Here's the thing, though. What makes a good relationship isn't the amount of sex had in it.

It's compromise.

Healthy compromise. Not just pressuring and badgering a person until they give in to what you want (that's not compromise for the record—that's *sexual coercion*[2]). It's negotiating your priorities and your comfort zones and finding a solution that works for you both.

Some allo partners may find that they can live without sex, and prefer their ace partners to feel comfortable rather than doing certain things they're not inclined to do.

Some ace partners may not be into sex that much personally, but are okay with doing it once in a while if they feel their partner needs sex to feel close or comforted in a relationship and they're comfortable providing that.

Some may feel the need to "broaden" their relationships, choosing to remain in a romantically committed relationship, while exploring "open relationships," which include sexual relationships with other people.[3]

Some may explore polyamory[4] or polyfidelity,[5] openly negotiating multiple sexual/romantic relationships simultaneously, ideally with the knowledge and consent of all parties involved in or affected by the relationships. (I would not recommend stepping into these options *lightly*. Each would require *a lot* of research and discussion with your significant other/s, and preferably conversations with people who have had experiences with those options.)

In reality, there is a large number of possibilities, with a large number of emotional, physical, and romantic combinations that can, like a Rubik's Cube, be twisted in any number of configurations that suit you and your partner/s personal sensibilities.

And if you find that you and your partner/s have incompatible orientations/libidos, then it might also be worth considering terminating the relationship if a compromise cannot be found.

And while that idea may sound heartbreaking, it might be a more considerate option than putting yourself or your partner/s in a situation where neither of you will be happy or satisfied.

As Angela Chen wrote:

Of course, just as one person has the right to say no forever, the other has the right to prioritize their own sexual needs. Sexual mismatch can be a source of real pain, and claiming that sex shouldn't matter at all or judging someone for wanting to leave is not helpful. If sex is important, let sex be important. It's okay to leave and have sex with someone who wants to have sex with you. Just remember that leaving for sexual reasons does not mean the other person was wrong.[6]

While I can't guarantee that finding or sustaining a relationship when ace will be easy, I can also promise you it's not impossible.

I know many aces who have or have had fulfilling romantic relationships where their aceness wasn't the "breaking point," but simply another fixture of the relationship, like being a couple that chooses to go out all the time or prefers to stay home and watch TV.

If you are an ace who is interested in sexual experimentation, or you come across a situation where your partner is, then it might be useful to be aware of a consent model that goes beyond the overly simplistic "yes means yes" and "no means no" binary.

Sex researcher and educator Emily Nagoski, author of *Come As You Are: The Surprising New Science That Will Transform Your Sex Life*, suggested a framework with four types of consent:

Enthusiastic consent:
When I *want* you.
When I don't fear the consequences of saying yes OR saying no.
When saying no means missing out on something I want.

Willing consent:
When I care about you though I don't desire you (right now).
When I'm pretty sure saying yes will have an okay result and I think maybe that I'd regret saying no.
When I believe that desire may begin after I say yes.

Unwilling consent:

When I fear the consequences of saying no more than I fear the consequences of saying yes.

When I feel not just an absence of desire but an absence of *desire for desire*.

When I hope that by saying yes, you will stop bothering me, or think that if I say no you'll only keep on trying to persuade me.

Coerced consent:

When you threaten me with harmful consequences if I say no.

When I feel I'll be hurt if I say yes, but I'll be hurt more if I say no.

When saying yes means experiencing something I actively dread.[7]

The last two, if you couldn't tell, stray into the territory of sexual harassment and assault, while the first two make room for aces who are indifferent or favorable to having sex.

Also, if you need a simple refresher course on consent, I would recommend checking out the short film *Tea Consent*.[8] Hint: Just as you wouldn't force a cup of tea on someone who doesn't want to drink it, you shouldn't pressure someone into having sex if they don't want to have it.

Other Useful Things About Sex that You Might Want to Know

★ Get a mirror and look down there.[1] Even if you don't want to play with your genitals, having an informed spatial understanding of where certain parts are aligned is a pretty decent knowledge to have, especially if you want to be more health-conscious, medically speaking. For example, noticing something *down there* that might be not usually be there that could require medical treatment, such as certain types of cysts or genital warts.

★ Masturbation as a source of self-pleasure not only allows you to have a better understanding of what feels good to *your* body but can also help to teach you how to navigate pleasure in partnered sex (knowing what turns you on will help the other person/people understand too). Masturbation in itself can be a pleasant, personal activity for the purposes of "getting off" or stress relief.

★ Lube is your friend. Don't be ashamed to use it.

★ Repeat after me: VIRGINITY IS A MYTH! There is no physical marker on the body to show whether a person has had sex or not. The hymen is a small piece of skin or partially closed membrane found inside the opening of the vagina; it does not "break" (regardless of popular opinion) but can stretch and can be disrupted by more than sex, including inserting a tampon or exercising. You can even have sex without ever "breaking" the hymen.[2]

★ The only reason the concept of virginity exists is to exert societal shame over sexual practices and control over more marginalized (i.e. women's) bodies.

★ Orgasm shouldn't always be the goal of sex. While much of media (and porn) makes the "big O" look like the final end goal of sexual activity (cough *Sex and the City* cough), sex (whether solo or partnered) can still be pleasurable without that "big finish."

★ Most (consensual) kinks are just other facets of human sexuality.[3] They operate on terms of "extreme consent" and carefully negotiated boundaries, which many aces and non-aces are attracted to. Many of us don't choose the kinks that attract us, but as long as we operate through the lens of ethical and respectful consent, it's not something you should judge yourself or others too harshly for. Note: I would *strongly* recommend doing your research before stepping into "new territory."

★ "Arousal nonconcordance" is a thing. If you've ever found your body "responding" (i.e. being aroused) by something you find a mental "turn-off," this might be what's happening. What the genitals can find "sexually relevant" or "sexually appeal-ing" may be different from what the brain actually wants. You can be turned on without wanting to engage with what turns you on. As Emily Nagoski stated, "My genitals do not tell you what I want, or like. I do."[4]

★ What can I say, human sexuality is complicated and messy.

★ "Lubrication is not causation."[5] Sexual arousal and genital response are not the same thing. "Being wet" does not mean you are consenting to sex.

★ You can stop sex at any time during sex. Period.

★ "Blue balls" is not a real thing. Being sexually aroused for an extended period of time without having an orgasm or ejaculation may be uncomfortable, but it's not medically dangerous. If any partner tries to pressure you into having sex because of "blue balls," tell them to take a hike or jump into a shower and use their own toys or hands. They're there for a reason.

★ You never owe anyone sex. EVER! Not to strangers or friends or date mates or spouses. Your body is yours, and it belongs to you and only you.

★ Being a sexual assault/abuse survivor does not "damage" you or make you unworthy of having a relationship or finding pleasure in your own body. What happened to you was NOT your fault. (If you are a survivor, I am so sorry for the harm inflicted upon you, and wish you nothing but the best.)

★ Clothing is never an invitation for unwanted touch.

★ "You were born entitled to all the pleasure your body can feel. You were born entitled to pleasure in whatever way your body perceived it, in whatever contexts afford it, and in whatever qualities you want it. Your pleasure belongs to you, to share or keep as you choose, to explore or not as you choose, to embrace or avoid as you choose."[6]

★ There is more than one way to feel pleasure, and not all of them are sexual.

★ Take your time, don't rush into anything you don't want to do, and have fun!

Miscellaneous Sex Education Resources

Because asexuality does not equal no sex or celibacy, here are some useful (and ace-friendly) sex education texts for exploring sex, sexuality, and relationships, should you be inclined. Note that this is not a fully comprehensive list, and more and more inclusive resources are being created by mainstream and independent sources every day.

★ *Come as You Are: The Surprising New Science That Will Transform Your Sex Life* by Emily Nagoski
★ *Drawn to Sex: The Basics* by Erika Moen and Matthew Nolan
★ *Drawn to Sex: Our Bodies and Health* by Erika Moen and Matthew Nolan
★ *Oh Joy Sex Toy* (Multiple Volumes) by Erika Moen and Matthew Nolan
★ *A Quick & Easy Guide to Sex & Disability* by A. Andrews
★ *A Quick & Easy Guide to Consent* by Isabella Rotman and Luke Howard
★ *What Does Consent Really Mean?* by Pete Wallis and Thalia Wallis

Sex Education YouTube Platforms:

★ Planned Parenthood

★ Hannah Witton—UK content creator who makes videos about "sex, relationships and disability"

Podcasts:

★ Sensual Self with Ev'Yan Whitney—hosted by Ev'Yan Whitney, a Black asexual non-binary sexuality doula®.
★ Supernatural Sexuality with Dr Seabrooke—a fictional sex and romance advice radio show set in a world where monsters are real.

Websites:

★ www.scarleteen.com—inclusive, comprehensive, supportive sexuality and relationships info for teens and emerging adults.
★ www.autostraddle.com—digital publication and real-life community for multiple generations of LGBTQIA+ humans (and their friends).

On the Erotic and Intellectual Merits of Fanfiction

For a long time, the term "fanfiction" has been synonymous with something frivolous and artificial, something that takes someone else's original ideas and hard work, and twists it into meaningless pomp, play-acting at writing. The people who enjoy fanfiction are often assumed to be immature readers who get off on lip service that caters to childish fantasies about romance or vapid pornography.

As a result of negative attitudes like this, the many people who write and read fanfiction are afraid of admitting it, knowing the ridicule and criticism they will receive, accused of being over-enthusiastic fans who need to get a life of their own, or salivating smut-creators (as though smut were a bad thing).

But here's the thing.

I love fanfiction.

I love nearly everything about it. I love the shipping. I love the tropes.

Give me the full wonderful range of possibilities, from post-canon exploration of my favorite fandoms to AUs (alternate universes) (and yes, I am a sucker for Flower and Coffee Shop AUs). Give me Fluff, Hurt/Comfort, Angst, Longing, Touch-Starved, and, yes, Smut.

Contrary to popular belief, not all aces are uncomfortable with or repulsed by erotic or "sexy" material.

Just as asexuality itself is a spectrum, so are aces' attitudes and comfort levels around sex and sexual material.

As Yasmin Benoit eloquently put it:

> Not all asexual people squirm at the sight of sexual material. In fact, quite a lot of us are either neutral to it, or are quite into it. Keep in mind, that it isn't uncommon for asexual people to—wait for it—have sex, and we can actually enjoy it. Not to mention that asexual people are fully capable of pleasuring ourselves if need be. Not experiencing sex attraction can make achieving sexual pleasure a little different for asexual people, but that doesn't make it impossible. Sexual attraction or the desire to have sex with someone are not essential for the appreciation of pornography, erotica, sex toys, kink culture, or anything else along those lines. In fact, it can be a healthy substitute for actually participating in sexual intercourse, allowing us to experience and experiment with different layers of sexuality without taking the so-called "deep dive."[1]

For me, sexy fanfiction acts as a great way to dive in without drowning in deeper waters, to experiment and figure out what turns me on without actually having to "get it on" with anybody else.

And the general reality is that fanfiction is pretty incredible, reaching an impressive number and range of readers, while the writers, who spend hours on this time-consuming project, do so with little or no intention of making a profit, but simply create for the joy of it. And while the current literary market is dominated by cis white men, with evidence suggesting that simply having a feminine name can limit a writer's opportunities,[2] the majority of fanfiction writers are female and/or non-binary.

In fact, fanfiction can be a LGBTQIA+ person's paradise, a place to explore one's gender identity and sexuality (or asexuality) in a safe, controlled environment. Fanfiction communities are often a safe place for young, queer writers to begin navigating their identity. When it comes to young queer fans, Kristina Busse, the founding co-editor of *Transformative Works and Cultures* and scholar of online fandom, referred to online space as the "only place they can be out... They are still negotiating what they want to be called—like what their pronouns are—and coming out as trans online allows them to explore that identity."[3]

And while traditional publishing can gatekeep certain identities, such as asexual, fanfiction provides free grounds for writers of all orientations and identities to write the type of stories they wish to see, reflecting who they are. And for readers who may not have the means (if they're afraid of guardians discovering their queer reads at home) or funds to access validation from bookstores, fanfiction provides a means of joyful escapism from a place of protective anonymity, all without any financial cost.

Fanfiction even works to fill in the holes left by mainstream media when it comes to queer representation. Examples of this can be found in slash fiction, fanfiction that focuses on interpersonal attractions or relationships between persons of the same gender. When the majority of couples in mainstream movies and television are heterosexual couples or, worse, inflict queer-baiting (that annoying trope of teasing a potential queer relationship, but never actually confirming it), fanfiction provides a chance to see the couples we only ship in our imagination play out on the page, validated by the same readers who engaged in those fictional universes, confirming that we aren't the only ones shipping those characters. Furthermore, when censorship or time limitations prevent in-depth focus on queer relationships, whether the physical (seeing queer characters kiss on screen or having the screen fade to black during more "intimate" scenes) or simply wanting to see more scenes of domestic relief, fanfiction offers us access to that content.

When it comes to sex-shaming comments about fanfiction

being "too sexy," there's actually nothing wrong with that, as fanfiction allows a safe space to explore our needs and desires. Many people like erotica, and fanfiction plays into the field of literotica, engaging with the reader's desires intellectually. In many senses, fanfiction is a form of safe play, a vicarious method of pleasure in which we are engaged in the content, but still separate from it, choosing when to engage and enjoy certain scenarios or moving away if we don't.

Furthermore, while there are those who can be nasty in the world of fanfiction (what media outlet doesn't have its jerks?), in my experience, fanfiction communities, such as Archive of Our Own, are generally welcoming and respectful. Fanfiction writers often provide common courtesy toward their readers, featuring specific content warnings at the top of each piece to warn readers about subjects, such as violent content, that could potentially discomfort or trigger them. In addition, readers can often provide encouraging comments to fanfiction authors, as well helpful advice in terms of editing and content, engaging reciprocally in a positive parasocial way.

When I was an English major in college, my syllabus consisted of works by Edith Wharton, Mark Twain, William Shakespeare, John Milton, Jacques Derrida, and so forth. While all these authors have produced brilliant and acclaimed works, it can be mentally exhausting if that's what you have to read all the time. When I was tired from school or needed a reprieve from my own anxious mind, I turned to fanfiction. There I found well-written and lovingly crafted fiction involving the characters I loved, simultaneously engaging my geek side and my queer side.

In their poem "Fantastic Breasts and Where to Find Them," poet Brenna Twohy speaks to what they love about erotic fanfiction, how it provides a safe, fun alternative to the degrading and misogynic rape culture often found in mainstream pornography. Twohy emphasizes the agency found in the leads of fanfiction, whereas in other sexual media certain (often female) individuals don't exist beyond their sexual utility to someone else (often male).[4]

Truthfully, a major part of me is turned off by regular porn or even graphic content in mainstream film and television, which often features gratuitous, cis-heterocentric, and frankly boring depictions of sex. As someone who identifies on the asexual spectrum, contrary to popular misconception, I still sometimes like "sexy" content, and my favorite content often appears in fanfiction, where I can read about characters whom I admire for their beauty, courage, and intelligence as they engage in both emotionally and physically intimate scenarios. I can figure out what I enjoy fantasizing about, as well as the types of relationships I might wish to engage in, based on the same foundations of affection, humor, consent, and respect. With or without sex, these characters exist three-dimensionally in a story that leaves me feeling satisfied, relaxed, and happy.

Ultimately, fanfiction can be engaging and empowering, a powerful tool that fans can use to engage with the media given to them, taking source texts and deconstructing and reconstructing them until we produce the content we desire, bringing diverse headcanons to life, such as trans, Jewish Peter Parker or bisexual Steve Rogers, focusing on characters that look, love, and live like us. In this sense, fanfiction can resemble alchemy, providing something fictional and powerful. American author Lev Grossman has written about the active, subversive nature of fanfiction, in which an audience can engage with producers and their content, writing that "culture talks to them, and they talk back to the culture in its own language."[5]

Until the day when there are enough stories to capture every facet of human reality and fantasy out there, fanfiction will continue to be written, providing much-needed fictional nourishment and validation to a starving community.

On Intimacy

Often when it comes to intimacy, the first things we're trained to think of are those of the sexual variety. Red silk sheets, heated breath, va-va-voom music, all that jazz. As most of us know, Hollywood likes to make a big deal of sex, using it as a plot device that indicates a major shift in a scene, a climax (ha!) in the narrative between characters. Having the majority of romantic narratives in mainstream media associated with sexual intimacy can contribute to the misleading idea that all intimate relationships (at least romantic relationships) are invalid without sex. And for many aces, especially those who are sex-repulsed/averse, for whom the idea of sex may be undesirable, this idea is heartbreaking.

Many aces (as well as others who have complicated relationships with sex) worry about intimacy in romantic relationships, scared that if they will not or cannot have sexual intimacy with their partner/s, their relationships will be seen as lacking, their bond less legitimate.

However, intimacy in itself doesn't necessarily have to be sexual, or even physical. The word "intimacy" refers to a sense of closeness or familiarity, a personal connection that connotes a level of proximity and trust that isn't easily achieved off the bat. Intimacy need not only be found with sexual and/or romantic partners, but also with anyone with whom one has a close bond, such as friends and family.

Intimacy doesn't have to be relegated to a sexual act in the bedroom (or any other space) or even related to grand romantic gestures. Intimacy can be as soft and simple as sharing a meal or having a heartfelt conversation (digitally or in person). Intimacy can be related to things you can do together, such as dancing, or doing individual activities while sharing the same space (parallel play).

What's more, the ways we can establish intimacy, the ways in which we can show care and affection, are infinite and diverse.

Below is a list of fifty acts of non-sexual intimacy, which you can pick and choose depending on your personal preference, physical ability, and comfort level.

Fun fact: Many of these activities don't even have to be done in person, thanks to technology, which includes phones and video conferencing.

1. Holding hands (that Beatles song "I Wanna Hold Your Hand" is still a classic for a reason)
2. Trading/sharing secrets
3. Listening to music together/sharing playlists
4. Learning something new together, such as painting or studying another language
5. Kissing (cheeks, lips, shoulders, other body parts)
6. Sleeping together (literal sleeping—sharing the same bed and snoring together)
7. Playing games/sports together
8. Reading together (this is one of my favorites)
9. Sharing a meal/feeding each other

10. Cooking a meal for your person/people
11. Hugging
12. Massages
13. Drawing/painting/making art (not love!)
14. Writing together/to each other
15. Attending events together (concerts, book talks, etc.)
16. Watching TV/movies together
17. Head scratches/back scratches
18. Tracing skin
19. Tickling
20. Caring for them when they're sick
21. Helping with their treatment or medication (e.g. if your trans partner/friend is scared of needles, offering to help with their hormone injections can be appreciated)
22. Putting on their makeup/watching them take their makeup off
23. Running errands together
24. Meeting each other's families/spending time with family
25. Shopping together (whether as a pleasurable activity or for moral support depends on you)
26. Sharing clothes (if possible); alternatively, tailoring and/or making clothes for the other person
27. Compliments
28. Crying (trust me, nothing says trust like an ugly cry)
29. Open and honest conversations
30. Speaking/signing to them in your heritage language and/or familial tongue (there can be a world of difference between "I love you" in English and "I love you" in the words your abuela/lola/babushka/bubbe uses for you)
31. Providing moral support (e.g. going to the doctor together)
32. Sharing responsibilities (e.g. child care, chores)
33. Rolling together (whether on rollerblades or in wheelchairs)

34. Hair care (washing, styling, brushing, braiding)
35. Bathing/showering together (nudity ≠ sex)
36. Dressing/undressing each other (see #35)
37. Looking into each other's eyes
38. Play-wrestling or play-fighting
39. Inside jokes
40. Laying your hand on their shoulder
41. Traveling together (car rides can be deeply bonding experiences)
42. Making memories (e.g. taking photos together)
43. Listening (without judgment, reservation, or unsolicited advice)
44. Listening to/feeling the other's heartbeat/breathing
45. Exercising together
46. Being still together
47. Painting nails (read Elizabeth Acevedo's poem "You Mean You Don't Weep at the Nail Salon?"—I guarantee it's worth it)
48. Listening to each other's stories
49. Respecting each other's personal space/boundaries
50. Learning your person's specific love language

Interview with Ev'Yan Whitney

This is a transcript of an audio interview. This interview has been condensed and edited for clarity.*

Michele: So, my first question is, how would you define yourself as well as your place on the asexual spectrum?

Ev'Yan: Oh, that's an excellent question. I mean, that's something that I'm still trying to figure out for myself. I mean, that's something that I'm still trying to figure out for myself. I mean, I recently came out so I am not sure how to describe myself. If I should just say that I am an ace person, or if I should also identify that I am demisexual, and I feel like my demisexuality, as well as my aceness in general, really intersects with my queer identity and my Blackness as well.

Michele: It's interesting that you are a sex educator. Most people wouldn't really imagine that being in line with an asexual person.

Ev'Yan: I'll think I'll be honest with you and say that I think that's one of the reasons why it took me so long to come out to

---

* Credit to J Rei Photography, who took the photograph this illustration is based on.

myself and also see the reality and the truth of my own sexuality. Because I also thought that in order to be a sex educator, that means that sex educators couldn't be asexual. That those two things kind of counteract each other or go against each other. But the more that I listen to ace people's stories and their experiences of sex or not having sex, the more I realized like, "Wow, this is exactly who I am," and how can I integrate and honor my ace identity within my sex education.

And the truth is that I've been doing it all along, even before I knew that I was ace in my work. I've been doing this work for eleven years now. I have always sort of gravitated toward the "unconventional" or "non-normative" ways of sex education. Like I was always talking about sensuality and connecting to the body. I was always highlighting the importance of being your own person and figuring out who you are, and also not having sex unless it was an absolute YES for you. Like it's okay to say no to sex that you don't want to have. So I think that coming out has been an experience of both "wow, this is a really new thing," and also "it's not so far off" because I've been teaching and coaching and facilitating in this way for a long time.

Also, I'll say that one of the things that I was worried about when I was coming out was that people would see that, and that would sort of dismiss or undo all of the lifelong work that I've done in my sex education. And actually I've been very surprised that when I came out, a lot of folks who have been following me for years were saying things like, "I am ace" or, "Wow, your experience of talking about your sexuality and the different ways that you desire sex and interact with sex is opening up this new world for me about my own sexuality and it's given me courage and permission to also identify as ace."

My experience of coming out has been a lot more well received than I thought it was going to be. I had a really big fear that people weren't going to get it, because there's still a lot of misinformation and misunderstanding about what it means to be asexual and who gets to claim that as an identity, and I've been really happy that it's been received so well, that folks have been really receptive. And that my coming out has also impacted and inspired folks (even folks who don't identify as ace) to re-examine what sexuality is, and what sex is, and what that looks like.

It really felt like when I came out, it was like I was coming home to myself as opposed to rediscovering this newfound thing that I am. It's been a really interesting and beautiful process.

Michele: Can I ask how you came into the realization of this part of yourself?

Ev'Yan: Well, two things. One, I think I've always known and I think that I had been fighting against my asexuality for many, many years. I kind of came into my work as a sex educator, wanting to "fix" myself. And in a lot of ways that desire to "fix" myself was warranted. I had a lot of insecurities about sex, a lot of shame and trauma around sex. So my sex education came from that place of wanting to know myself better and heal parts of myself. But the one part of myself that I don't think that I've ever quite "healed," for lack of a better word, is the nuances of my sexuality. Like the fact that sex isn't like the top priority for me, that I could go without sex and not really bat an eye, and that I also don't really experience sexual attraction. And so I remember in my work, I would be trying to sort of figure out like, "Okay, what are the ways that I can put sex on the map and try to have more sexual desire?"

I was always sort of curious about why it is that my desire is low or sex isn't really on the map for me, and I would try to do things and try all these hacks and tweaks to get my libido up, and I figured, "Okay, maybe those things aren't working," and I just kind of put those things aside and didn't really mess with it much. And then I read Angela Chen's book *Ace*, which was like the second piece that made me realize that I was definitely ace.

I mean, I think within the first page of her book, I had to put it down and just like take a breath and really come to terms with the fact like, "Wow, this person is talking a lot about their own experience of attraction and desire and sex, and all of these things, and it's really resonating with me, and they identify as ace. I think that I might be ace, too." It just gave me a lot of permission to stop shaming myself or trying to be someone that I sexually wasn't, because she really opened up this definition of what it means to be ace outside of sex-repulsed people, you know?

Michele: I want to touch again for a second on what you said about "fixing." I think that's a really key word in our community because so many believe they're "broken" until they come into the realization of the word "ace." And I don't think it's just ace people. I want to talk about how much of this world just gives us this limited perception of how to be a sexual person or enjoy sexuality.

Ev'Yan: Yeah, I think about that a lot. In our world, there's a lot of room for variation. We understand that there are many different types of people who have different types of preferences and personalities and shapes. Like we understand that. But in other ways, particularly with gender or with sexuality, those things are still really fixed. Like there's still a one-size-fits-all label that is slapped on all of us.

And it's so interesting because so much of my work has been about reclaiming different ways of being sexual and giving myself and other folks permission to be the full expression of who they are, even if it's counter to the narratives or the standards that we've been given about what these things should look like. But for whatever reason, when it came to attraction and desire, even as a sex educator, like I will admit that my own scope of these things, of this variation, was really, really limited because, I think, because of the culture that we live in, and also a lot of the sex education that I received around aceness or various desire levels and different ways that people desire. It wasn't like I wasn't given those messages either. It was very much like it's black or white. You either love sex or you hate it. And if you hate sex, there's something wrong with you and here's how we can "fix" that. And I feel so liberated actually that aceness is a thing, because I feel like it's giving me and other folks permission to be the full spectrum of who we are as sexual beings without it being pathologized or stigmatized.

Michele: Within the ace community, there's such a range of perspectives around the subject. There are sex-repulsed aces who are not interested in the act of sex or maybe uncomfortable around sexual material. And then there are sex-neutral aces who...maybe it's not their favorite thing on the menu, but they don't mind "sharing a meal" with their partner if it makes them happy.

Ev'Yan: I certainly fall into that camp. But I also have noticed that that can change. There are some days where I feel like really, *really* ace, where I'm not into sex at all. And then there are other days where I do want to experience sexuality with another person or with myself. But I think that's what I love about aceness as a spectrum, that it just gives us so much fluidity and flexibility to go up and down on that scale without any shame or stigma or this need to "fix" ourselves to be one or the other. That's been really liberating for me.

Michele: What does having an ace-informed lens around sex do for us as a community?

Ev'Yan: I think it just allows us to expand our definitions of what sex is, and what sex looks like, and what a sexual person is, and what a sexuality looks like. It really just blows open this one-size-fits-all model that we've been given, like, "This is the way that you are supposed to desire sex and have sex and experience sexuality and desire." Again, I just think it gives us a lot more freedom and fluidity to move and just be who we are.

I feel like coming to the realization that I'm ace has allowed me to experience my sexuality in deeper ways because I'm no longer in this space of trying to "fix" myself.

I feel really grateful that I am on this journey so that I can also help guide folks and give them the tools to ask themselves questions to figure out, like, "Are you ace or not?" And it doesn't matter if you are, but I want for people to just give themselves the space to be who they are, even if it goes against what society and culture have told them their sexuality should look like.

Michele: I think coming into asexuality myself did give me a set of tools, like how to define certain types of attraction.

Because, as you might know, there's sexual attraction, romantic attraction. There's sensual attraction, which is described as the desire for touch, and that might not necessarily be a sexual thing. Sometimes you just want to hug or kiss a person without sexual intent being behind it.

Ev'Yan: That's right. I have noticed that as I and others have been coming into these realizations around ace identity, I think it's giving us a lot more space to really define for ourselves, like what we desire, what we're attracted to, and how can we accentuate that and bring that into the relationships that we have in ways that are outside of the lens of what we've been given about what sex and love and intimacy looks like.

Aceness is kind of a superpower because it gives us the ability to relate to people in different ways that are outside of this binary system of sexlessness or sexfullness. It's like, no, there are many different ways that we can explore intimacy with other people.

I think that I have now started to see aceness as a kind of superpower that enables us to explore and experience different methods of connection and intimacy and sensuality with people that I don't think we would have been given or have been given through conventional sex education or the role models of sexuality that we have today.

Michele: It's interesting because what I've noticed within the ace community is that when you de-center a certain thing that's been taken for granted as "natural," you start to break down the scripts for other things in life.

Ev'Yan: I mean, it really just highlights how everybody's experience is different. Like their experience of their bodies is different. Their experience of gender. And the way that they relate to other people is different and, as such, so is the way that they experience sexuality. In the work that I do, I really want to hold space for all the different ways that sexuality or lack thereof can look, and affirm that that's okay.

Michele: I think that by deprioritizing sex as the ultimate pleasure, it allows us to value other forms of pleasure and intimacy.

Ev'Yan: I've experienced that as well. I think the moment that I realized that I was ace, I was starting to pick up on all the different ways that I experience, you know, physical intimacy, sexual intimacy, and sensual intimacy. Because for the longest time, I think all of us have been given this message that sex is at the center of a relationship. So realizing that I was ace allowed me to make more room for the different ways that I can show up to intimacy with myself and with my partner.

Michele: I'm so glad that it has opened more lines of communication and pleasure for you and your partner, because oftentimes as aces we're scared that because of our complicated nature with sex, we can't have happy fulfilling relationships with other people.

Ev'Yan: I feel really, really lucky that I'm in a relationship with someone who is able to hold all of the nuances of who I am and not see that as a detriment to my ability to be loved or my ability to receive and give intimacy to someone. And I know that that's not the case for a lot of people.

Michele: The way I see it, sometimes being ace can make it harder to find certain relationships. But then I see other aces who are in monogamous relationships where sex isn't a factor. Or maybe they're in open or polyamorous relationships where they're able to negotiate what they're comfortable with and find a happy compromise. It's possible to find connection with other people when you're ace.

Ev'Yan: Yeah, absolutely.

Michele: I want to talk for a second about the word "sensual," because for me, when I think of the word "sensual," I don't necessarily think of sexual. I think of music that really makes me feel in tune with my body. Or how amazing it is to get into a warm bed after a shower. Like the pleasure connected to my senses rather than just sexual vitality. And I'm wondering how would you define sensuality?

Ev'Yan: You are probably the first person that I've talked to that has defined sensuality in that way. Like most of the people that I speak to are like, "Sensuality means sex, right?" Like if you are being sensual, you are being sexual. So exactly the way that you describe it is how I experience sensuality. It's how I teach it. You know, this idea that sensuality and sexuality are not synonymous. They are each their own unique experience. That sensuality has been over-sexualized in our culture. And that it's really about a connection with yourself. These private experiences that you have with your own senses, with being in your body.

And sensuality can absolutely overlap in sexuality. But one of the things that I stress a lot in my work is that they're not the same, and it's important to create a relationship with sensuality outside of that sexualized lens. I really feel that gives so much information about the pleasure that is our birthright, and not just pleasure from a sexual lens, but just what makes you feel good on a day-to-day basis. What are the things that soothe your soul and bring ease and delight to your body and senses? To me, that is the practice of sensuality.

Michele: Yeah, it's not always sex toys and lingerie, although you can still enjoy those things as an ace person. But for me, I think it also has to do with a pleasure that can be accessible to anyone.

Ev'Yan: One of the things I say in my work is that if you have a body, you are a sensual being. Sensuality can live in a thing. Lingerie, candles, sex toys, stuff like that. And I think that those are tools that can conjure up some essential feelings, but sensuality doesn't live in those things. Sensuality is about what you experience in your own body, and I think that we are all sensual, and that sensuality and the pleasure that comes from it is our birthright.

Again, there are so many different ways to experience pleasure, just as there are so many different ways to experience sex and desire and intimacy and connection. So yeah, we should all hold space for the nuances of all of those things, even if we think that we are sort of "standard model," you know, like it doesn't fit for us. Like I want to encourage all of us to just ask ourselves, you know, *Who are we really?*

Michele: A lot of asexuals have an interesting relationship with self-pleasure. Either thinking about it as a way to take care of an "itch" because some asexuals have a libido, and use masturbation as a way to just "drain the pipes," so to speak. And other times, they just like the relaxation of it.

Ev'Yan: Yeah, I've heard that, too. And I've also actually experienced that, you know? Like sometimes having sex isn't supposed to be so deep. Like it's not always supposed to be so sacred and spiritual. Sometimes it's just "getting off" and maintaining your own body. I've certainly got experiences where I'm like, I just need to have an orgasm so I can go to sleep, or so I can get rid of this headache, you know? And yeah, I also want people to not take sex so seriously or at least not take orgasm so seriously. I mean, for some folks, it means a lot, but I think that in my work, I've seen a lot of people put a lot of importance on sex. Especially me since I was raised in purity culture. So the idea that sex was like "spiritual" and "holy" and "sacred" and "intimate" and all of those things. It's been really nice to be like, "Yeah, sometimes it's like that," but a lot of times it's also just like let's just "get off" and call it a night, you know? And that's okay. That doesn't mean that I'm any less of a person. It's just there's different ways to experience it.

Michele: I want to talk about that for a second, like the people who do find it important for themselves. Oftentimes there's this idea that a liberated person means being someone who is able to have lots of sex with people, or is able to be this sexual master like Samantha from *Sex in the City*, and that makes a lot of aces or a lot of people who don't prioritize that feel less "liberated." And I'm wondering about your thoughts on that.

Ev'Yan: Yeah, I think that that's one of the reasons why I ran away from my own ace identity for so long because of tropes or expressions of sexuality like Samantha from *Sex and the City*. That's what sort of set the standard of what sex should be like and what sexual empowerment is in particular. The idea that you are sexually liberated if you have lots of sex and you want lots of sex and you talk about how much you want and are having lots of sex. I certainly tried to do that with myself. I came up against that a lot in my personal experience of having an open relationship and realizing that I was queer and wanting to explore my queer identity within an open relationship, and it became very obvious to me that to be queer, there's this automatic assumption that if you're queer, then that means that you're having sex or there's like this...it's not an understanding, it's more like a pressure that I felt that if you are queer, that means that sex is at the center of it. And that was really difficult for me because my queer identity isn't wrapped up in sex, and I think it really frustrated a lot of the folks that I dated, because they were coming to that place thinking, "Oh well, we're both queer, and queerness is about having sex and getting raunchy with each other. Why don't you want that?" And that also made me question, like, "Am I queer if I don't want lots of sex, or my queer identity isn't centered around having physical sex with people?" I feel like there are a lot of ways that I have dismissed or not taken seriously my own identities because so much of these identities is wrapped up in the kind of sex we have, whether or not we have sex.

Michele: I think it's because historically for so long sex has been weaponized against us. Like during the AIDS crisis, gay men were shamed about the amount of sex they had. So sex became part of their identity, partly because of the way it was pushed on them, but also as a way to reclaim their own humanity against a world that tried to neuter them.

But the thing is, for me, queerness can come in so many forms.

I think we need to give ourselves room in order to have multiple ways of being queer, multiple ways of being ace. Or having multiple ways to be a sexual or sensual person. To say that there's not just one way to exist or to feel in this world, but that there are multiple ways and none of them are more valid than the other.

Ev'Yan: That's right.

Michele: So my last question is, what would you like to see for the future of the ace community?

Ev'Yan: I want to see more representation. I want to see more representation of ace folks that don't look like white cis men, you know? I also want to see different expressions of ace identity that aren't just like "I don't have sex." And that's not to diminish or dismiss the ace folks who do have that experience, but I want to see more people who are on that spectrum who are aromantic, but have sex, or say that they're asexual and they have a high libido. Like I want to see more variants in what an asexual person can look like.

And not even just when it comes to aceness. When it comes to sexuality on the screen, I want to see different ways that people are experiencing sex and having sex, and experiencing intimacy with their partners. And I want to see more representation where sex is the thing that people have, but it's not the center of every conversation and that's okay.

I want to see more variants of what a sexual person looks like and also what an asexual person looks like.

Ev'Yan Whitney (they/them) is a sexuality doula®, sex educator, and sensualist. Since 2011, their work has focused on decolonizing, unshaming, and liberating sexuality at the intersection of identity, trauma healing, pleasure, and embodiment. Ev'Yan is the author of *Sensual Self: Prompts and Practices for Getting in Touch with Your Body,* a self-guided journal that will help you prioritize your pleasure and come home to yourself through your senses. They also host a beloved podcast of the same name. For more about Ev'Yan's work, go to www.evyanwhitney.com and follow them on Instagram @evyan.whitney.

Interview with Courtney Lane

This is a transcript of an audio interview. This interview has been condensed and edited for clarity.

Michele: Okay, thank you for taking the time to meet up with me today.

Courtney: Thank you for having me.

Michele: So my first question would be, how would you describe yourself and your place on the ace spectrum?

Courtney: Well, that can be a very complicated answer, actually. There was a period of time, a significant period of time, where I would have considered myself to be a heteroromantic asexual. However, in recent years, I have very much started to question the nature of that. I do believe that I am pretty squarely in the aromantic spectrum as well, probably somewhere in the realm of demiromantic, but that took quite a bit of unpacking to figure out, and it's not a label that I have identified with for long. So asexual is just kind of my personal all-encompassing label that I'm comfortable with. I use queer quite often. Because my spouse is agender and I have never had a connection with another person in the same way I have with my spouse who is also asexual, which no doubt plays a part in our connection. So once you get into asexuality and non-binary genders, you really sort of break the whole system wide open, and it leaves a lot of room to question, well, what does heteroromantic actually mean in this sense? And does it actually apply to me? And so it's complicated.

Michele: What you said about breaking down the whole system is something that a lot of the aces I've been talking to have also described, how dismantling your ideas about one thing just leads to dismantling ideas about other things?

Courtney: Well, absolutely. And I've never really publicly or sincerely identified with anything in the biromantic spectrum. However, I think I do have some level for capacity in gender fluidity. And one of the first people I ever really kissed as a kid was a girl and I didn't like it. So I kind of just said, "Well, I don't like girls." But then I started kissing boys. And I didn't really like that either. [Laughs.] But there was still some level of compulsory heterosexuality that took its toll on me, so to speak. So I still just sort of stuck with that because it was the simpler answer, even though it honestly well and truly did not fit.

Michele: It really is so interesting that you and your spouse are both asexual. Did that come as a surprise to you when you discovered it?

Courtney: I knew right from the get-go. In fact, if we were not asexual, we probably would have never met in order to fall in love. Because it was a wild chance, happenstance on a dating site of all things, where...oh, gosh, should I go into this whole story? [Laughs.] It's a bit of a long story. Where I wasn't even interested in dating necessarily. And at the time, Royce lived several states away from me, so there wasn't anything practical about it. But somehow Royce's profile got on my radar and this just looked like such an interesting person. What I was reading on the profile was so interesting. And right at the bottom, I read, "I am heteroromantic asexual." And at the time, that was the label I had for myself, and Royce was presenting male at the time. So it all just seemed to be perfect and I needed to reach out to this person. And I suppose the rest is history, as they say. But I would have had no inclination to reach out if I didn't know that right off the bat. So I had not put on my profile that I was asexual even, because I didn't want to deal with what comes from putting that out publicly as a young woman on a dating site. That can open you up to a lot of harassment. So I am just so grateful that Royce was the bold one to put that publicly so that we could get to where we are today.

Michele: That's sweet. I've actually had a little bit of experience with dating apps. You know that OKCupid feature where you can list asexual as a feature?

Courtney: You can now, yes! I'm very happy about that. At the time we met, we could not do that.

Michele: So my experiences were not too bad necessarily, but I did have guys ghost me when they asked, "Oh, what's asexual?" And then I told them, "Well, look it up," because I'm so tired of explaining it at this point. And then they proceeded to ghost me.

Courtney: I wish I could say I'm surprised about that.

Michele: Which brings me to another point, about how dating as an asexual is awful. Sometimes it can be really hard.

Courtney: Yes. Definitely awful.

Michele: So as a romantic ace, what would you want to say to other romantic aces looking for a connection, and who are fearful that their orientation might make that a little more difficult?

Courtney: I would say the number-one most important thing is to really do the self-reflection and to learn what it is that you want and need. Because far too often, we have seen younger members of the ace community just sort of feeling hopeless, and expressing concerns that they want a romantic relationship, but just do not think it's on the cards for them.

And it absolutely can be and there are so many ways that it can work. There is, of course, the option of dating and romance with allosexual people. And that can work for some aces. But it also doesn't work for everyone. And usually in the narrative, it's "Well, if you want to date, you probably have to date an allo—here are ways to do it." And that often includes things like open relationships, polyamory. Which is fantastic and works for some people. But I've also seen more monogamously inclined aces really leery and concerned about that, because it's not for everybody. And I don't want people to feel like they have to settle or build a relationship structure that is outside of what they are comfortable with. And if you really know truly what you want, stick to that and look for it. In my instance, it was pure happenstance, because I did not think it was possible. So I was not looking. And it was a wild coincidence that got me to what I needed, and I am happier than I could have ever hoped for. And I do want people to know that it is possible. And it may be difficult. And it may involve using the tools available at our disposal, dating sites and being very, very open and honest, right from the get-go. Don't waste your own time. Of course, experiment if you're not quite sure what works for you yet. But it is possible and there may be some compromises that do need to be made. But that is, again, really knowing yourself and what works for you. Because perhaps you do want to experiment with an open relationship. Or perhaps you're willing to compromise on location. A lot of aces are concerned that in order to establish a relationship it will have to be with someone who is non-local. And honestly, that's what I did and it worked for me. I know relocation isn't going to work for everybody, but explore all of your options and really know what you want and what you're willing to compromise on.

Michele: I want to touch on the word "compromise." Because I feel a lot of times—what you said about allo relationships and asexual relationships—a lot of times the asexual person is expected to compromise. And in that instance, it's not really a compromise—it seems more like they're expected to give in to the allo person's supposed "wants." Which means sex, and that doesn't really seem fair to just prioritize one person's wants and needs over the other's.

Courtney: Absolutely. And I think that that can especially be an issue for women. Because even if you aren't an asexual woman, there are many cultures that I grew up around that definitely expect the woman to be the one who submits and gives so much of herself for the comfort of her partner. And it's a really ugly, messy culture that has led us to this point. But if you're both a woman and asexual, or if you have any other number of intersections, there can just be everything in the world telling you that *this* is your job to compromise. And this is what society expects you to do. So there can even be this thing that happens where you may not even necessarily be directly pressured by your peers or your individual partner, but there is sort of a larger societal pressure that can become so ingrained and deep-seated in you that you don't even approach the conversation because you just already feel like *this* is what I need to do.

Michele: You could definitely internalize a lot of negative messages from your environment that you have to do this one thing in order to be "happy," or in order to make someone else happy, which ends up making you feel miserable.

Courtney: Yes, definitely. And that's honestly what I did. For the longest time. Royce is the first relationship I've ever had with a fellow ace. And luckily, we struck gold and it worked. But all of my previous relationships were with allos. And there was always just something "wrong" that didn't work for me. And in some of those cases, it was because I was putting on the masquerade of the "good girlfriend," the "good woman," the allo...well, I guess I never really posed as an allo...

Michele: The accommodating asexual.

Courtney: The accommodating asexual. [Laughs.] That's a good one.

Michele: Well, I'm glad that you found such a lovely relationship with your spouse. I am always glad to hear love stories like that work.

Courtney: Thank you. We found that our story does help others. And that's why we do what we do with our podcast and talk about who we are. Because we don't want anyone to feel like it's completely hopeless, because it's not.

Michele: Speaking of your podcast, a lot of the other stuff that you talk about regularly there, besides your relationship, is also your disability and your intersection with asexuality and disability. I was wondering if you wouldn't mind talking about that, what it means for you to exist at the intersection.

Courtney: Absolutely. So asexuality and disability is such an interesting and difficult intersection both for me personally and as someone putting my story out publicly. Come to think of it, both my asexual identity and my disabled identity are things that have definitely been present throughout my entire life. And there are signs that I can think back on and point to with my asexuality. It's sort of picking a crush in elementary school because I thought that's what everybody did, or it's kissing a girl and deciding I didn't like it, but also I didn't like it with boys. But with my disability, I knew how to relocate my own dislocated elbows before I could even speak fluently. And I was constantly in and out of doctor offices, and I was constantly developing new symptoms, and I would have doctors writing notes to get me out of gym class and making me wear braces on my joints. But the word "disabled" never crossed the lips of any of my doctors, or any of the adults in my life. As I was growing up, it was right when I reached early adulthood that I decided to put labels on all of the very difficult complicated things in my life that were growing more and more clear that this is not the typical experience.

So that included research into asexuality and really pinpointing, "Yes, 'asexual' is the word for me." Funnily enough, it was the word I'd already had in my brain. I just didn't know other people were also using it. So that was a nice coincidence as well.

But in terms of the disability, it actually took me a little bit longer to get comfortable with that label. I'm sort of a natural educator. So as frustrating as it is for ace people to always need to be explaining their sexuality to other people (and I can get tired of it too in some cases), I'm much more willing to be the first one who's presenting information to someone. So if someone's never heard of asexuality, I'm game to explain it to them. But with the label of "disabled," people already know what that means, or at least they think they know what that means. And it often comes with a lot of internalized prejudice and ableism. And so it was a little more difficult to embrace, but countless doctor's appointments and several diagnoses later, I finally had to come to terms with the word "disabled," and it was really ground-breaking, and it was very freeing, because that was unpacking some of my own internalized ableism as well, and it allowed me to view my own experience with so much more clarity.

And when I began this journey of what is this internalized ableism, I started thinking about all of the little things I've been told over the years when explaining asexuality, and so many of them boiled down to "Well, maybe you're sick. Have you been to a doctor? Maybe there's something wrong with you." And every time, I would shrug it off. Like, "No, I'm in and out of doctors constantly for all of my other things. This is not another symptom of that."

Michele: It seems like people are trying to pathologize your asexuality in relationship to your disability.

Courtney: Oh, absolutely! They pathologize it. And I mean, pop culture and media do not help. In fact, a decade ago, I think every ace is familiar with the dreaded *House* episode. I actually saw that episode the day it aired. And it was just a couple of weeks after I decided to come out as asexual.

Michele: That sounds awful.

Courtney: I had decided in my head, "This is a comfortable label for me, I'm going to start the process of telling people." And I hadn't said it aloud yet when I sat down and watched that episode. And, of course, I was dealing with all of my own medical issues, and I had been my entire life, so it did complicate factors. It gave me a lot more to think about. But I'm grateful that I proceeded with the process of coming out just a couple of months later all the same.

Michele: I think there needs to be space within the asexual community to acknowledge that identity can be complicated.

Some aces do find their asexuality is possibly affected by or possibly a result of their disability. And then there are aces who find it two completely different things. And I think that both of those things can be valid as long as we know that we're coming to that place from our own personal knowledge.

You know, we aces are in our heads all the time. Like thinking about whether we are actually ace or not, because of society telling us we can't be. And so after we've gone through all the tests, all the medical tests, all the mental testing, if you come to the conclusion that asexuality feels like the best fit for you, then I'm all for people embracing whatever makes them *feel* right. But to say that someone can't be asexual because they're disabled or that your disability automatically makes you less legitimate is something that we really need to talk about as a community.

Courtney: Yes. Well, and the two communities—the asexuality community and the disability community—have historically seemed to be at odds with one another. And when I first started publicly presenting myself as not only an asexual person but also a disabled one, I very quickly saw the two communities try to distance themselves from me. And I understand the reasons for that, because asexuality is so often medicalized and it is pathologized. And so in the fight to have our orientations seen as something that is legitimate in the eyes of society, many aces want to distance themselves from that label. And they want to say, "We're not disabled, there's nothing wrong with us." And we still have just sort of community trauma from that dang *House* episode. Like no, it doesn't mean we have cancer, we're not just lying about this.

Michele: And from the disability community, who has been desexualized for so long, the word "asexual," which in general has been used as an insult, they want to distance themselves from that, too.

Courtney: Absolutely. And that goes back decades, centuries even. It has a very nasty root in eugenics, where society will say, "If you are disabled, if we deem that there's something wrong with you, you should not be able to reproduce, you should not be a sexual being." And in the ugliest sense, that has led to forced sterilization. So there's so much trauma in the disability community as well, that a lot of modern disability activism has sort of come to this place of putting yourself out as a "sexual being," and it's very sexually charged. And there's nothing wrong with that for individuals to say, "I am a sexual being," but...

Michele: But then it doesn't leave enough space for people like you who are also asexual, or people who may be celibate and are not interested in anything sexual.

Courtney: Exactly. There are these broad sweeping statements from both sides. The disability community saying, "Yes, we all have sex because we're human." And the asexual community on the other side says, "We are not disabled, our bodies are not broken. There's nothing wrong with our brains."

Michele: It's a double-edged sword, right?

Courtney: It absolutely is. Yes. And so early on, that actually affected the way I did my activism because I felt like to be a "good activist" for either of these communities, I, too, had to separate these parts of myself very, very staunchly and clearly. I had to say, "Yes, I am disabled and I am asexual." But these are two totally different identities that exist in me in parallel, but they do not intersect. They do not influence one another. And over the years, I've talked to more and more disabled aces who do say, "Well, I do think my disability and asexuality influence one another in some ways." And I realized that by sort of yielding to what these two communities were telling me, what they wanted out of my activism, I was inadvertently hurting others who did have that experience. And now I'm very much of the mind that we just need to meet people where they are and accept their word for it and believe their own unique experiences.

Michele: If I may offer up my own parallel example, I'm Jewish. That is a very strong ethnic cultural identity for me. And I also experience anxiety, and so you see stereotypes in the media about the neurotic Jewish person, especially the neurotic Jewish woman, which is very tangled in antisemitic misogyny in my own personal opinion And so it's hard for me to deal with that word "neurotic" because it feels so stigmatized for me. But at the same time, there is a strong history of trauma within the Jewish community. My family has a strong history of trauma happening to them, and which may or may not have affected, you know, the way that my brain works or the way that I react to things in real life. And so sometimes I can't separate what my response is to pain versus what has historically been done to my community.

Courtney: Absolutely, and I think that can happen with any intersection. I think society really wants us to split ourselves into pieces and put ourselves into boxes, but it's a lot more difficult to do than I think any of us give ourselves credit for.

Michele: So I think this is just a point that I really tried to reiterate in the book. We need to understand that identities are intersectional, that we all come from different roads of class and ability and race and religion and culture, and that none of those ways of existing are less valid than the other, but it can make certain others more marginalized. And then we need to make an extra effort of not stigmatizing them, but protecting and validating them.

Courtney: Absolutely.

Michele: So I guess what I want to ask now is, what do you want to see for the future of the ace community?

Courtney: Ooh, that's a big one. I would like to see the ace community focus more on celebrating our own lived experiences rather than putting on a show, and subscribing to a brand, and making ourselves seem as "palatable" as possible to outsiders.

Michele: The allosexual society.

Courtney: Absolutely. Because I have seen so often, time and time again, and there have been different iterations of where the broader community as a whole will sort of decide what is the "easiest" take, the easiest definition. And we all try to subscribe to the brand. Because we all want to be "good asexuals." We want the allo who's hearing about our orientation for the first time to have all the "right" information. But if we all individually brand ourselves, it's going to be very superficial, and it is not going to really celebrate the lush diversity that does exist within our community.

Michele: Definitely. And I want to thank people like you for just giving a voice to that diversity, for giving a face to your experiences. Because no matter what people say, I feel like having disabled aces and having aces of color and having aces of faith discuss their rich, multifaceted experiences only helps broaden the idea of what asexuality can be.

Courtney: Absolutely. Thank you. That means a lot to hear because it is not always easy to put oneself out in what can sometimes be a very hostile reception.

Michele: Of course, and I want to say thank you.

Courtney Lane (she/her) is an award-winning Victorian hair artist, internationally renowned historian, and self-proclaimed professional weirdo. Through her company, Never Forgotten, she creates bespoke works of Victorian hairwork for clients, lectures on the peculiar history behind this art form, and even teaches classes on how to perform these nearly forgotten techniques. A fierce asexual activist, you may know Courtney as one half of The Ace Couple and cohost of the podcast by the same name. She is the founder of such community projects as Disabled Ace Day and Aspecs Committed to Anti-Racism, and has utilized her extensive knowledge of accessibility while serving on the board of the International Asexuality Conference in conjunction with World Pride.

PART V

DELVING DEEPER

To Be "Queer" or Not to Be

Content Warning: This chapter includes discussion of acephobia, sexual assault, and intimate partner violence.

Note: The A in LGBTQIA+ is understood to represent all identities under the "a" prefix, including asexual, aromantic, and agender. The A has never stood for ally, though allies are always welcome for support!

When it comes to asexuality and queerness, there's a bit of an impasse for some on whether the first qualifies as the latter.

For many of us who grew up learning about the queer community (and those of us who only came into such knowledge later in life), the first letters we come to learn about are often the first four of the LGBTQIA+ acronym (emphasis on the L and G), only learning about other identities, such as intersex, pansexual, and, of course, asexual, later on, almost as an afterthought.

Of course, it definitely doesn't help that asexuality is considered the "invisible" orientation because of its lack of visibility in mainstream culture and media.

According to the Q+A section of the website for the organization PFLAG, the word "queer" has come to mean "an umbrella term for sexual and gender minorities."[1] And according to an allonormative world, where allosexuals are considered the social majority, asexuals definitely could and, in my opinion, should be considered under the umbrella of queerness.

Yet given the fact that much of mainstream media often leaves the portrayal of non-straight, non-cisgender identities lacking, much less the handful of ace characters on screen or in literature, is it any wonder, when "seeing is believing" (especially to the sighted), that aces who don't see themselves reflected back in the media they consume, who don't see themselves as part of the larger picture, mostly end up feeling alone? Erased. Invisible.

Not to mention the fact that some aces may encounter other LGBTQ+ folks who don't consider asexuality to be a form of queerness, who insist that aces aren't "queer enough."

Many acephobes within the LGBTQ+ community might try to use "history" as their argument, arguing that asexuals have never had to fight for their civil rights like the gay community has had to, or face discrimination directly on the streets, such as a same-sex couple holding hands might. Some might argue that because being asexual isn't as "visible" as, say, being gay or trans, asexuality doesn't count.

Yet that's exactly the point of invisibility. Invisibility is erasure, the denial of existence, which in turn creates marginalization.

When we are invisible, no one recognizes the need for support, for protection. As Julie Sondra Decker noted in their book *The Invisible Orientation*, "it's very easy as someone who is not in the affected population to say 'I see how my oppression affects me, but I don't believe yours is affecting you because it is irrelevant and invisible to me, so I refuse to consider it real.'"[2]

And the ace community does have its own forms of oppression. In addition to lack of ace-inclusive sex education, ace-ignorant medical biases, lack of representation in the media, and general acephobia (see examples above), there is also a noted prevalence of sexual harassment and abuse.

In their article "Asexual Perspective: When Violence is as Invisible as Orientation," Lithuanian writer Alice Michelini writes about how some partners may feel a sense of entitlement over their ace partners' sexuality, feeling as though they are "owed" sex. In some cases, they may even go as far as to initiate corrective rape to "fix" their partner's orientation. "Domestic and dating violence against asexual women can degenerate in the form of forced sexual intercourses, perpetrated with the idea that the 'beneficiary' of the act will be initiated to the magic of sex, enlightened on its beauty and eventually healed."[3]

Again, as scholar Julie Sondra Decker notes in their book:

> Asexual people in relationships—especially women—face coercion and are at higher risk for sexual assault, which is often overlooked because outside observers may believe the aggressor deserves sex or that people who are in relationship are in a constant state of consent and therefore are not capable of sexually assaulting each other.[4]

Unfortunately, corrective rape as a hate crime, in which a person is assaulted as a result of the perpetrator's attempts to "correct" the victim's perceived orientation or gender identity, is not uncommon in the LGBTQ+ community. Coined in South Africa after some well-known corrective rape cases involving lesbian women were publicized, the term became popularized by activists to raise awareness of similar cases involving LGBTQ+ people around the world.[5]

As of 2019, in terms of anti-discrimination laws in the U.S., only one state (New York) explicitly mentions asexuality. According to Asexuality Archive, "Many states have anti-discrimination laws that protect people on the basis of sexual orientation, but then go on to narrowly define sexual orientation in a manner that excludes asexuality."[6]

So yeah, on the question of whether aces face discrimination and oppression, I would say, yes, we most certainly do.

But here's the thing.

I don't want to define queerness by oppression or trauma. Those things are certainly part of the history of the LGBTQIA+ community, but they shouldn't be the standard or the hallmark of identity. Queerness shouldn't be an oppression Olympics. And even if aces weren't oppressed, then how could that be seen as a bad thing, a deterrent for being welcomed by a community that is supposed to be built on diversity and inclusivity, welcoming to those who've also felt like outsiders from the mainstream hetero-cis-centric world.

I want a world where people, regardless of whether they are trans or bi or ace, don't have to be scared or hurt for who they are.

On the question of whether asexuals should be counted as part of the queer/LGBTQ+ community, asexual activist David Jay answered:

> Definitely! ... While I wouldn't say that every ace is queer (plenty don't identify that way), I don't think you can draw a complete picture of the queer community without us. We share too many struggles and too many goals, our experiences of sexuality are too wrapped up with those of other forms of queerness.[7]

Indeed, many aces are what I would call multiply queer, occupying more than one space on the LGBTQ+ bingo board. In addition to identifying as asexual, many aces can also align with a number of romantic orientations, ranging from heteroromantic to biromantic/panromantic/polyromantic/etc. to aromantic. Not to mention that asexuals are just as likely as anyone else to identify as trans and/or non-binary.

And one may ask, so where does that leave cisgender heteroromantic aces? Could they still be counted as part of the queer community?

In my opinion, absolutely!

Even cis heteroromantic aces who experience opposite-sex attraction are still oppressed in an allonormative society, where those who experience sexual attraction are considered the "normal ones." The heteroromantic sex-repulsed ace boy is still the one who's shamed for not wanting sex, because in Western culture "real red-blooded" men are the ones who are always ready to "sow their oats" and chase after the next hot meal. The heteroromantic sex-neutral wife is shamed for her lack of attraction, thinking as a "liberated" woman she should want to desire men as much as men desire her, that to be anything otherwise is a "prude" or frigid. Just as the patriarchy hurts men, enforcing rigid, unforgiving gender roles that define who gets care and respect, allonormativity and compulsory sexuality, even when aligned with a hetero identity, still work to hurt asexual (and even many allosexual people) by reinforcing a definition of "normal" that is unachievable.

Before queer was known for its modern definition today as anything not straight or cis, the original meaning of queer was something akin to "strange" or "peculiar," something that deviates from the familiar, the so-called "norm."

In fact, the concept of sexuality as identity (i.e. identifying as a gay man versus as a man that has sexual/romantic relationships with other men) is a relatively modern invention. If you don't believe me, try looking into queer theory, particularly *The History of Sexuality* by Michael Foucault. But to save you the trouble of going into Queer Theory 101, one of Foucault's major theories was that during the Victorian era, sexuality as a system of classification was codified into science and law, defining a certain sexuality (heterosexuality) as a "normal" sexuality, while categorizing all other sexualities that deviated from such "norms," such as homosexuality, as "deviant" sexualities.[8]

So yeah, when something is placed on a pedestal as the standard for normal against which everything else is compared, a backboard against which everything else is criminalized and/or stigmatized, someone's going to fail to measure up.

Some heteroromantic aces may feel uncomfortable with identifying as queer because they feel it "takes resources away" from the queer community or that there's not enough space for heteroromantic aces at an already crowded table.

But here's the thing. The problem isn't that aces are asking for accommodation or space. It's the fact that there are limited resources at a table that never existed in the first place. Rather than fighting with each other about who gets to be designated as the "most legitimate" type of queer, why not instead make queerness a thing that is infinite, one that has room for multiple definitions and nuances, and makes space for everyone?

And why don't we try to understand that everything exists in context? That perhaps the challenges that a white cis gay man faces will be different from those an Asian biromantic ace cis woman faces, and perhaps that will be different from the challenges a heterosexual Black trans person faces. None of these people or their struggles are any less legitimate than the other, but as American scholar Kimberlé Williams Crenshaw suggests, there is the necessity for intersectional feminism, of understanding how overlapping systems of oppression—classism, racism, sexism, etc.—can work to marginalize some more than others.[9]

We need to acknowledge that while we may all be involved in the same battle for equality and acceptance, some of us are often historically placed on the frontlines more than others, especially QTPOC* people, and that we can move to help those who are more targeted or at risk, while still acknowledging our own needs.

And the way I see it, the ace community has more in common with the general queer community than it doesn't.

There's a quote from writer Ocean Vuong that goes:

* QTPOC: Queer and Trans People of Color.

Being queer saved my life. Often we see queerness as deprivation. But when I look at my life, I saw that queerness demanded an alternative innovation from me. I had to make alternative routes; it made me curious; it made me ask, "Is this enough for me?"[10]

To me, ace is exactly that. Discovering that I was asexual and learning about asexuality helped open my eyes to new ideas about the world and people. It led me on the path to learning about concepts like compulsory sexuality, allonormativity, and amanormativity. And maybe I could have learned about these things if I was straight/allosexual, but perhaps it would not have meant as much to me or have been as significant. Asexuality made me question the scripts and cultural messaging that I was brainwashed with from the moment of my conception, and made me ask, "Is this enough for me?" And by saying no, I found some things that were even better.

And when we think of queerness, perhaps we can borrow renowned scholar bell hooks' definition of queerness as "not about who you're having sex with, that can be a dimension of it, but queer as being about the self that is at odds with everything around it and has to invent and create and find a place to speak and to thrive and to live."[11]

Being ace and being queer can often feel like being at odds with the heteronormative, allonormative world around you. But it also can mean making space for new inventions. For creativity. A chance to make a world that is more tolerant of difference and diversity, and that finds the beauty in those things.

So maybe take this rule of thumb: if you're ace and feel comfortable identifying as queer, then you're queer.

And if you don't, no worries!

You do you.

On Gatekeeping and the "Gold Star Asexual"

Gatekeeping: "The activity of controlling, and usually limiting, general access to something."*

Imagine a tall, wide gateway. Heavy iron bars. Behind that entrance lies the golden ticket: resources, validation, a sense of acceptance.

Now picture the gatekeeper. The bouncer standing in front, looking you up and down, deeming you "worthy" or "unworthy" of entering. This is what happens when any party, whether a person of that community or outside it, decides they get to say who is valid, who deserves approval and legitimacy, and who doesn't.

* "Definition of gatekeeping in English." Lexico.com, www.lexico.com/en/definition/gatekeeping.

While plenty of allos have a lot of say about who does or doesn't qualify as asexual (often without ever actually having met one), for this section I want to address the reality of gatekeeping within the asexual community, to address the ways that we gatekeep each other, whether intentionally or unintentionally. Because while there is much I love about the ace community, I would be doing it and other aces a disservice by only viewing it through a rose-colored lens.

Because I have personally witnessed this gatekeeping happening in real time.

In the summer of 2021, I had written an article for the feminist media organization Bitch Media titled "It's 2021. Why Are Doctors Still Trying to 'Cure' Asexuality?" The article was written to address the issue of medical bias surrounding the asexual community.

Originally, I had been inspired to write the article based on my own experiences, as well as reading those of other asexuals, who had less than stellar experiences with doctors. For the article, I interviewed a number of asexuals, including one openly disabled and asexual woman. Overall, while many people responded positively to the article, finding it informative and relatable, there was, of course, the exception of a few critics.

And while as a writer, I would understand that not everyone would be a fan of *my* work in particular, the majority of the criticism wasn't intended for me. Instead, it had been directed toward someone else.

To my horror, I learned after the interview was published that the person I'd interviewed, the disabled asexual person who had been so generous in sharing their experiences with me, had been harassed by both acephobes *and* members of the asexual community. The latter specifically targeted her for speaking as a disabled ace person, claiming that she was not a "good" spokesperson for the asexual community, that she was invalidating the community simply by speaking up about her own personal experiences as a disabled person, and ultimately saying she should not have spoken at all.

Instead of appreciating a valuable voice that had strengthened the article by speaking to the intersectional diversity of the ace community, as well as the multilayered oppression of medial bias faced by those within the ace and disabled communities, they instead attacked and maligned her for existing as who she was.

Unfortunately, this person is not the only one who has faced this sort of malicious behavior.

Yasmin Benoit, a Black British asexual model and activist, has been repeatedly trolled over the years for her image, both as a woman of color and as a lingerie model, receiving racist and misogynistic vitriol. While many see Yasmin Benoit's presentation as a way to knock down the limitations of what an asexual person can look like (Yasmin Benoit literally invented the hashtag #thisiswhatasexuallookslike in order to showcase that there is no "standard" look for an asexual), some detractors bashed her as an "inappropriate" role model for her dress, using cutting slut-shaming remarks for the "revealing" clothes she sometimes wore, while others were blatantly racist in their disapproval of her.[2]

Unfortunately, just as it is systemic in wider society, the ace community is not immune to ableism, racism, or any other -isms or types of social prejudice.

While it is definitely no excuse, perhaps a large part of this ignorance stems from the lack of diverse representation in the mainstream picture of asexuality. When your only note of reference for asexuality is either Todd Chavez from *BoJack Horseman* (a white, despite the Latinx last name, cis man) or David Jay (another white cis man), then you might possibly get a limited idea of what asexuality can look like. And no matter how lovely the representation or representatives are, if they only come from a limited demographic, then they can only represent a limited demographic.

Just as general queer representation has been dominated by stories and images of white cis gay men, erasing the presence of other letters within the LGBTQIA+ acronym, the asexual community has, until recently, been predominately depicted through a narrow gaze, itself an imprecise reflection of a wider, more diverse audience.

And, of course, there's also the issue of the "Gold Star Asexual."

"What is the 'Gold Star Asexual'?" you may ask.

In 2010, a blogger named Sciatrix coined the term "Gold Star Ace" (presumably taking inspiration from the term "Gold Star Lesbian," meaning a lesbian who has never had sex with a man) to refer to an asexual who has no "quality about oneself that might allow some person to challenge our asexuality."[3]

And believe me, those who identify as asexual have faced *many* challenges from other people with regard to our identity.

Many times, when an ace person first comes out to the world, we are instantly met by a rebuttal of our identity by allosexual trolls (not referring to the allosexual allies who are lovely and respectful) who try to invalidate our asexuality for some reason or another.

Many acephobes will try to reason away our orientation through various explanations, claiming that we are either too "young" (for those that are young at least—for older aces, the argument may be different) to know who we are, or that this is a "hormonal issue," trying to pathologize asexuality as a "medical condition," and even trying to imply we are only asexual become someone has "hurt" us, as if asexuality could only stem from the abusive actions of an outside party (the fact that random strangers feel entitled to ask about this is horrifying in itself).

As a result, many in the asexual community become guarded and wary of this type of treatment and comments, and we constantly feel on the defensive, arming ourselves with a metaphorical shield of reasoning to deflect any criticism we might face. Like others in the LGBTQIA+ community feeling pushed to claim the "born this way" narrative in order to avoid having their identity attributed to something negative, such as poor parenting skills or child abuse, we try to avoid any connotations of pathology or other unfavorable origins that could "delegitimatize" who we are.

Yet according to Sciatrix's comments, the "Gold Star Ace" must be a person who not only has never experienced sexual attraction, but also has never had sex, has never desired sex, has never even masturbated, who has also never had a record of disability, chronic illness/pain, and/or neurodivergence, or history of trauma or abuse, while also being presumably young, cis, white, and conveniently "attractive" (in order to dispel any notions that they only identify as asexual because no one else has found them "desirable").

Honestly, the list is bullshit.

Because, according to this list, the field of those who would qualify as "legitimate" asexuals would be *extremely* narrow and limited.

The reality is that aces come from all kinds of backgrounds and can be of all shades, shapes, and sizes.

There are aces who happen to be disabled, as well as aces who also happen to be non-white. In neither case does one identity cancel out the other.

There are also many aces who have a sexual history for various reasons. Perhaps some asexuals who come out later in life (likely because they didn't have the resources to understand or recognize their own asexuality) have already had sex because they felt obligated to. And some aces have sex for others reasons, whether it's to consensually please their partner, to procreate, and so on.

Many aces have a range of libidos and desires. Some may find they have a high libido, others low, and many have those that are in between or fluctuating.

Some aces may even enjoy things that seem sexual in nature, like erotica, kink, masturbation, etc.

And none of this makes any of them less ace.

As for the idea of the validity of asexuality based on a pure "origin," that asexuality must not be caused by illness or trauma or any other extenuating circumstances in order for it to count, nothing in life is clear-cut.

As each of us goes through life, we accumulate a number of experiences, some good, some neutral, and some not-so-great.

Some asexuals are born disabled, while others become disabled later in life. Disability activist Judith Heumann once pointed out that the likelihood of someone "acquiring a disability, temporarily or permanently, is statistically very high."[4] It is estimated 15% of the world's population—more than one billion people—experience some form of disability.[5] And with asexuals estimated to make up at least 1% of the human population,[6] there's bound to be some overlap.

As for those who identify as asexual and have experienced trauma (physical, emotional, etc.), let me say this...

While there are those who consider their asexuality and their trauma to be two separate facts, others may feel that their asexuality is somewhat rooted in the latter.

In this world, there are some experiences we cannot untangle from the core of ourselves, no matter how much we may want to. Sometimes we are the web of our experiences, each thread of one identity inextricably bound to other threads. So while one thing—trauma or disability—may not be the entirety of who we are, nevertheless we are still shaped by these things, as well as the things that have happened to us.

So while the fear of ace invalidation through medical pathologizing or trauma blaming is very real, by saying that we are asexual because we are not "this, this, and this," we may also accidentally invalidate those who are.

And the real problem isn't the aces with complicated backgrounds or "too many tangled threads." It's the naysayers, the acephobes, who are looking for any excuse to make us feel nullified. As Angela Chen stated, "The obsession with the origin of asexuality, this pressure that makes proving asexuality nearly impossible, comes from—you guessed it—the belief that every person should be sexual, whether that comes from the general public or is enforced within a particular community."[7]

In our world, being allosexual or straight or cisgender is considered the "default." And placing those identities as the default places every other identity under suspicion, making anything else seem like a "glitch," a failure.

Heteronormativity is the reason why orientations such as homosexuality were put under the microscope for so long, why scientists questioned whether someone was gay because they were "mentally ill" or sexually abused. Until 1973, the American Psychiatric Association listed homosexuality as a "deviant and immoral" mental illness in its *Diagnostic and Statistical Manual* (DSM) until queer activists campaigned to change it.[8]

Today (in more liberal areas at least) it would be considered outrageous to suggest that someone is gay because of abuse, and even more ridiculous to suggest that someone heterosexual is straight because they weren't abused.

But it also doesn't change the fact that both gay and straight abuse survivors exist.

While many aces do not associate their asexuality with their history of trauma or abuse, there might be those who do.

And that's okay, too.

Identity doesn't exist in a vacuum.

Aceness doesn't exist in a vacuum.

Simultaneous truths can coexist. When I walk out into the world, I walk out into it as someone who is both marginalized and privileged. Marginalized for being queer/ace, and AFAB, while at the same time *literally walking* without a physical disability and with a sense of "safety" because of the color of my skin, and at the same time knowing, because I am also Jewish, how white supremacy makes that privilege *very* conditional.

Rather than suggesting that aceness should conform to a simplistic "check one box" criterion, we can acknowledge intersectional identities, acknowledge that there is a natural diversity and complexity of self that refuses to be stamped down by the temptation of simplicity or the "Gold Star Asexual" myth.

Because "Gold Star Asexuals" are just that. A myth.

Although the ace community is so used to the pain of being discredited by others, when we begin to turn on each other and discredit a person's asexuality based on the color of their skin, disability/mental illness, or anything else that "complicates" the ace narrative, we become the worst, most carnivorous versions of ourselves.

While it has long remained a playful (if edged) joke within the lesbian community, the term "Gold Star Lesbian" has recently been called out for its more pejorative nature, and its potential to invalidate and demean other queer people. As non-binary comic artist Archie Bongiovanni said about the expression, "2009 called, it wants its transphobic biphobic slut-shame-y lingo back."[9]

Instead of trying to conform to the "Gold Star Asexual" trope, perhaps it's better to admit that reality is more complicated. That maybe all of us human beings are both a product of nature and nurture. That identity can be complicated and innate and fluid. And that while many of the circumstances of one's life are out of one's control, we can still lay claim to the identities we choose. And that anyone who uses your pain or your other identities to invalidate who you are as a person is someone who is doing a disservice to an already vulnerable community.

Rather than fighting for space, for recognition, for resources at an imaginary table (when in reality the table doesn't exist), why not make a bigger space so that everyone may get the help and support they need?

And instead of favoring those who might be more privileged in the ace community (white, cis, non-disabled, etc.), we can do the work of including everyone and uplifting those voices that may have been sidelined, giving them the space, credit, and care they deserve.

It's a harsh world out there.

Let's just try to be kind to each other instead.

Tips for Coping with Acephobia and Other Garbage

Content Warning: This chapter includes discussion of acephobia and general bigotry.

While there are many things I love about being ace, dealing with acephobia is not one of them.

Acephobia, otherwise known as aphobia, acemisia, or ane-antagonism, refers to the prejudice, hostility, and/or oppression experienced by asexual people. This can take many forms, from the absence of protective legislature for aces within law, to discriminatory medical biases, to plain ignorant comments from assholes.

While the consequences of the latter may seem less intense than the former, the ramifications of ignorance, as any person who has experienced bullying would know, can still be severe.

I think by now everyone knows that the saying "sticks and stones will break your bones, but words will never hurt you" is complete and utter bull. While the physical effects of "sticks and stones" may be more visible on a tangible level (i.e. bruises), the emotional effects of words can have just as long-lasting (if not longer-lasting) outcomes, such as anxiety and depression.

As therapists and authors Susan Forward and Craig Buck have written, "Verbal abuse is as damaging as physical abuse, and in some cases, it does even more damage... Insulting names, degrading comments and constant criticism all leave deep emotional scars that hinder feelings of self-worth and personal agency."[1] Although the authors wrote this in the context of abuse inflicted by toxic parents, I feel their words are applicable to anyone who has ever been on the receiving end of toxic attitudes that dismiss one's identity and humanity. Especially when they come from those you care about.

One of the strongest examples of acephobia I've experienced in my life came from a relative. Although I won't go into detail about the event (my brain has blocked most of it out of self-preservation), essentially after I came out to this family member, they proceeded to tell me that asexuals don't exist and that people who claim otherwise were immature and mentally unsound. To say that this incident doesn't still sting to this day, even years after that conversation, would be a lie.

In that moment, I had told someone I'd considered family (and still do) a personal truth of mine, had opened myself up to vulnerability. I would have been fine if they had just looked at me with a blank expression and said, "Okay." If they had just moved on, without ever bringing the subject up again. Instead, that person had reacted with contempt and acidic remarks, mocking something that was important to me. My identity.

In that moment, I was sad and angry, feeling disappointed at their reaction and hurt by their ignorance. And while it's so easy to get caught up in those hurt feelings, to let the other person's comments stick and solidify into a thorn that will rip flesh every time that memory moves in your brain, there are some things you can do to help mitigate that pain and hopefully heal from it.

So based on my own personal experiences and other advice I've picked up, here are a few coping strategies that I would recommend for dealing with acephobia:

Remove Yourself from the Scene

If you can leave, do it. Go away. Now.

Take yourself far from the people who are actively causing you distress and harm. If the acephobia is happening online, log off whatever social media platform you're on, and stay away from the phone/computer for as long as you can. While I know a part of you might want to defend yourself, in my experience of this type of situation, the people who are arguing against you have only one opinion they value, and it isn't yours.

Most likely in the case of social media, the people who are spouting acephobia are most likely trolls, people who, no matter what clear or logical arguments you may present, will have no sense of empathy or reasoning to hear your side. Instead, they simply enjoy wasting your time and energy. So rather than fighting a battle you can't win (because this isn't a war that can be resolved in one day), it's better to disengage than waste your energy and mental effort on someone who won't listen.

Acknowledge the Stressor/Deal with the Stress Cycle

You might notice your body and mind going through a number of things after dealing with a case of acephobia, such as racing thoughts, tight muscles, shortness of breath. And if that all sounds like stress, it probably is.

In their book *Burnout: The Secret to Unlocking the Stress Cycle*, authors Emily and Amelia Nagoski identified something common in a lot of modern-day people known as the "stress cycle," in which the body and mind after a harrowing encounter (or stress built over time) are running on anxiety and cortisol, which need to be released from your system; otherwise, they will build up over time and burn you out. Basically, imagine being chased by a lion, and your body goes into fight-or-flight mode, and you do whatever you can to put yourself out of danger. Now convert that to a less physical, but still emotionally draining context. Maybe you can escape the lion, and think, "End of crisis, end of stress cycle." But in cases that have a more ambiguous ending (perhaps the stressful situation is still ongoing in some way), the crisis isn't over, and your body is still responding as though it's under attack.

If you've experienced acephobia, you have been attacked. Perhaps not physically, but emotionally and mentally? Definitely. Because unlike an attack by a literal lion, which is most likely done out of instinct (e.g. hunger or feeling threatened), an attack by an acephobe feels more personal because it is. When someone attacks your identity, they are attacking your sense of self, the most intimate part of you. And while the lion might eventually lose interest (or eat you), the effects of acephobia, of stigma and negative attitudes and insults, might last longer, eating away at your insides instead.

So instead of dismissing acephobia as "just words," letting the effects of that hurt fester and rot silently inside you, acknowledge it for what it is—a stressful and painful form of bigotry. That way you can name the stresser (aka the "lion"), and begin the resolution of the stress cycle, the process of soothing and healing.

Ways for Dealing with Stress

Breathe

The first thing you can do is breathe. Cliché, I know, but it's a cliché for a reason. Just as you would need to breathe after being chased by a lion, your body needs oxygen after going through something mentally exhausting.

One breathing exercise you can do is breathing in slowly for five seconds, holding that breath for five more seconds, and then exhaling for five seconds. And then repeating as needed.

While breathing may sound overly simplistic, it does something for the nervous system that almost nothing else can, and it teaches you "mindfulness," which basically translates to awareness of your surroundings and yourself.[2] Mindfulness activates the parasympathetic nervous system—your body's "rest and digest" system—and once that's activated, your heart rate and blood pressure will lower, reducing anxiety in the process.

If you're having trouble being mindful on your own, there are meditation apps, as well as free guided breathing exercises available online to help teach you. And if the idea of needing to teach oneself to "breathe" might sound a little silly, sometimes the chaos of life can make us all forget how to do basic functions, so it doesn't hurt to have a reminder every now and again.

Crying or Screaming into a Pillow

Know that building pressure behind your eyes or the hot angry feeling in your chest that's trying to get out? Let it.

While polite society might suggest it's immature to do those things, saying stuff like "big girls/boys/enbies don't cry," sometimes it's truly necessary to feed into the emotional instincts we try so hard to repress so that our body can self-soothe and use its natural mechanisms for handling stress. Tears were designed for the purpose of lubricating the eyes and cleansing stuff out like dust and dirt, so let your body use tears as a way to cleanse the stress hormones and toxins from your system.[3] As for the screaming, well, there's almost nothing as primal as yelling or howling out loud for a temporary release from anger or frustration.

Just maybe go somewhere private for that, like a bedroom with a pillow, or somewhere where a scream won't attract attention.

Laughter Is the Best Medicine

Again a cliché, but a cliché for a reason. Other than just feeling really good, scientists have studied the physical and mental benefits of laughing, including releasing stress hormones, reducing physical tension, releasing endorphins (feel-good chemicals), increasing blood flow which helps long-term in promoting cardiovascular health, etc.[4] (I'm not kidding, look it up.) So go to YouTube and pull up clips of your favorite comedian or that comedy series you love (a personal favorite of mine is *The Nanny*) and just lose yourself in the laugh track for a few minutes. You might find yourself coming back to a mental space that's more hopeful and less hostile.

Hit Up a Friend

After a nasty encounter with an acephobe, it's nice to turn to someone friendly, someone you actually want to be around. After the encounter with my family member that I described earlier, I called one of my best friends, who, while not ace, was an ace ally and was willing to hear me kvetch about what happened in a non-judgmental manner, offering his sympathy and support. And after I was finished (for the moment at least) processing what happened, we talked for a bit about nerdy stuff, which might have helped me as much as the venting did. Whether meeting a friend in person, video-calling, or texting, having someone who you know as a safe space can be almost as good as having a literal safe space.

Affection

While this may not always be applicable, physical affection from others, whether a hug from a loving family member, friend, or partner, or cuddling with a pet, can do wonders for the body. Hand-holding, kissing, stroking one's back, and other examples of affectionate, non-threatening touch help release a bonding hormone known as oxytocin (the same hormone that bonds new parents to babies), which in turn makes you feel good and releases toxic stress from the body. You can even alter the type of physical affection according to physical ability and comfort levels, including self-compassion from yourself.[5] Examples include placing your hand over your heart (corny, but studies show that this one small gesture can release a good amount of oxytocin), softly squeezing one hand in the other, or gently rubbing your chest, all of which are self-soothing, stimulatory motions that teach mindfulness, as well as help you feel safe and comforted.

Physical Activity

While, to many people, physical activity might not sound appealing to many (who knows—maybe the person reading this is a gym rat), it can be a pretty effective way of managing stress.[6] Many of the same things spoken about in the previous sections—focus on breathing, endorphins, mindfulness—can be found in exercise. When done carefully (it might be best to stay away from any risky activities when you're angry or upset), exercise forces you to pay attention to your body, to its movements, and its breathing patterns, while drawing your attention away from stressful thoughts. Not to mention it can be pretty damn cathartic punching or kicking when you're upset (especially if you imagine the target as acephobia or any other garbage you have to deal with on a day-to-day basis).

Even something as simple as taking a walk can give your mind something to focus on instead of the crap you've just faced.

In whatever way you enjoy or tolerate motion—swimming, martial arts, running, etc.—my advice is if your blood is already pumping, give it a healthy outlet.

Creativity

Painting, writing, sewing, playing music... If you're more artistically inclined, perhaps try turning toward your imagination for help. As a writer, I can say it has definitely been helpful to put my feelings down on paper (or on a computer), processing my thoughts (and hurts), and editing things to my satisfaction. If you're a poet, write a poem. If you're a singer, sing something (maybe even death metal like in *Aggretsuko*). If you like to sew your own cosplay, why not try working on a pattern for that animated character you love? If there's a creative endeavor you enjoy and/or find emotional release from, why not do it?

Of course, you don't always have to make something or be productive to find the benefits in creativity. I am a big advocate for indulging in one's imagination (and fandoms) just for the sake of it.

If you're the type of person who enjoys crafting something, why not combine the best of both worlds and try knitting a scarf while binge-watching *The Owl House*?

In Conclusion

Please understand this...

Acephobia hurts. If someone says or does something acephobic to you (no matter how "small" it might seem), it's okay—no, natural—to feel hurt because of it.

And if someone, specifically the acephobe themselves, tries to tell you whatever comment they made was "not a big deal," don't believe them. That is them trying to invalidate and gaslight your pain, taking away their responsibility for hurting your feelings, for hurting you. Your feelings are valid, and your pain is real.

Even after dealing with the initial stress, it can still hurt. For me, while I may have dealt with the incident with my relative using some of the strategies described above, I can't say the memory still doesn't hurt from time to time. Or that the other times I've experienced acephobia don't hurt. Or that the times I may face it in the future won't hurt. All I can do is acknowledge that hurt for what is, while taking care of myself. To which I have to say...

It is not indulgent or immature to take care of yourself. In fact, it could be one of the most emotionally mature lessons you can learn, to acknowledge pain and learn how to process it through non-destructive coping mechanisms. Which brings me to...

Placing Boundaries

Remember that thing I said about temporarily removing yourself from the stressor? Sometimes you might have to go a step further.

The truth is, some people might always be rooted in their prejudices. As much as you might want people to understand and accept your asexuality (or at least for people not to be jerks about it), this isn't something you can control. That's why I'd advise working with what you can control—your personal boundaries.

If the situation takes place online and applies to social media, there's a reason the block feature was invented. Remember, you don't have to engage with every fight an acephobic troll brings your way.

And if the acephobic person is a loved one, then, first of all, I want to say I'm so sorry you've had to deal with that. No one should have to put up with that crap, especially from someone they care about.

The truth is, while perhaps some people might come around, taking the appropriate measures to acknowledge how they have hurt you and working on educating themselves to make sure it doesn't happen again, it's not something I can guarantee.

In cases like this, something you need to know is that just as you can't squeeze blood from a stone, you can't force acceptance from other people. Sometimes it may just be easier to accept other people's limitations.

But remember, just because you accept something, that doesn't mean you have to forgive it. It just means you can try shifting the weight of their ignorance so that it will weigh less on you. In those cases, it's up to you to be a good judge of character and decide if and how you want to engage further with the people who have hurt you.

For me, that meant deciding not to engage with my acephobic relative on anything related to asexuality. I continue to see them during family get-togethers, but I limit my interactions with them and stay mum about asexuality around the more conservative members of my family. Other times, it has meant cutting out "friends" who've put me down because of their ignorance. It's not perfect, but it saves my sanity, which is very precious these days.

Only you can decide how to define your limits around those you engage with (though I would advise speaking with a trusted counselor and/or supportive friend/family member if you feel you need a second opinion or guidance on the situation). Which brings me to...

Find Your Community and Allies

One of the best things I did for myself as an asexual person was to reach out to allies and other ace folks for guidance and support.

Find people who relate to you in terms of asexuality, who have the vocabulary for understanding what asexuality is, and for knowing what it's like to be ace in an allo-majority world. Finding solidarity through community can be a healing experience, and perhaps knowing that others have gone through the same things you have will help remind you that you are not alone in your experiences or your identity.

I would recommend looking up AVEN as well as ace-specific meet-up groups in your geographic area, such as Ace Los Angeles or Aces NYC. And while physical interactions with other aces may be limited, let me just say that living in a digital age has allowed for connections in various spaces.

(Please remember to exercise caution and personal discretion, as you would in any situation engaging with new people, whether in person or in cyber space. If you are meeting with someone IRL for the first time, please do so in public spaces with a trusted family member/friend knowing where you are. If online, please keep personal information limited and privacy settings on, and follow other general practices for internet safety.)

Remember that while being ace isn't always easy, there are people out there who are willing and able to support you. Sometimes these might look like unexpected allies who can surprise you in all the best ways, like the friend I mentioned who was there for me and is currently learning all he can about the LGBTQIA+ community. And sometimes it might mean finding fellow aces who understand and get what you're going through.

Just know that you are valid in who you are, and no one can take that away from you.

Am I Repressed?

That's probably one of the first questions many aces ask themselves. Am I actually asexual? Am I too old-fashioned, too prudish? Am I not feminist enough, liberated enough, sex-positive enough? Et cetera, et cetera, et cetera.

And the truth is...

In some ways, we all have a little bit of repression in us.

Or, to paraphrase the song from *Avenue Q* (ahem, cue music), "Everyone's a Little Bit Repressed!"[1]

Think about it.

If we define repression as a form of restriction and oppression, then every human on this planet is "repressed" in one way or another by various systems, including medical, legal, and religious, as well as by conscious and unconscious expectations of social etiquette and behavior. French philosopher Michel Foucault proposed the *panopticon*, "a central observation tower placed within a circle of prison cells" as a disciplinary model for human society.[2] As the Ethics Center puts it, "from the tower, a guard can see every cell and inmate but the inmates can't see into the tower. Prisoners will never know whether or not they are being watched."[3]

Sounds intense, right?

Academic psychologist and author Meg-John Barker best summarized the panopticon theory as follows:

Foucault, however, used the panopticon to illuminate the ways in which people in contemporary societies become so aware of the various critical gazes upon them that they end up self-monitoring their own actions through fear that they might not be acceptable to others. This has developed into a culture where everyone polices themselves through fear of punishment, ridicule, and disapproval.[4]

Sound familiar?

While Foucault first developed this theory in the 1970s, it would seem that the panopticon model is still relevant today, especially with the advent of surveillance technology and social media.

In a world where we are put under literal constant observation, of course we would develop some form of self-consciousness through fear of being judged by others for our thoughts and actions.

Especially when it comes to sex.

Frankly, society has always been obsessed with sex. With how we have it as individuals, in our own relationships, and how others have it as well.

For those of us who live in the West (I can only speak to my own experiences living in North America), we live in a culture that is both puritanical and sex-obsessed, flinching away from it while also being (nonconsensually) voyeuristic about it.

Just look at the hypocrisy of a society that does its best to restrict access to birth control and comprehensive and accurate sex education (which unfortunately is not always legally mandated and varies from state to state and county to county), yet nearly every billboard, advertisement, television show, and film has readily available sexually suggestive content that only stops short of the actual act itself.

Historically, the way we've treated sex—how we've depicted it, lambasted it, restricted it, and celebrated it, and back again, as well as made it the center of political debates and social revolutions—can make anyone's head spin.

During more sexually repressive times, when sex as an act was legally restricted within the confines of a monogamous heterosexual marriage and sexual agency (particularly for those AFAB) was limited, there were reverse movements for sexual liberation inspired by the ideals of sex-positive feminism.

But what does sex-positive liberation look like?

Does it look as some characters from *Sex and the City* would suggest—where everyone has sex all the time, where women can "fuck" like men (or how we think "men" have sex), having sex aggressively with as many people and orgasms as possible, without emotional attachment?

Does sexual liberation look like having the "wildest" sex possible, trying out every toy and fetish and scenario known to humankind, never stopping until we check off every point on a never-ending to-do (both in terms of activities and partners) list?

And if so, does sexual liberation mean shaming the person who isn't interested in any of that? Does it mean laughing at the woman who wants to wait until marriage to have sex? The eighteen-year-old boy who hasn't gotten "laid" yet and is not even sure if he really wants to, if he ever wants to? The non-binary aromantic asexual who would rather have a platonic cuddle session with their best friend while watching a movie and drinking a cup of tea?

I don't think so.

To want to have sex, in whatever manner or with however many people you want, is one thing. But to embarrass or shame people into thinking there's only one "right" way to have sex, to be a sexual person, or even to be a person at all? To force someone into thinking they're "broken" or "prudish" if they don't experience desire or attraction in the way everyone else does (or the way mainstream society thinks everyone else experiences those things)?

That doesn't really sound very revolutionary to me.

If a man (or anyone) were to say to me right now, "Hey, you're not really asexual," tell me that I'm just sexually repressed or oppressed, and suggest they could "fix" that by having sex with me, that wouldn't be liberation. That would be a *manipulation* of the idea of sexual liberation, disguised as something else in order for the other person to get what they want (without focusing on what I actually want or need).

For so long, we have compared ourselves with each other, trying to work out what is the "best" way or the "right" way to have sex, to figure out what is normal and what isn't.

Yet the idea of "sexual normativity" has hurt so many people.

It is the reason why monosexism exists, "operating through a presumption that everyone is, or should be, monosexual (attracted to no more than one gender),"[5] and how biphobia happens, shaming those whose reality doesn't follow that presumption. It is the reason it takes lesbians years, if not decades, to come out, because of compulsive heterosexuality,[6] believing that they must be "straight" because no other possibility is allowed to exist. It is the reason why many asexuals are terrified to admit they're asexual, because it means going against the cultural scripts of sexuality that have been forced down our throats our entire lives.

While I can understand how confusing (and frustrating) it can be to untangle the influences of toxic patriarchy, of cis-heterosexism, and all the other crap that potentially makes us feel ashamed and terrified of our bodies and minds, I also believe that forcing oneself to do something just because other people say it's the "right" thing or the "liberating" thing to do, despite our actual comfort levels, can be like giving in to peer pressure. To twist your body into a shape that you know and feel is "wrong" for you.

Ultimately, it's up to us to trust in our own self-awareness, to know what feels good and natural for ourselves. But in order to have that, we need to be given the space to experiment, to figure things out on our own without the pressure of shame or coercion.

And to be clear, while there has been much debate within feminist movements (there have been several waves and branches of feminism throughout the years) of what can be considered "liberating" versus "degrading" (look up the anti-pornography movement of the 1970s and 1980s) as well as current debates over sex work (historically, the criminalization of sex work has primarily done more to harm women and femme-identified people, particularly trans women/femmes of color), what was essentially underlying the sex liberation movement was the drive for a world free of patriarchal violence and restriction.

To allow sex to be more than just reproduction, letting those who have been historically restricted from pleasure feel entitled to it. To ensure that women weren't considered the property of men, that husbands couldn't "legally" rape their spouses and get away with it. To give everyone, regardless of their gender, access to family planning and birth control.

Ultimately, full liberation means allowing other people to define what "liberation" means to them, whether that's having consensual sex around the clock or never having sex at all.

So if you're ace, and someone thinks that makes you "repressed," it just means they don't understand what asexuality really means or they don't want to understand what that means. And that's their problem. Not yours.

Remember, no one but you has the right to dictate what happens in your bed or between your legs or any other part of your body. Even if they buy you dinner.

Sacks of Yellow Fat

Ever seen that show *Crazy Ex-Girlfriend?*

Despite the awful name, the show is actually pretty brilliant, dismantling sexist, ableist tropes, like the "crazy ex-girlfriend" trope, in addition to thoughtful commentary on subjects such as mental health, Jewish identity, and more. And much of it through the lens of musical comedy.

Among the show's many hit bops is the unforgettable song "Heavy Boobs,"[1] in which protagonist, Rachel Bunch, talks about (or rather sings about) some of the downsides to being "busty."

As a person who isn't exactly flat-chested, I felt a hilarious sense of vindication at a song that pointed out how big boobs could be a pain sometimes (literally!) rather than just the perky accessory most people think they are. At various points, she even calls them "sacks of yellow fat," reminding people that their original biological purpose was to feed children.

Aside from how troublesome it can be finding affordable bras for larger sizes—despite what its modeling campaign suggests, Victoria's Secret does not love big-breasted women—there are other drawbacks to these "sacks of yellow fat."

Such as how, from the moment I turned eleven, I felt the need to hide my body. To hunch over and cover my curves with excess layers, even on hot days. To know that everyone, from family members, to school administrators, to strangers on the street, suddenly had something to say about this new "development," whether it was good or bad.

It wasn't just the physical weight of breasts that dragged me down, even though exercise soon required an industrial-strength sports bra and sleeping on my stomach became more complicated. It was the mental weight of it as well.

Of having creeps leering at my chest, yelling obscene things about my body when I walked my dog down the sidewalk. Of feeling shamed for wearing clothes that allowed my skin to breathe and me to feel comfortable in 100°F+ weather. Of the pressure to never leave the house without a bra and being unable to take one off for seven or more hours at a time, even when the underwire pressed painfully against my ribcage.

Now, not all asexuals will have the same relationship with their body as I do. A person's relationship with their physical form is a deeply mental, emotional, and personal thing. Many aces, like non-aces, love their heavy boobs, seeing it as an affirmation of their gender identity and a signal of their sensual appearance, which is completely valid.

But I don't think it's out there to say there's a certain weight existing as an asexual person in a hypersexualized body.

In fact, Western society has a certain fixation with breasts, especially in a gendered sense.

Why else would breasts be so heavily focused on in modern media, such as television and film, but the people who have them are so heavily disciplined? Dress codes penalize female students just for showing bra straps[2] (the mere suggestion of boobs being enough to distract the other male students, *rolls eyes*) or parents being shamed for breastfeeding in public (even though advertisements with models who look as though they would fall over if they just leaned a little further with their spilling cleavage show far more boob most of the time).

My point is, this one body part is put so far under the microscope that I'm surprised there's not a permanent bruise from the indent.

And this situation is even worse for people of color.

Non-white bodies have been hypersexualized for *centuries*, the curve of their bodies being subjected to appearing in freak shows (as seen in the case of Sara "Saartjie" Baartman, nicknamed the "Hottentot Venus"[3]), to colonial and post-colonial exploitation, as well as sexual and racial fetishization. Examples linger in jokes about the oversized bodily proportions and sexual prowess of Black men, which are so common that many forget the darker undercurrents of this type of humor, of how these jokes are tied to an overly aggressive sexuality thought to threaten the "innocence" of white women. Or how Black and brown women, when they are not desexualized as "Mammy" figures, have been classified as "Jezebel" types,[4] considered to have such insatiable sexual appetites as to render void any physical crimes committed against their bodies (and their autonomies).

And aces of color have to deal with all this and acephobia, too.

It's undeniable that when it comes to being seen and accepted as ace, many aces of color have a harder time of it, both within and outside the asexual community. Due to the lack of diverse ace representation in mainstream media and the persistence of racialized sexual stereotypes tied to hypersexualization, many people think Black and other people of color are inherently unable to be "asexual," even claiming asexuality as a "white thing," despite the overwhelming evidence proving otherwise.

Personally, I can't speak to the

multiple margins of oppression that aces of color face on a continual basis, but I don't have to.

Aces of color have been doing that on their own.

Take the essay "The Antithesis of Malehood: Being Asexual as a Hypersexualized Being" by M'Jean Mason, in which the author discusses how their existence challenges stereotyped perceptions of Black masculinity created through white supremacy, toxic masculinity, and acephobia. In their piece, they speak about "living as a Black ace man maneuvering through life in the face of the stigmas against all identities encompassed as one."[5]

Or how Yasmin Benoit, a Black asexual lingerie model, challenges the claim that a body that is "desired" must inherently be sexual, instead embracing a sensuality that is equal parts making a living, embracing her own individuality and aesthetic appearance, and pursuing a mode of activism challenging expectations of what an asexual can "look" like.

When I or any other asexual person steps out into the world with these "sacks of yellow fat," or our bodies in general, we are entering a web of hypersexualization that is further complicated by racism, sexism, misogyny, fatphobia, capitalism, and other threads of oppression.

But what I can say is that no matter how you choose to present your own aesthetics, or how your body manifests in this world, you are worthy and deserving of bodily autonomy, consent, and respect, even when the world may say otherwise.

It's 2023. Why Are Doctors Still Trying to "Cure" Asexuality?*

In a 2012 episode of *House*, titular protagonist Dr. Gregory House (Hugh Laurie) attempts to disprove a couple's claim that they're asexual. In House's view, the only people who don't "want" sex are "sick, dead, or lying." The episode resolves with the doctor discovering that the husband has a pituitary tumor that affects his sex drive (note: lack of sex drive ≠ asexuality), and that his wife was just lying to preserve her husband's pride. In other words, House was right: asexuality isn't real and is often a symptom of a medical issue. Unfortunately, House's mentality is all too common in the real world. "As discriminatory as this is in fiction, it's really not too far from what I've actually experienced," ace artist Courtney Lane says. "Not only does it lead to fear and mistrust, but it does real, tangible harm diagnostically and financially."

Lane has a disability, the nature of which she doesn't disclose, that requires her to undergo an above-average number of X-rays in a given year. Before the X-rays are conducted, she has to take a mandatory pregnancy test, even though she's repeatedly shared that she's asexual. "I've quite literally been sitting in my doctor's office having difficulty breathing and urgently needing a lung X-ray to check for

* Originally published as Michele Kirichanskaya. "It's 2021. Why Are Doctors Still Trying to 'Cure' Asexuality?" Bitch Media, June 21, 2021, www.bitchmedia.org/article/doctors-still-mistreat-asexual-patients.

pneumonia while waiting on a urinalysis to come back and tell my doctors the obvious," she says. "It's humiliating to not be believed by the people I'm supposed to trust to oversee my health, but it's also tremendously expensive when all of these little costs throughout the year add up." Because of doctors' assumptions, Lane's been forced to pay out of pocket for certain procedures, such as urine tests, and has endured unnecessary emotional stress. "My disability has riddled my medical history with question marks, and not all physicians are prepared to diagnose or treat something so rare and under-researched," she says. "I've seen first-hand how harmful it can be when doctors try to pathologize your illness when they've run out of ideas. I don't want doctors to pathologize my illness, and I don't want doctors to medicalize my sexual orientation, but I find that the two often go hand in hand. It's exhausting."

The pathologizing of LGBTQ+ people isn't new: Until 1973, the American Psychiatric Association equated queerness with being "crazy" in its *Diagnostic and Statistical Manual* (DSM).[2] Although the DSM no longer lists "homosexuality" as a mental illness, the manual's fifth edition relates asexuality to a condition called hypoactive sexual desire disorder, or HSDD, defined by "low sexual desire accompanied by marked distress or interpersonal difficulties."[3] Whether this distress is attributed to having "low sexual desire" or is associated with existing as asexual in an allonormative/acephobic society[4] is the question. When people in the asexual community come out, they're often met with incredulity and/or skepticism from family, friends, and even medical practitioners.[5] Lane says they've experienced "burdensome biases from healthcare providers" throughout their life, which has contributed to a "culture of distrust in medicine when it comes to patients who are women and/or exist within the LGBTQ+ spectrum."

According to the Asexual Visibility and Education Network, an asexual person is defined as a "person who does not experience sexual attraction."* It isn't equivalent to celibacy, and while some asexual people may not experience sexual attraction—demisexuals** and graysexuals*** can be an exception—they can experience other types of attraction, including romantic, sensual, and aesthetic, as well as other types of human connection. Contrary to popular belief, asexuality isn't the same as aromanticism, the orientation defined by a lack of romantic attraction,[6] though there are aces who identify as both asexual and aromantic (otherwise known as aroaces). As one of the most under-represented groups—asexuality is often termed the "invisible orientation"[7]—within the LGBTQ+ community, asexuals face a number of challenges, including being discriminated against by medical professionals. Because they may be pathologized, many asexuals fear going to the doctor's office, particularly when they're seeing a physician about their sexual or reproductive health.

In her 2021 book *Ace: What Asexuality Reveals About Desire, Society, and the Meaning of Sex*, Angela Chen explains extensively the medical bias asexuals (both disabled and non-disabled) face. "Medical authority can be powerful even when it is imaginary," she writes. "Doctors encourage aces to ask ourselves if we're sick and doctors also diagnose and make declarations without caring what an ace person might think."[8] I experienced this first-hand a few years ago, when I visited an ob-gyn for a clinical breast exam and routine check-up, and decided to share that I'm asexual. I couldn't tell if I wanted to gauge my doctor's reaction or if I just wanted to be fully honest with the medical practitioner tasked with helping me take the best care of my body. After I told her, she offhandedly mentioned the idea of prescribing me medication. A chill that had nothing to do with my exposed chest went through me. I was

* www.asexuality.org.
** "Demisexual." AVENwiki, https://wiki.asexuality.org/Demisexual.
*** "Gray-A/Grey-A." AVENwiki. https://wiki.asexuality.org/Gray-A/Grey-A.

relieved when I learned I didn't have to return to that same office for reproductive care. To this day, I can't remember exactly what kind of medication my practitioner wanted to prescribe me, or exactly what it was for. But I do remember her tone, the way she so easily suggested treatment as if there were something I needed to be cured of, as if my asexuality needed to be cured.

I'm not alone in this experience. "I've had to find a new primary care provider a few times...and every time I do, they ask a bunch of questions about my sexual history," said S., who didn't disclose their last name. "I always flinch a little. It catches me off guard that I'm apprehensive about talking about my lack of sexual activity, even with my care provider, because of a few experiences with non-medical folks that make me fear [my asexuality] will be ridiculed or believed." Some asexuals I spoke with for this article said some doctors have expressed disbelief before offering hormonal therapy and other unwanted treatments that invalidated their identity and needs. Some were told their orientation stemmed from a psychological issue such as trauma, and/or referred to services equivalent to conversion therapy.[9] Some doctors default to prescribing medication to their asexual patients, believing their asexuality may be a mask for other health issues.[10] Others automatically assume a patient's low sex drive is a symptom of hormonal imbalances or some other ailment, or a side effect of medication. (For the record, asexuality is defined by attraction rather than sex drive or libido, which asexuals may experience to varying degrees.)

As such, when many asexuals disclose their identity, doctors attempt to "treat" their asexuality as though it's a medical issue instead of a legitimate identity of which they claim ownership. When a system is calibrated in favor of a supposed "majority," the system then neglects and harms minority groups. Take, for example, healthcare's noted racial biases,[11] which create treatment disparities between white patients and patients of color, or queerphobic biases which leave those who don't have sex with cis men at a noted disadvantage.[12] Trans people seeking trans-inclusive medical care often face obstacles, from legal targeting[13] to a lack of respectful clinical training.[14] The fear of being misgendered is enough to keep some trans people from going to the doctor, afraid of the dysphoria that will trigger more pain instead of decreasing it.[15] "It's hard to feel safe talking to a medical professional whose priorities may be so different from yours," M. Rodriguez, an asexual woman and medical practitioner, explains, going on to say:

> For example, people have tried to deny me needed medications to save my nonexistent libido and sex life, attempted to refuse me treatment for fear of damaging an impossible pregnancy, and derailed entire appointments about other things to try to fix some aspect of my asexuality despite my protest. I have always been lucky enough to be able to advocate for and get the care I needed in the end. But it should have never been that difficult in the first place.

I've had to learn about asexuality mostly on my own. There was no mention of it in my sex education classes in high school or college, so I combed through various websites and books to find stories that matched my own and helped validate that I was not strange, weird, or "broken," as so many people in my asexual community grow up believing about themselves. I'm now at a point where I'm in community with other asexuals and can even claim pride over this part of myself. But the idea that I might step into a doctor's office and be told I need to be cured of something I've just learned to be proud of is heartbreaking and exhausting. Thanks in part to Yasmin Benoit, David Jay, and other activists, there's a growing awareness about the needs of the asexual community. Asexual people are also becoming better advocates for themselves, but that burden shouldn't be entirely on our shoulders. People like me shouldn't have to be afraid of going to the doctor, of having unnecessary tests, procedures, or medications pushed on us because of assumptions made about our sexuality and/or lack of sexual activity.

By creating uncomfortable environments for their patients, doctors reinforce the idea that patients will not be able to trust their medical providers. And by not trusting our medical providers, ace and other queer-adjacent folk will be less inclined to go to them for assistance, which puts our lives at risk. Medical establishments treating both physical and mental health need to expand their education, constantly update their terminology, and work to provide inclusive care. When I revealed to my therapist that I was asexual, she was affirming and positive about my orientation. In turn, I felt safe in our sessions, which allowed me to open up more. While no one can expect their healthcare providers to be aware of *every* issue, doctors and other medical professionals should be open to learning—and to admitting they're not the ultimate authority on their patients' needs. It's up to the medical establishment to become more inclusive and to learn about the sociopolitical issues that could be affecting their patients' mental and/or physical health. Most importantly, the medical community must learn and constantly understand that asexuality is a real identity. Asexuality isn't an internet sexuality[16] or a medical dysfunction. Asexual people aren't broken—and doctors shouldn't treat us as if we are.

PART VI

RELIGION AND IDENTITY

Thoughts from a Nice Jewish Ace

To be honest, I hadn't originally intended this as a section in this book.

Religion has often been a complicated subject for me. As someone raised in a Ukrainian-Jewish American household, where I did not grow up practicing many of the "traditional" aspects of Judaism (i.e. attending Temple services, observing Shabbat, keeping kosher, etc.), I sometimes questioned if I was "Jewish enough," especially in comparison to other more traditionally observant Jews.

Not to mention that for many in the LGBTQIA+ community, religion has been a bit of a controversial subject. Organized religion (i.e. the structured system of faith or worship, which in itself may be considered separate from one's personal spirituality) has a complicated relationship with those who identify as queer. Undeniably, there's a long legacy of those in power abusing their positions to hurt those who are more vulnerable, justifying their hate through scripture, as well as running campaigns to strip away our civil rights.

And yet there are many of us who can't separate ourselves from religion, who consider our faith/spirituality to be a core element of our identities.

As an ethno-religious identity, being Jewish is a strong part of who I am. Even if I would not say I was the most steadfast at practicing certain elements of Judaism growing up (this stems in part from my family coming from a secular post-Soviet Jewish background where religion was, and continues to be, a complicated subject), being Jewish has definitely informed the way I grew up in the world, as well as the values that have enriched my life, such as a dedication to learning, community, food, survival through adversity, and more. And over the years, as the concept of identity has become more politicized, learning more about my heritage and the Jewish community, as well as standing firmly in my Jewishness, has definitely become more of a personal priority.

So while there is undeniably a history of faith being used to hurt, I also think it would be simplistic to say that everything about religion is "bad" or that we as modern members of the LGBTQIA+ community must write it off altogether. Especially when there are so many interesting conversations to have about the intersection of the two identities.

In 2020, I wrote an article for the Jewish feminist website Hey Alma titled "Notes from an Asexual Jew" taking about what it meant to be both Jewish and ace (at least what it meant for me).[1] To my surprise, more than a few people reached out to me, telling me how much the article had meant to them in reflecting and resonating with their own experiences as Jewish asexuals.

Which gave me food for thought.

Since coming into the ace community, I've read about and encountered other aces of faith: Christian, Jewish, Muslim,[2] etc., all of whom had intriguing things to say on the subjects of asexuality and spirituality. Some coming from more conservatively strict backgrounds described how certain religious institutions limited their access to knowledge of non-heterosexual orientations. Others found the instructions to abstain from "lust" and "wait until marriage" hilariously easy, until the time came when they were expected to marry and suddenly transform into sexually viable partners. And also, quite beautifully, some aces explored and interpreted their identities through the lens of their faith, finding both poetry and affirmation.

So I thought, why not talk about this a little here? Why not talk about the times when being Jewish and ace can be hard, such as dealing with the pressures of rit- ualized amanormativity that can some- times underlie Jewish culture? Or the other times when Jewish theology and mythology have enlightened me about the more queer-affirm- ing aspects of Judaism, allowing me to find metaphors and stories that have signaled recognition and belonging.

So in this section, I want to talk about some of the nuances of what it means to be ace and Jewish. For example, is there such a thing as "kosher sex"? What concerns would you have dating as a Jewish asexual person? How can we reconcile old traditions with new ideas that expand our definitions of what it means to exist in this world as an ace person of faith?

Plus, have you ever heard the expression "two Jews, three opin- ions"?[3] One of the things I find most fascinating about Judaism is the diversity of thought within the Jewish community. Judaism is itself considered a "divine argument," in that there are so many interpretations and opinions that can be had. One of my favorite memories to highlight the miscellaneous nature of being Jewish was when a non-Jewish friend of mine came to me for advice on how to write a Jewish character. Because the word "Jewish" wasn't really enough to tell me what kind of Jewish character he was looking to write, I asked questions about the branches, sects, and ethnic origins of the character—whether they were Reform, Conservative, Orthodox, etc., and if they were Ashkenazi, Sephardic, etc. I then laughed at my friend's stunned response as to how many types of "Jewish" there were. As a Jewish person from a Ukrainian-Jewish immigrant family, the type of Judaism I might align with the most is secular/humanistic/Reform Judaism. And even then I can't speak for all Jews who align with that specific type of Jewishness. At most, my voice can only be taken as one in a larger conversation about Jewish faith and identity.

On "Kosher Sex" and Judaism's Thoughts on Sexual Relationships

Note: I am not an official Jewish scholar or professor—please take these thoughts and considerations on Judaism with a grain of salt.

Okay, I think I know where your mind will be going with this, and no, this isn't going to be about a conversation about circumcised body parts or "kosher meat," so please get your mind out of the gutter.

No, this is going to be a contemplation on sex and relationships, on what that might mean and look like for someone who is ace and Jewish.

As far as I can tell, for many Jews, religion acts as a lens through which every aspect of life is filtered, negotiated, and debated, from food to dress code and, yes, sexual and marital relationships.

My first glimpses of this were through film and books. In the 1983 movie *Yentl*, directed by and starring Barbra Streisand (who, even if you're not a practicing Jew, you might have heard about in some capacity), a young woman secretly enters a Yeshiva dressed as a man in order to study Talmudic law. The titular protagonist discusses intimacy with the character Haddas (a woman who has no idea initially that Yentl is a woman, but I digress...). The two touch upon the idea of sexual expectations for marriage, and Haddas worries about her "wifey duties" of providing sex. Yentl assures Haddas that "according to the Talmud, a woman has the right to refuse her husband." If that wasn't enough, as the two continue to study the Talmud together, Haddas touches on the idea that a woman also has permission to request pleasure: "When you told me I had the right to refuse me, you didn't tell me I also had the right to demand you."

Wild, right?

After learning this, I had skimmed Jewish law and perspectives on sex, and learned that the film was right. The Torah not only made room for consent but emphasized it, and certain Jewish rituals prioritized having sex for the sake of pleasure and companionship (at least within the legally sanctioned space of marriage) rather than just procreation.

As someone who grew up around Christian-centric culture (even though the United States does not have an "official religion," anyone who is a religious minority living here is often aware of the way Christian-centric views can take up space), these ideas seemed mind-blowing. A religion that affirms sex as a "good thing" and makes room for pleasure seemed really cool.

However, no faith is perfect, and that includes Judaism.

While the idea of highlighting sex for pleasure (both for the woman and the man, since the Talmudic laws for sex were originally written with heterosexual couples in mind) seems cool in theory, as Jewish feminist scholar Melanie Malka Landau points out, the reality is more complicated. Suggesting that "not only is married sex potentially holy, but, in fact, it is part of the husband's martial duties"[1] places certain gendered pressures on the husband to "perform," while simultaneously and implicitly suggesting the woman's duty to "receive"—"a woman's refusal to have sex is also a woman's thwarting of her husband's attempts to fulfill the commandment of giving her sexual pleasure."[2]

As Landau points out, by intertwining religious obligation with compulsory sexuality—as traditional Judaism considers sexual relations between a married couple to be a mitzvah, a good deed, or "religious duty"—there's a danger of compromising consent, even when consent is understood in principle.

Of course, I'm not a student on Rabbinic law, and interpretation changes based on time, location, and level of observance, but the idea of constructing sexuality as a matter of a "form of service," of being spiritually obligated to have sex as part of one's marital duties, doesn't sit right with me.

Perhaps one of the best ways to sum up Judaism's take on sex is through Rabbi Dana Ruttenberg's words:

> So are Jewish attitudes about sex enlightened or problematic? Is Judaism an earthly religion of the body or a patriarchal institution? Both, of course, and neither. As with most things, there are many shades of gray between these two extremes. Jewish sexuality is nothing if not complex.[3]

Regardless of how observant you are or what religion you follow, whether you're asexual or not, married or not, male, female, or non-binary, you are NEVER obligated to have sex if you don't want to, under any circumstance. A good marriage or relationship (whether romantic, sexual, platonic or otherwise) depends upon good communication and mutual consent.

And make no mistake about it, Judaism *heavily* emphasizes consent. As Landau states, "The halakhic system attempts to legislate for humanized sexual relationships."[4]

Coerced sex, whether within or outside marriage, was (and still is) heavily frowned upon within Judaism, and religious texts, such as the Babylon Talmud tractate Nedarim 2b, list among the conditions for unacceptable intercourse *all* forms of coerced sex, whether one "consented" out of fear (*eimah*) or was aggressively forced to have sex (*anusah*). Even back then, consent was recognized as more complex than a simple yes or no, and emotional manipulation, such as pressure, bullying, and intimidation, negates any form of meaningful consent.

So how, then, can we describe "kosher sex"?

Elliot N. Dorff, a Conservative rabbi and professor of Jewish theology, wrote that while "waiting until marriage is the ideal," Judaism was "not only for those who can live up to ideals," and that for a couple who did want to engage in a sexual relationship before marriage, "they need to abide by the same values that apply to sex within marriage, including mutual respect, honesty, modesty, health, safety, and holiness."[5]

And, honestly, that doesn't sound too bad to me.

Judaism recognizes sex as something that can be more than "sin," seen as an intentional act and a "divine gift" that can be sacred and holy. And for many people that is true.

But sex, in itself, doesn't make marriage holy or a relationship more legitimate.

So, if I may only take it a step further, I would advocate that in calling for humanized sexual relationships, we also call for humanized *asexual* relationships, in which those who are asexual do not feel pressured or obligated to have sex if they don't want to (and that goes for everyone else as well), whether out of a religious obligation or for any other reason.

Owning Your Truth Is a Mitzvah

It seems appropriate that I'm currently writing this section as Purim approaches.[1]

For those of you who might not be familiar with Jewish traditions outside of Hanukkah (since that seems to be the only holiday mainstream media seems to recognize, *rolls eyes*), Purim is the story of a young Jewish queen named Esther. Now, in the beginning, Queen Esther wasn't really open about the fact that she was Jewish to her husband, Ahasuerus, the King of Persia (though, to be honest, there's never really been a *great* time in history to be openly Jewish). However, upon hearing that Haman, the king's adviser, plotted a massacre of the Jewish people, Esther, horrified at Haman's plans, became conflicted about what to do. Should she stay quiet about her Jewish identity and let her people be destroyed, or should she reveal herself, her full self, to her husband, and risk losing not only her marriage, but her life? In the end, Esther comes out to her husband about being Jewish, foiling Haman's evil plans, and her people are saved to live and fight another day.

Today, Jewish communities around the world celebrate Esther and her bravery in a joyous celebration filled with costumes (think Jewish carnival or Mardi Gras[2]), noise, music, and sweets (I swear hamantaschen cookies are one of the best desserts on the planet), celebrating life during a day when we could have lost it.

I mean, come on, how cool is that?!

In addition, Purim is also literally a coming-out story.[3]

Many queer Jews have interpreted Esther's story as a coming-out allegory, relating to the oppression she faced, the fear and terror of living in a hostile world that would hurt them for being open and true about themselves.[4] Really, it's no wonder that Purim is considered the "gay Jewish Halloween" within the queer community—let's just say there's a lot of cross-dressing and drag at Purim parties.[5]

Being ace in an allonormative, amanormative society means living in a world that emphasizes conformity. That emphasizes there only being one way to exist. That tries to punish us for existing any other way.

And, in a sense, that reminds me of what being Jewish means, too—having to fight against assimilation, against people who would prefer I didn't exist.

However, as Queen Esther's story says, it is a mitzvah, *a good deed*, to remain honest in a world that encourages dishonesty.

To be brave enough to be oneself even in a world full of bullies.

And even if you do not "come out" to the whole world, simply coming out to yourself, holding and acknowledging your own truth, is a blessing in itself.

Resources for Further Reading

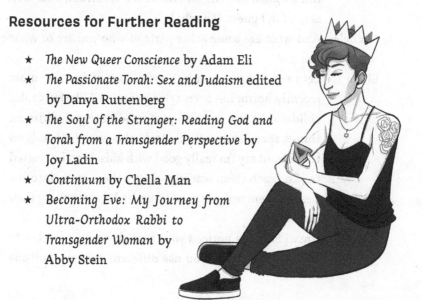

* *The New Queer Conscience* by Adam Eli
* *The Passionate Torah: Sex and Judaism* edited by Danya Ruttenberg
* *The Soul of the Stranger: Reading God and Torah from a Transgender Perspective* by Joy Ladin
* *Continuum* by Chella Man
* *Becoming Eve: My Journey from Ultra-Orthodox Rabbi to Transgender Woman* by Abby Stein

Interview with Ellen Huang

This is a transcript of an audio interview. This interview has been condensed and edited for clarity.

Michele: So my first question would be, how would you describe yourself and your place on a spectrum?

Ellen: So I would be asexual aromantic. Like I guess I don't want to say full asexual, but full asexual, like the far end of the spectrum. Like zero, zero of it, I guess. [Laughs.]

Michele: And what are some other parts of who you are or what you do?

Ellen: Let's see... I am a writer. I write a lot of fantasy; most recently, horror has been a thing of mine. I like fairy tales, children's lit too, and also poetry. So I guess all different things, speculative fiction. And I also work with kids on the side. I'd say I'm really good with kids; I can be trusted to just teach them reading and get them really into stories, get them really into being excited about writing their own stories.

Michele: Great! So I first noticed you through your ace poetry. In one of your poems, you use different card symbolisms in an *Alice in Wonderland* poem. So I was wondering how that came about, you exploring identity through your art and your poetry?

Ellen: Yeah, I remember that poem was called "The Fifth Ace or Asexual in Wonderland." I couldn't decide between the titles [laughs] and yeah, I don't know that that idea came because I think *Alice in Wonderland* is just like a really cool cultural theme for a lot of us for different reasons. And then I just thought the Ace, the cards thing, would have been funny. So I guess I just sort of put that together. You have four different cards and four different identities can be explored through that. And they're just all questioning themselves. But then, also, what if Alice returned to Wonderland? I think in a way, while I was writing that, Wonderland became a metaphor for questioning. So like "Wonderland," you're "wondering" about yourself, and then I think a lot of us are in a place of just "wondering" about ourselves so much and then we can just like tear ourselves apart if we're there by ourselves. Just isolated in a "world of my own." But then if you had someone come and visit your Wonderland, you have other friends in the same boat in the same Wonderland as you. It makes it okay. Like, "Wait, this is a wonderful place!" This is a beautiful place to be. Let's just sit and have tea and we'll like enjoy, I don't know, being in a different world, different norm. We're going to enjoy being outside of the normal for a bit here.

Michele: I love all that. "Wondering" about yourself in Wonderland. That's such a really great metaphor for what being an ace is like, trying to shift through all the pieces of ourselves in a world that doesn't give us much vocabulary for it, and then just trying to conceptualize who we are.

Ellen: Absolutely, yeah.

Michele: Another thing that attracted me to your online profile
            was the way that you discussed religion. You identify as
            an ace Christian, correct? Would you mind describing
            what that means for you?

Ellen: I think I've been thinking about that a lot myself. I con-
            sider myself, I guess, Liberation theology Christian—like
            on the more progressive side. And then I also believe in
            a very creative G-d. I believe that G-d created different
            ways to love and different aspects of personality, differ-
            ent ways to relate, and that G-d is about that relationship.
            Not just what we mainly see in mainstream media, like
            the "normal way" to define family and all that stuff. It's
            more expansive than that.

            So it's just like there's all of these other ways to love.
            Ways to have family, adopt, choose, cultivate those rela-
            tionships. And for me, the aspect that I feel more leaning
            toward is I am all about the platonic love. So all about
            friendships and I feel that wholeheartedly in day-to-day
            living when I think about, "What am I grateful for? What
            am I praying for? What am I spiritually caring so much
            about and wanting to show people?"

            I think that's one way for me to say what it means
            to me. Like, it's not just that it *can* coexist, but that it
            should coexist. Like, what we call the kingdom of heaven
            or family is not limited to nuclear families or who you're
            gonna marry (and leave everybody else for). The way I
            see it, I believe in going to heaven and all of that, and
            the reunion of everyone, and reconciliation of everyone
            personally. Well, there's not a wedding there in my book.
            It's more like...well, it's more expansive than that. It's

the ability to see this divine or good or love or spirit of like all these different people and to care for them, even beyond attraction, one set family, that's us against the world. I feel like I'm kind of rambling. [Laughs.]

Michele: No, no, no, it's great. I'm still defining myself as who I am, both as an ace person and as a Jewish person. So basically my family comes from Kiev, which was a part of the former Soviet Union. So religion...definitely had a complicated history there. Ethnically, we were Jewish, but we weren't allowed to practice a lot of the traditional facets associated with Judaism. And it was also used as a form of discrimination against us because literally on my family's passports they were defined as "Jewish." So it's not just a religious identity for me, it's also an ethnic and cultural one.

And so nowadays, there is a cultural heritage that I have, and there's also a spirituality that I'm still learning to process because it's there for me in academia and art and music, and so I'm still trying to figure all that out.

Ellen: That is a lot. I mean, it's a lot of things happening at once. I guess it's its own Wonderland in a way because you're wondering about it, identity-wise, and then also like maybe on a larger scale sometimes. Like you're thinking about history, heritage, and possibly spirituality.

Michele: Exactly. And so, what gets me, as people in the LGBTQIA+ community where religion has often been weaponized against us, how do we reconcile being aces of faith?

Ellen: That is a big question. Yeah, I don't know. When I think about the way religion has been used, honestly, to erase, to murder, to justify things that feel so antithetical to what faith is supposed to be, I don't think I really have an answer for, "Why did that happen? How could that happen?" I don't think people who have a surefire answer can really be trusted.

So I hold some complexity with that. And I sometimes think about some people who share a similar belief with me. I do get complicated feelings inside. I'm like, "Are we talking to the same G-d?" Because I don't know how you seem to have this, like, almost romantic relationship with G-d, talking about things like "provide for me," and then I'm over here and I'm just like, "What about me?"

But then on a personal level, I think it comes from, how do we reconcile that? It's almost a different religion in a way if you are religious and also queer *and* love yourself, which feels...

Michele: It feels kind of revolutionary, sometimes.

Ellen: Yeah, revolutionary. I like that. Oh man, that's a much better word than what I was trying to say. [Laughs.]

Yeah, it's almost a completely different faith. It's a different font than the one that's been used to justify persecution of you.

Some people on the flip side can say, "How can you be queer and also still be religious at all?" And I go, "Well, they shouldn't be contradictory."

Michele: It's like, "Why are you trying to contradict something that feels natural to both parts of myself?"

Ellen: Exactly. So it's like the queer part feels undeniable because that's just how you are. So, well, I can't deny that. And the faith part is more like...well, that shouldn't be contradictory because anyone should be allowed to believe in something that they can't see, should be allowed to believe that there's miracles, or maybe there's a reunion with loved ones, or maybe there's guidance for a love that is bigger than us. People should be allowed to believe if they want to, like in an afterlife or an ancestral connection.

Michele: Because it's still comfort.

Ellen: Yes, exactly. So I feel like, for a lot of people, that is a comfort that they can have in a very terrifying world. So people from any background, any sexuality should be allowed to believe in something. People should be allowed to feel that there's something bigger in life.

It's sad to me how much we, the queer community and religious communities, see that as a contradiction. It should not be.

Michele: For me as a Jewish version, I honestly see some things in faith that actually affirm queer identity. Within Judaic law, there has been recognition of gender diversity,[2] recognizing people whose bodies didn't fit the binary and how religious theology made room for that. It may not have been the same understanding of gender diversity as it is today, but it was there. Scholars didn't ostracize these people; they worked to include them in the community. As well as the story of Purim, Queen Esther. Her story is a coming-out story! About how acknowledging her truth saved her community. And so, in that way, I see all these beautiful examples of how faith can affirm queer identity and how we're constantly making room to affirm queerness today in the modern world, like with the B-Mitzvah,[3] which is the gender-neutral version of a Bar and Bat Mitzvah. So the Jewish community has in a sense—I'm not saying that it's always been liberal—but there has been a sense of activism and revolution. That has always been there, and it still continues to be there because it's an evolving practice. Literally, the idea of Judaism is called a "divine argument." And so we keep arguing about different texts. We keep talking about different versions of the same story because we want to make that conversation not just a passive thing but an active one. We keep adding to Judaism because that's the nature of what it is. Something that is a constant evolution.

Ellen: Wow, that's amazing! I actually didn't even know about the gender-neutral ceremony. That's amazing! Wait, that's so cool! Thank you for that insight! I didn't even know about that.

Michele: This is why we need conversations like this. Because even though I'm not religious the same way you are, there's certain things in other religions that I can find really beautiful. I may not understand all of it, but I can see the worth of it. You know?

Ellen: Yeah, totally. And that reminds me of what you said about the divine argument? Like constantly arguing because there's so much more that gets revealed and then it's almost like faith is a living thing. It's not the same with each generation, with each century. It's supposed to grow. That reminds me of something I heard once, like the kingdom of G-d is like bread. It's like it's bread and (religion) like the dough and you put it in the oven and then it expands, and then there's more over time. and I think that's supposed to be still happening today. Like the more we discover about people, the more we're going to also discover about faith, then that expands as more gets revealed over time. It's not like, "Oh no, we're going to still stick to the flat earth and stuff." It's like, "Oh wait, there's more, oh wait, there's space!", and even *space* is literally expanding.

So I think that's really cool to think of faith or questioning of faith as something that's alive and growing, instead of something that is, I don't know, a ring in a box or something, and they just keep it that way.

Michele: I think a lot of the problem with organized religion is the strict fundamentalism of it, like people saying there's only this one version and it has always been that version without considering the context of time and how societies have revolved around the patriarchal lens, and how at that time certain forces interpreted things one way versus a modern world that is interpreting things in a different way.

Ellen: Yeah, absolutely.

Michele: I also think there's something to be said about the expectation around sex and sexuality when you're a person of faith. Speaking as a Jewish person, I've written about some of the amanormativity within the Jewish community, because a lot of Jewish culture is structured around familial dynamics, oftentimes the nuclear family dynamic. I feel some of that pressure in the way I engage with the world and with other Jewish people.

As a Jewish woman, I'm expected to carry on the line, not only through the biological sense of reproduction, but teaching it to the next generation as well, which is a pressure that I think people don't stop to think about. Like what it means to tell a woman, "Oh, you have to preserve your culture in this way or otherwise you're failing it," you know?

Ellen: Yeah. That's real. Amanormativity isn't just a media expectation. It's very personal, like family expectations, and then faith is often used as a reason for it, too. That stuff's real. I think the pressure might be different for me.

Michele: The "be fruitful and multiply" proverb?

Ellen: Yes, the "be fruitful and multiply" thing and it's like...it boggles my mind actually how much that has been taken so literally. Like the only way to be "fruitful" is to literally have sex and be like bunnies. [Laughs.] Like have a whole bunch of kids and then you raise them...just so you have more people of your faith. What do you call it? Salvation anxiety/conversion agenda?

Michele: Unfortunately, a lot of the repopulation concern for the Jewish community is tied up with intergenerational trauma.

Ellen: Right, that is different.

Michele: I think we've talked about this before. Like after the Holocaust, there was such a decimation of the Jewish population. I think part of the mentality moving forward was that there's an added pressure toward marriage and procreation. Of "We need to make up for this tragedy that has happened to us," and so having bigger families has been seen as a victory against it or survival against that. And when you consider the historical context of that, that is a very valid point to make. But it also puts another pressure on maybe someone who is Jewish and falls in love with someone who's of another faith, or maybe they don't want kids. Like, what does that say? Are they "betraying" their community? Or are they just trying to figure out how to be a Jewish person in this world, while reconciling that we are in a very diverse, multifaceted world? So not everything is clean-cut.

Ellen: I think that's what I mean by there's a huge difference between the contexts in that way. Unfortunately, I think the evangelical side of things is very power-based. Like, "Let's permeate the world, so that we are the majority somehow." It's very colonial, unfortunately.

Michele: Versus Jewish people who are like, "We don't want our religion to die out."

Ellen: Like it's preservation. Staying alive and keeping something alive after senseless tragedy. And that is really hard because then I would imagine that, overall, it's a very valid thing that people want for their people (repopulation). And then at the same time, the pressure of that would probably be a lot more heavy.

Michele: Yeah. Like that idea you brought up earlier, of being fruitful in other ways.

Like for me, I'm also a writer. So I want to contribute, in the possibility that I don't have kids one day, I can still contribute to the world in other ways. I can still write stories, and there are artists there who can draw, and musicians who can compose.

And so I want there to be a larger conversation on how there's not only one way to exist in this world as a Jewish person. There's not only one way to preserve the Jewish faith. Like there's multiple ways of existing in the world that don't compromise your personal comfort.

Ellen: I think especially just for queers of faith, too, when many of us are not going to have kids, you know, the biological way at least, there are more ways to "be fruitful and multiply." I mean, adoption is the number-one thing I can think of. But even if you don't want kids, like you find other ways to be so alive, and feel the presence of something, and to contribute to the world and to give to a community in other ways by being exactly who you are.

I think it's very valid to try to find the balance in that and try to find your own way to express, "Well, I am still of my culture or my faith." It's going to look different. I think similar to what you said about Jewish history, there were different peoples, different genders, different ways that people looked. And they were still people. We're not writing them off as this mythological creature. They were still people and they were in the history, and we are in the history as we speak now.

So if you exist, that itself is already a gift. And then that multiplies just naturally in other ways besides just physically, sexually. We don't exist just to be passing it along as soon as we can.

Michele: I love that. That we're existing in history. That we're actively changing the world as it is. So why not change it for the better? Why not use our faith and our other qualities to make the world kinder, more empathetic, more invested in education, in the arts. Those are all qualities I associate with being Jewish itself, beyond anything else. So those are the qualities that I want to affirm and continue in the world.

Ellen: Absolutely. And I think as even as a writer—especially as a writer—that's what we do.

We send things out. These are things from the heart, from the existence of a soul that speaks to another. That is passing on a light. So I just want to affirm that as well. Being writers, that's one way we're already making such a contribution.

Michele: I love that. So I guess one other question I have is, what do you want to see for the future of the ace community?

Ellen: That's a good question. Big question. I think I'd like to see us have fun. I want us to be comfortable in our asexuality, in our different ways of relating to people and the world. I think anyone in the queer community also can relate to this, like I want it to no longer be a "big coming out" where we have thread upon thread of educating people on the same things over and over. Where it's a big shift from the default was straight, and that you're automatically going to get married and have kids with the opposite sex. I want to see a future where that's not a conflict so much anymore. Where we're all just laughing and creating and comfortable with it.

Like we have time and humor and friendships and community. I would hope that the ace community gets to a place where hopefully we're not fighting so much anymore just to define the word for people.

Unfortunately, so much of what I see in ace representation so far, and it's not the aces' fault—it's just we had to fight for existing, I guess. So much of what I see when I look up ace representation is a lot of response to acephobia, to amanormativity. I don't know, straights being weird. Allos being weird. Even the queer community just being like, "Oh, oh no, no, that's wrong."

And then it just takes up so much time. It takes so much energy.

Michele: I would love to see more conversations like this happening. Talking about how we can integrate aceness into art or aceness into faith. Like, let's talk about all the other cool stuff in our lives.

Ellen: Absolutely. I would hope that we can. And you know, I think we are getting there. I think at least in the past year or so, I'm seeing an explosion of more representation. I know different people are working on different books and podcasts and art and stuff like that. So I know it's happening. So I would hope that, you know, this plants the seed in the future, where there's going to be more conversations like this. Where it's no longer the entire video or interview being, "So, what is asexuality like?" all over again.

Michele: Let's make this a non-issue so that we can just exist in the world as we are.

Ellen: Absolutely. Just like what you said, let's make it a non-issue. I'd hope for a much more comfortable, expansive, and fun world really, where being ace is just another way to exist. It's another color that you see and that's cool. It's like people are seeing the color purple for the first time or something.

Ellen Huang (she/her) is an aroace Taiwanese American writer of the semi-spiritual, the whimsical gothic, and some quite eccentric fantasy. She was named in "5 Poets of Color to Watch in 2021" (*Luna Luna Magazine*). Her poems "Aromantic Jesus" (*miniskirt magazine*), "Split Attraction," (*warning lines*), and "You Might Not Be Struck by Lightning As You Wish" (*The Rising Phoenix Review*) were nominated for Best of the Net 2021. Additionally, she is listed on Invisible Cake Society as an ace Christian resource. She is currently authoring her asexual horror anthology *NOPHOBIA* and her fairytale chapbook *Chiaroscuro*; much of her work is grounded in themes of platonic love. For more, find her watching movies religiously at https://worrydollsandfloatinglights.wordpress.com, or being up way too late as @nocturnalxlight on Twitter.

PART VII

CONCLUSION

Queerness, Labels, and Ambiguity in the Search for Self

Picture this: it's 2015 and you are standing in the center of a crowded nightclub, dark except for the strobing lights emanating from the small stage at the front of the room. The lead performer tonight, a badass non-binary singer, whose lyrics with the intensity and vulnerability of broken glass have soothed your own young heart many a time, is hyping up the room, creating an energy that can only be described as electric. The room and its people are unapologetically queer, girls dancing with girls, femme and butch and androgyny taking up equal space and measure. A random femme on the side of the stage pulls up their shirt and flashes the crowd. The audience roars in appreciation as a silver shine bounces off their freed nipple ring. Everyone is moving, their arms, their hips, free and open. You (the type who usually prefers sitting back and watching other people move) try dancing, too. The lesbian next to you, who you briefly chatted with along with their partner in the line for the coat rack, is also moving and smiles when they see you dancing. In an unspoken moment, you are suddenly dancing with the other person, a rare moment that you, as a closeted kid just beginning to understand their own sexuality, didn't usually get to have. You are unsteady and nervous and trying to find your rhythm (which you're not sure even exists) when you feel their hands on your waist, moving quickly down. In a moment of panic, you break away, and they apologize. You forgive them, knowing the gesture was not predatory, simply a misreading of signals. But you stand in the room, in a mess of queer tangled bodies, and where you hoped to find queer comradery, you almost feel more alone than ever.

Now back to the present.

Over the years, as you studied the LGBTQ+ alphabet, wondering which letter you are, you increasingly run into a number of stumbling blocks that leave you feeling lost and confused. You are drawn to the pink, purple, and blue of the bisexual flag. But that doesn't feel right either, the "sex" in bisexual tripping you up.

School is a mess of pheromones, your fellow students chasing each other, crushes and horniness popping up at every turn, yet you largely remain neutral, content just to study and read in your own little corner. But as you move through the world, you realize it's not just school. It's the advertisements on billboards, the shows on TV, of sweaty bodies moving in ways you don't know how to relate to, much less be turned on by.

Luckily, by chance, you stumble in a random Google search across the word "asexual," and some things click into place. You are soon relieved, knowing there is a word out there describing how you feel, how you relate to the world in a way that others don't seem to. But as much as you appreciate the word "asexual," on its own it doesn't seem quite enough to describe the full picture.

Within the queer community, there is often a quiet (if not overt) pressure to pick and choose your own label quickly. Because, let's face it, finding your label is considered one of the ultimate moments of queerness, of self-discovery, the moment when you can proudly say to the world who you are (at least part of who you think you are). After years of living in a world that practically brainwashes you into thinking straight is the default, finding a word that says otherwise can feel like a revelation.

But what happens when one word doesn't feel right anymore, or even enough on its own? What happens when you do feel attraction to other people—boys, girls, and non-binary people—but so rarely that you can only count the number of times it's happened on one hand? When much of your identity has been about wanting and not wanting at the same time, an orientational paradox that leaves you feeling as though you've been pulled in too many confusing directions.

In some ways, moving throughout an allosexual/alloromantic world (allosexual meaning someone who experiences sexual attraction to other people, alloromantic meaning someone who experiences romantic attraction to other people) feels like attending a silent disco. It is one of those things that once seemed like science fiction, where people dance in a room listening to music transmitted completely through wireless headphones. Except you are the one without headphones, or if you are wearing them, they are tuned into a completely different frequency, and you are standing at the edge watching other people move silently to a sound you can't hear.

That feeling has touched me in many places, both straight and queer.

At times, it has felt jarring and lonely to feel ambiguous in a world that requires simple and solid definitions. You listen to other people describe the times when they kissed their first person, touched their first significant other, and you, as a person with relatively little romance/sexual experience, are made to feel like a child. You are told by others that you can't know yourself until you've found the "right person" to prove your orientation, like some convoluted Peter Pan who only grows up after fitting into the expectations of their society. And it is enough to make you scream, scared you'll never find someone who will understand or accept you as you are.

But then you discover places that do understand or are willing to try to understand.

For me, I discovered that within the comic *Shades of A* created by Tab Kimpton (a hilariously queer parody of *Fifty Shades of Grey*). In the comic, there's a discussion in which the lead character, Anwar, is panicking to his friend about how to describe his orientation, saying, "Labels are difficult." In response, the friend says to him, "Labels just help find people like you, they aren't perfect descriptions of the human condition."

In that one page, I found a valuable start to an important lesson. That while labels are important, helping me make space for the feelings I was beginning to identify, they don't have to be all-encompassing or everlasting. That labels can be like pieces of fabric, clothing that, when it fits, can feel like the coat you need to stay warm in an unforgiving blizzard. And that, like clothing, a label can be tailored to fit you: a tuck here, a loosening there in the form of mirco-labels. Or, if necessary, something you can shrug off when you outgrow it in exchange for something else or possibly nothing at all.

Today, I am someone who stands as part of the asexual community, simultaneously at home and still searching for a specific space to call my own. And honestly, that is okay. Perhaps I will remain comfortable with the labels that I choose today, or maybe my identity will always be in a state of flux, while still being valid in its own complexity.

Maybe I can try, as Rilke says, to:

Be patient toward all that is unsolved in your heart and try to love the questions themselves, like locked rooms and like books that are now written in a very foreign tongue. Do not now seek the answers, which cannot be given you because you would not be able to live them. And the point is, to live everything. Live the questions now. Perhaps you will then gradually, without noticing it, live along some distant day into the answer.[2]

Maybe it's as Zora Neale Hurston wrote in *Their Eyes Were Watching God*, "There are years that ask questions and years that answer."[3]

Maybe as you move through your years of questioning, you'll come to your years of answering. And maybe you'll never find the exact answer, but at least you can still enjoy the questions and the journey along the way.

Ace Quotes

For this book I asked a number of aces to tell me in their own words what they find joyful or enlightening about being asexual or part of the asexual community.

The thing I love the most about being ace is the ace community. It has allowed me a space to explore and discover the specifics of my sexuality as well as provided a mostly supportive community that has helped me so much on this journey. I would have been felt so broken without my friends in the ace community.

– Maria R, She/Her

I never want to stop exploring what it means to be asexual. For me, coming into my ace identity meant freedom, freedom from the burden of expectation or the desperation to understand why I felt the way I did. I'm happy. I'm married. I'm asexual. At last, I'm me.

– Dill Werner, They/Them

The greatest joy for me in being ace is the feeling of living authentically. I'm not trying to be something I'm not. I'm not attempting to behave in ways that aren't true to me. Being ace is being fully myself, and that's a liberating and joyful thing.

– Cody Daigle-Orians, He/They, author of I Am Ace:
Advice on Living Your Best Asexual Life

Being Ace has gifted me a golden opportunity to think and expand on preconceived notions of what human sexuality and relationships can look like in a society that has so many assumptive ideas of what they "should" or "must" look like under the power dynamics of compulsory sexuality, amatonormativity, and cisheteropatriarchy. I love examining the ways in which asexuality and aromanticism can expand our understanding of humanity and culture. These are theoretical, academic interests, of course. So on a more personal note, without asexuality, I would not have the beautiful spouse, profession, or home that I currently do. I love my life and I would not be where I am had I not come out as Asexual when I did.

– Courtney Lane, She/Her, co-creator of
the podcast The Ace Couple

For me, being ace is enlightening because it gives me a wider perspective of life. I think more openly and see things differently. I think the best thing that's come from me coming out as ace is being able to understand that in life, if you get rejected it's not a statement on who you are and it's a chance to explore other forms of relationship styles that others see as less than. People assume if you're not having sex with someone your value decreases and that's not true—platonic, sensual, alterous, aesthetic, etc. all matter and are just as important as sexual attraction and being ace has taught me that.

– Kimberly Butler (The Asexual Goddess), She/They

What I find joyful? That we have a community now. When I was a teen I didn't, and these days we have ace elders and parents and teens and adults and we're just living our lives. But also that we're doing things: writing and making art and being activists and teachers and humans who make mistakes, who grow, who don't have to only be defined by our complex relationships to attraction and sex. That's joyful stuff.

– Jen Ferguson, She/Her, author of
The Summer of Bitter and Sweet

As someone who spent the first decade of my adult life as part of a couple, it took quite some time to understand I didn't have to leave my dreams behind when I became single again. Our society is steeped in the notion that certain dreams can only be fulfilled by couples. Yet as a single aspec person, I've traveled, bought a house, and even become a parent, as well as deepened my relationships with friends and family. Moreover, I feel stronger as a single person than I ever did as part of a couple.

– Lisa Jenn Bigelow, She/Her, author of
Hazel's Theory of Evolution

My favorite part of being Ace is the freedom it gives me to be who I am sexually. Since I came out, I've been walking around feeling so much lighter because now I know that there's nothing wrong with me, and it's been astonishing to realize how much space that anxiety and inadequacy were taking up in my brain. Embracing this part about myself has given me so much peace around my sexuality and it's also enabled me to be a better educator to folks who have similar experiences with the way they are sexually (or not). I love that through my own knowledge of being Ace I'm able to be a possibility model for other folks who are questioning themselves and curious about the different ways that sexuality can look. I never thought that I'd say this because the idea of being Ace used to terrify me so much (it's one of the reasons I ran from it for so long)—but I'm really really proud to be Ace.

– Ev'Yan Whitney, They/Them, creator of the podcast
Sensual Self with Ev'Yan Whitney

Being ace for me has meant a life of a lot more time, love, liberation, and imagination than I could have originally thought before I came out to myself. Not everyone pays attention to it, but while not everyone needs romantic or sexual love, everyone needs platonic love, even allos. Maybe just by existing we help people turn their eyes to that and notice such a need, like seeing more stars when the brighter lights don't block them out. I also exist on a different timeline than most, it seems, which expands my life to not wait for a complementary match as permission to just go enjoy things. Also, we have fun. I don't know if you've noticed, but aces have some refreshing kickass sense of humor, a creativity that just comes with being created differently, and seeing the world differently. When we look up from the norms, we may find there is so much more life full of love and without fear, just waiting to be discovered!

– *Ellen Huang, She/Her*

I think that the most joyful thing about being ace is that once you come out to someone it's like there's a barrier that's like taken down and you can be like totally free.

– *Druu Hadjez, She/Her*

What I feel joyful about being on the ace spectrum is a deep affirmation of my view of relationships: One that prioritizes and deeply values emotional intimacy and personal connection over sexual attraction and sexual activity. It is empowering and liberating. It is confirmation that I do not need in any way to buy into normative views of relationships, love, romance, and sex that are restrictive and reductive. At first I felt like there was something wrong with the way my need for intimacy manifested itself. Now, it's a source of pride, not shame.

– *Justin, He/Him*

My favorite thing about being with other aces is feeling like I don't have to explain myself and what I say about myself will be believed. Which I realized is horrifying if you think about it, because it wasn't until I said that out loud that I realized that, until I found the aces, if I talked about what the world was like to me, I could expect to be misunderstood or invalidated. Now that I spend most of my social time with other aces, I've tuned out a lot of things that didn't work for me or didn't make sense to me, and I've stopped pretending to do stuff just because other people expected it. It feels like I shed a weight I didn't realize I was carrying.

Making friends with other aces is a lot less stressful. When

I meet people, I'm often worried about them getting the wrong idea. But when I meet people at an ace meet-up, we as a community have to throw out a lot of assumptions about what people are looking for. I can spend a lot of time with someone and really enjoy their company, and when I say I want just friendship, I know people will believe me.

— Stacy Strobel, She/They

Being ace helped me ponder how unconsidered norms might be shaping my choices in other areas of life. My ace identity is interwoven with being queer and with being non-binary. Each identity helped open the doors of possibility for the others.

— Maia Kobabe, E/Em/Eir, author of Gender Queer

It is because I am ace-spec that I have found my precious person. Ever since I was young, I told myself that I would not let someone's gender dictate who I love. By being ace I was able to choose my partner without the need or desire for sexual attraction. Ending up with my wife has been the best thing that ever happened to me. If I had another lifetime, and I was able to choose my orientation, I would choose to be ace all over again.

— Jen, She/They, co-creator of webcomic Novae

Being ace, I didn't have a lot of interest in sexual or romantic relationships when I was young. I feel the absence of those relationships in high school and college allowed me more time to explore myself and my interests. I had so many enriching experiences because I did develop those parts of myself and I'm proud of who I've become. Figuring out who I was also allowed me to be in a wonderful relationship I would not have thought possible when I was young.

— Kate, She/They, co-creator of webcomic Novae

When I first realized I was ace, I was positively giddy. All these pieces finally clicked into place. There was a name for what I was experiencing and tons of others who shared that experience!

I devoured the AVEN archive, reading every message board and story I could get my hands on until 1–2 a.m.

– Kai, He/They

Realizing I was demisexual freed me from trying to squeeze myself into the norms and expectations of dating life. It reassured me that I am not wrong for having different needs. I've been able to put my comfort and peace above all else, letting me take time to truly love myself as my own person before I decide to, eventually, share myself with someone else.

– Kiara Valdez, She/Her

What I find joyful about being aspec is the freedom to be me without expectations—which is what we should all be able to do! Before I realized I was aroace, I thought there was something wrong with me for not being interested in romantic or sexual relationships, that I was just too anxious and self-conscious and I needed to be putting in more effort, because sex and romance are something that *everyone* does so I have to do it, too. I couldn't understand why all the love and passion I put into platonic relationships wasn't good enough for people, why I needed to be spending my free time dating instead of pursuing all the other joys of life. But now, I love understanding who I am and knowing that I can pour all the love that's in my heart where I choose, how I choose, when I choose, and that those relationships are just as meaningful and beautiful.

– Kat, She/They

Being ace has allowed me to see the world more clearly. It has not only given me permission to be as I am—it has pushed me to imagine more than I thought possible.

– Angela Chen, She/Her, author of Ace: What Asexuality Reveals About Desire, Society, and the Meaning of Sex

What I find most joyful about being a part of the ace community is the acceptance. For most of my life I pretended to be something I wasn't because I was afraid of being ostracized;

now I know there are not only other people like me, but they're full of kindness and love for those who feel lost. It's like when something bad happens and you want to do something kind to make the world better—and the whole community is like that, really. It's pretty great. There are many things I like about being ace. More than anything else, the very nature of being ace is something I like being. I wouldn't change that I'm ace if given the chance to do everything over again—but I would introduce myself to the idea much sooner.

– Elle Rose, She/They

Being asexual has meant that I'm hyper aware of a lot of societal pressures surrounding relationships and expectations of adult life. At one point this was hard, but now that I'm older, I'm glad to have been faced with these pressures, and learned how to ignore them! I think my experiences from being asexual have made me much more secure and stronger in navigating relationships and social pressure, and I'm proud of that!

– Rebecca Burgess, They/Them, author of How to Be Ace: A Memoir of Growing Up Asexual

I possess a level of self-awareness that tends to confuse most people. I've always been extremely comfortable with myself and even though I didn't learn the term "asexual" until I was in my twenties, I had accepted that I was fundamentally different from my friends when it came to sex and relationships. I created a very firm list of everything I felt that differentiated me from them. Then one day, I found a list online that matched mine. Almost *perfectly.* Word for word, there it was. I've always been exactly who I am and who I'm supposed to be. And I finally had a name for it. It's a pretty surreal feeling to find where you belong.

– Claire Kann, She/Her, author of Let's Talk About Love

Ace Symbols

When it comes to the LGBTQIA+ community, we love our symbols.[1]

Within the gay community, a range of signifiers have been adopted for the use of self-identification and pride, from the green carnation popularized by the poet Oscar Wilde[2] to the pink triangle, used originally by the Nazis to brand queer male prisoners in concentration camps and later reclaimed as a symbol for queer protest and memorial.[3]

Among the Sapphic community, violets were commonly used as a code and symbol of affection between bi and lesbian women, inspired by the flower's appearance in various poems written by the queer Greek poet Sappho who lived on the island of Lesbos (I'm not kidding).[4] Fun fact: that famous catchphrase from the *Wonder Woman* comics—"Suffering Sappho!" —was inspired by this poet who openly wrote about the love and tenderness shared between women.[5]

Today one of the most ubiquitous symbols of the gay and general queer community is the rainbow flag, designed by Gilbert Baker to represent queer joy, as well as the diversity of the LGBTQ+ community.[6]

Below are some of the most popular symbols picked up by the ace community, as well as some notes on their possible origins and meanings.

Ace Flag

The ace flag, adopted in 2010, consists of four main colors: black, gray, white, and purple.[7] Like other pride flags, each color represents a different element of the asexual community:

★ black: asexuality
★ gray: gray-asexuality and demisexuality
★ white: non-asexual partners and allies
★ purple: community.

Similar flags include the demisexual pride flag and graysexual pride flag.

Cake

Depending on your familiarity with the asexual community, you may or may not have heard some aces joking around about "cake."* It's possible that the delicious dessert was adopted by the ace community in a 2004 forum survey on AVEN, asking what was "better than sex." Since then, the cake theme has taken off, spinning off into fun memes like, "You don't get asexuality? Let me explain it with a food metaphor," and today many in the ace community will even celebrate and welcome new members coming into the community by offering cake.

Despite the original innuendo behind the famous DNCE song "Cake by the Ocean," I gather that many aces would rather just have literal cake by the ocean. Biskvit happens to be one of my own personal favorites.

* "Cake." AVENwiki, https://wiki.asexuality.org/Cake.

Garlic Bread

Similar to the cake meme, some asexuals had another answer to the question "What's better than sex?", and landed on garlic bread. I mean, if you're having dessert, you might have well have some bread, too, I guess.

At this point, it's probably safe to say asexuals love a good food metaphor—sexual attraction = hunger, and aces not being hungry for...well, you get the rest.

Dragons

Just as the bi community has adopted the term unicorn, because, like unicorns, society believes bisexuality is just a myth (*rolls eyes*),[8] the asexual community has adopted the dragon[9] as one of its mythological mascots. And, quite frankly, like dragons, aces want to breathe fire whenever they get pissed, especially when they have to deal with acephobes.

Axolotl

Now I'm not sure exactly why this paedomorphic salamander is considered a symbol of the ace community. Perhaps some aces enjoyed the alliteration found in "asexual axolotl." Or perhaps it's because some people think they look like mini-dragons. Or maybe it's because there's an anthropomorphic axolotl asexual character named Yolanda Buenaventura in the show *BoJack Horseman*. Whatever the reason, I don't mind. They're cute as heck!

Ace Ring

If you ever find yourself at an ace meet-up group, you might spot a few members sporting a black ring on the middle finger of their right hand.* While the exact origins of the ace ring are a little unclear (it seems to have been a thing as early as 2005, as seen on some AVEN forums), the color black probably stems from the colors used in the ace flag. As a symbol, the ace ring is especially convenient in its elegance and subtlety. While not loud enough to attract the attention of queerphobes/acephobes, the symbol can still be recognized by those who are familiar with its meaning, signaling to other aces a sense of quiet recognition. Plus, it's the perfect accessory to have when flipping off an acephobe.

Similarly, some aromantic individuals have adopted a white ring as their symbol, wearing one on the middle finger of their left hand (the opposite position of the black asexual ring).

Playing Cards

Considering ace is a shorthand for asexual, is it any wonder that the ace community has adopted playing cards as their symbol? Interestingly enough, each of the aces in a traditional card deck represents a different group within the ace community:

♠ = aromantic asexual

♥ = romantic (alloromantic) asexual

♣ = grayromantic asexual

♦ = demiromantic asexual

* "Black Ring." AVENwiki, https://wiki.asexuality.org/Black_ring.

Ace Reading Recommendations

The following list features some of the best and most popular books with canon ace representation out today.

This is not a full and comprehensive list of all the ace books out there, and not every book might fit your individual taste. Luckily, more and more books with ace representation are being published (many by aspec authors themselves!), so you should be able to find whatever you're looking for someday.

Also, while every book features canon representation along the ace spectrum (including graysexual, demisexual, etc.) and some feature aromantic representation as well, not every book specifically uses that precise language on the page. All authors have either confirmed representation on or off the page.

Warning, some books may contain triggering material, so I would suggest researching the content warnings assigned to each book prior to reading.

Novellas

- ★ *Learning Curves* by Ceillie Simkiss (Adult Contemporary Romance)
- ★ *The Cybernetic Tea Shop* by Meredith Katz (Adult Romance/ Sci-Fi)

★ *Human Enough* by E.S. Yu (Adult Romance/Urban Fantasy)

★ *Soft on Soft* by Mina Waheed (Adult Contemporary Romance)

Novels

★ *Rick* by Alex Gino (Middle Grade Contemporary Realistic Fiction)

★ *Every Bird a Prince* by Jenn Reese (Middle Grade Contemporary Fantasy)

★ *Hazel's Theory of Evolution* by Lisa Jenn Bigelow (Middle Grade Contemporary Realistic Fiction)

★ *Radio Silence* by Alice Oseman (Young Adult Contemporary Fiction)

★ *Loveless* by Alice Oseman (Young Adult/New Adult Contemporary Fiction)

★ *Tash Hearts Tolstoy* by Kathryn Ormsbee (Young Adult Contemporary Fiction/Romance)

★ *Summer Bird Blue* by Akemi Dawn Bowman (Young Adult Contemporary Fiction)

★ *The Art of Saving the World* by Corinne Duyvis (Young Adult Sci-Fi)

★ *Every Heart a Doorway* by Seanan McGuire (Young Adult Horror/Fantasy)

★ *The Summer of Bitter and Sweet* by Jen Ferguson (Young Adult Contemporary)

★ *Aces Wild: A Heist* by Amanda DeWitt (Young Adult Contemporary)

★ *Forward March* by Skye Quinlan (Young Adult Contemporary/Romance)

★ *The Sound of Stars* by Alechia Dow (Young Adult Speculative Fiction/Romance)

★ *The Kindred* by Alechia Dow (Young Adult Speculative Fiction/Romance)

★ *Elatsoe* by Darcie Little Badger (Young Adult Speculative Fiction)

★ *A Snake Falls to Earth* by Darcie Little Badger (Young Adult Speculative Fiction)

★ *Fire Becomes Her* by Rosiee Thor (Young Adult Speculative Fiction)

★ *Tarnished Are the Stars* by Rosiee Thor (Young Adult Speculative Fiction)

★ *We Awaken* by Calista Lynne (Young Adult Speculative Fiction)

★ *The Black Veins* by Ashia Monet (Young Adult Fantasy/Adventure)

★ *The Witch King* by H.E. Edgmon (Young Adult Fantasy)

★ *Before I Let Go* by Marieke Nijkamp (Young Adult Contemporary Fiction/Mystery)

★ *All Out: The No-Longer-Secret Stories of Queer Teens Throughout the Ages* edited by Saundra Mitchell (anthology of Queer Young Adult Short Stories featuring two stories with asexual leads, both by ace authors—"And They Don't Kiss at the End" by Nilah Magruder and "Walking After Midnight" by Kody Keplinger)

★ *Let's Talk About Love* by Claire Kann (New Adult Contemporary Romance)

★ *Never Been Kissed* by Timothy Janovsky (New Adult Contemporary Romance)

★ *All the Wrong Places* by Ann Gallagher (Adult Contemporary Romance)

★ *The Charm Offensive* by Alison Cochrun (Adult Contemporary Romance)

★ *The Romantic Agenda* by Claire Kann (Adult Contemporary Romance)

Graphic Novels

* *Gender Queer* by Maia Kobabe (Memoir)
* *How to Be Ace: A Memoir of Growing Up Asexual* by Rebecca Burgess (Memoir)
* *Jughead* Volumes 1–3 created by Chip Zdarsky, Erica Henderson, Ryan North, Derek Charm, Mark Waid, and Ian Flynn (Contemporary Fiction with some Speculative Fiction elements)
* *A-Okay* by Jarad Greene (Semi-Autobiographical Middle Grade Fiction)
* *A Quick & Easy Guide to Asexuality* by Molly Muldoon and Will Hernandez (Educational Non-Fiction)
* *I Want to be a Wall* by Honami Shirono (Manga/Contemporary Fiction)
* *Our Dreams at Dusk* by Shimanami Tasogare (Manga/Contemporary Fiction with Some Magical Realism elements)
* *Be Gay, Do Comics: Queer History, Memoir, and Satire from The Nib* edited by Matt Bors, Eleri Harris, Matt Lubchansky, Sarah Mirk, and Andy Warner (Anthology of queer comics by queer and ace artists including "Birth Control is About More than Just Birth" by Alex Graudins and "Nothing is Wrong With Me" by Dylan Edwards)

Darcie Little Badger

Non-Fiction

- ★ *The Invisible Orientation: An Introduction to Asexuality* by Julie Sondra Decker
- ★ *Ace: What Asexuality Reveals About Desire, Society, and the Meaning of Sex* by Angela Chen
- ★ *The Invisible Orientation: An Introduction to Asexuality* by Julie Sondra Decker
- ★ *Ace: What Asexuality Reveals About Desire, Society, and the Meaning of Sex* by Angela Chen
- ★ *I Am Ace: Advice on Living Your Best Asexual Life* by Cody Daigle-Orians
- ★ *Sounds Fake but Okay: An Asexual and Aromantic Perspective on Love, Relationships, Sex, and Pretty Much Anything Else* by Sarah Costello and Kayla Kaszyca
- ★ *Ace Voices: What It Means to Be Asexual, Aromantic, Demi or Grey-Ace* by Eris Young
- ★ *Refusing Compulsory Sexuality: A Black Asexual Lens on Our Sex-Obsessed Culture* by Sherronda J. Brown

Angela Chen

Webcomics

- ★ *Rain LGBT* by Jocelyn Samara DiDomenick (Young Adult Contemporary Fiction)
- ★ *Rock and Riot* by Chelsey Furedi (Young Adult Historical Fiction)
- ★ *Aces Wild* by Sally Vinter (Educational Comic)
- ★ *Boo! It's Sex* by Danielle Corsetto/Monica Gallagher (Contemporary Fiction/Fantasy/Educational comic, warning: some NFSW content)
- ★ *Shades of A* by Tab Kimpton (Contemporary Fiction/Romance, warning: some NFSW content)
- ★ *The Mann and Lucky Channel* by Achiru et al. (Contemporary Fantasy/Romance)
- ★ *Friends with Benefits* by nezkovsou (Contemporary Fiction)

Sex Education

Because asexuality ≠ no sex or celibacy, here are some useful (and ace-friendly) sex education texts for exploring sex, sexuality, and relationships should you be inclined.

- ★ *Come as You Are: The Surprising New Science that Will Transform Your Sex Life* by Emily Nagoski
- ★ *Drawn to Sex: The Basics* by Erika Moen and Matthew Nolan
- ★ *Drawn to Sex: Our Bodies and Health* by Erika Moen and Matthew Nolan
- ★ *Oh Joy Sex Toy* (Multiple Volumes) by Erika Moen and Matthew Nolan
- ★ *A Quick & Easy Guide to Sex & Disability* by A. Andrews
- ★ *A Quick & Easy Guide to Consent* by Isabella Rotman and Luke Howard
- ★ *What Does Consent Really Mean?* by Pete Wallis and Thalia Wallis, illustrated by Joseph Wilkins

Acknowledgments

Well, it's gotten to that point of the book. The end credits and the award/acceptance speech nearly every writer dreams of writing, and is absolutely terrified to write.

Let's hope this doesn't turn out too cheesy.

(Though before we begin, this author wants to acknowledge that this book was primarily written in Brooklyn, New York, otherwise known as Lenapehoking, the Lenape name for the ancestral homeland of the Lenape people, which spans from Western Connecticut to Eastern Pennsylvania, and the Hudson Valley to Delaware, with New York City at its center. This author wishes to pay their respects to Elders past, present, and emerging, and extends that respect to all Indigenous readers who may be reading this book.*)

First of all, I've got to give credit where credit is due.

Thank you to Andrew James, formerly of Jessica Kingsley Publishers, for reading my proposal for *Ace Notes* and saying they were "very keen to develop this project further" with me. It was definitely a nice surprise receiving that email on December 3, 2021—my birthday, no less.

Also, thanks to Sarah Costello of the podcast *Sounds Fake But Okay* for introducing us.

Thank you to the team at Jessica Kingsley Publishers who have helped to work on and promote this book, including Laura

* "Lenapehoking." Brooklyn Public Library, https://www.bklynlibrary.org/lenapehoking.

Dignum-Smith, Victoria Peters, Alex DiFrancesco, Katelynn Bartleson, and the many others who've helped make this project a reality.

Thank you to my parents for their love and support, who kept me housed and fed while creating this book. Never underestimate the practical realities of writing.

Thank you to my sister, Nicole. As far as sisters go, it's nice to have you as one.

Thank you to my Babushka Yelizaveta whose love and strength inspire me always. Thank you for always giving me a safe place to stay.

Thank you to my beautiful dog, Foxie. You have been the perfect companion to have during this pandemic and while writing this book. Also, I have to acknowledge the puppy (even though you're not quite a puppy anymore) who was the perfect canine model for one of the illustrations in this book.

Thank you to those who are no longer physically here, but remain in heart and soul, including my Baba Roza, Dadushka Yefim, and friend, Lucy Fontana. May their memory be a blessing.

Thank you to my ace friends, who cheered for me when I told them about this project and who make me feel part of a community where I feel less alone in the world. Special thanks to Maria, Yoola, Dasom, Kai, and Stacy.

Thank you to Maia Kobabe, Shari B. Ellis, Ev'Yan Whitney, Julie Sondra Decker, Courtney Lane, and Ellen Huang, the aces who agreed to contribute to this project through their interviews. Your words have truly made this book richer and stronger.

Thank you to Darcie Little Badger and Angela Chen for granting permission to portray their personal likenesses in the Ace Reading Recommendations section. Thanks for expanding the field of Ace Lit!

Thank you to the many aces who contributed to the Ace Quotes section.

Thank you to Professor Bruce Ruben and Druu Hadjez for looking over the section on Jewish identity and asexuality.

To Professor Ruben, I'm really glad to have had you as a professor during my time at Hunter College. Thank you for helping to teach me about my own heritage and history.

And to Druu, I'm very glad to have met a Jewish ace friend, especially one all the way from Uruguay.

Thank you to Amelia Loken and my uncle Vova (Vladimir Kirichansky) for looking over the Deaf and wheelchair illustrations respectively. Those in the disability community have definitely enriched my life and I'm always grateful for your presence.

Also, Vova, I promised you I'd mention you in my book and I didn't break my promise.

Thank you to David Jay, for agreeing to write the lovely foreword at the beginning of this book. I was so lucky to have met you in person a few years back around the Ace & Aro Conference 2019 for World Pride. Thank you for helping make the ace community what it is today.

Thank you to Ashley Masog for the beautiful illustrations that are in this book. You truly went above and beyond with the designs. Here's to meeting amazing ace artists at anime conventions.

Thank you to the ace writers and activists who've made this book and the ace community possible.

Thank you to my teachers and editors, who found merit in my writing and showed me there was value in my words.

Thank you to my families, both the one I was born into and the one I've chosen.

Thank you to the readers reading this book now. I hope that you can take away something good from this book and know that you are not broken or alone.

References

Part II: Ace Basics
What Is the Ace Lens?

1 Sian Ferguson. "What Does It Mean to Be Allosexual?" *Healthline*, November 21, 2019, www.healthline.com/health/allosexual.
2 Melissa V. Harris-Perry. *Sister Citizen: Shame, Stereotypes, and Black Women in America.* Yale University Press, 2013, pp.28–35.
3 Sharon Lee De La Cruz. *I'm a Wild Seed.* Street Noise Books, 2021, p.52.

Coming Out as Ace

1 Briana Lawrence. "'Hue the Pride Turtle' Is a Gentle Reminder to Celebrate Those Who Aren't Ready to Come Out Yet." The Mary Sue, June 2, 2021, www.themarysue.com/pride-turtle-art.
2 Abigail C. Saguy. "Harvey Milk Day: The History of 'Coming Out' from a Secret Gay Code to a Powerful Political Movement." *The Milwaukee Independent*, May 21, 2020, www.milwaukeeindependent.com/syndicated/harvey-milk-day-history-coming-secret-gay-code-powerful-political-movement.
3 Jacob Tobia. *Sissy: A Coming-of-Gender Story.* G. P. Putnam's Sons, 2019.
4 Jacob Tobia. *Sissy: A Coming-of-Gender Story.* G. P. Putnam's Sons, 2019, p.102.
5 Jacob Tobia. *Sissy: A Coming-of-Gender Story.* G. P. Putnam's Sons, 2019, p.261.
6 Olivia B. Waxman. "The History Behind Why We Say a Person 'Came out of the Closet.'" *Time*, October 17, 2017, https://time.com/4975404/national-coming-out-day-closet-metaphor-history.
7 "Can We Say Bye-Bye to the Binary?" *Getting Curious with Jonathan Van Ness*, created by Jonathan Van Ness, season 1, episode 3, Netflix, 2022.
8 Desirée Guerrero. "Karamo Felt 'Betrayed' By His Son's Coming Out—And Then He Evolved." ADVOCATE, September 24, 2019, www.advocate.com/exclusives/2019/9/24/karamo-felt-betrayed-his-sons-coming-out-and-then-he-evolved.

Analogies to Explain Asexuality

1 *Sex Education*, created by Laurie Nunn, season 2, episode 4, Netflix, 2019.
2 *Yuri on Ice*, created by Sayo Yamamoto and Mitsurō Kubo, season 1, episode 3, MAPPA, 2016.

3   Helen Singer Kaplan. *The Sexual Desire Disorders: Dysfunctional Regulation of Sexual Motivation.* Brunner-Routledge, 1995, p.15.

4   Emily Nagoski. *Come As You Are: The Surprising New Science That Will Transform Your Sex Life.* Simon & Schuster, 2021, p.230.

5   Emily Nagoski. "I'm sorry you're lonely but it's not my job to help you: the science of incels." Medium, May 4, 2018, https://enagoski.medium.com/im-sorry-you-re-lonely-but-it-s-not-my-job-to-help-you-the-science-of-incels-25bf83e2aaa0.

6   "Asexuality Information and Resources." Duke University Student Affairs, https://studentaffairs.duke.edu/csgd/information/Ace-Resources.

7   "Potential and Kinetic Energy Explained." Tara Energy, https://taraenergy.com/blog/potential-and-kinetic-energy-explained.

8   Dill Werner. "Navigating the In-Between: Demisexuality in YA Lit." YA Pride, December 12, 2016, www.ya-pride.org/2016/12/navigating-the-in-between-demisexuality-in-ya-lit.

9   "Ace of Cupcakes." cupcakearrow, January 26, 2015, https://cupcakearrow.tumblr.com/post/109281781211/thestarlesswanderer-being-asexual-is-like-being.

10 "Ep 43: Yasmin Benoit—Asexuality." *FUBAR Radio*, January 21, 2022, https://fubarradio.com/episodes/ep-43-yasmin-benoit-asexuality/#.

How to Identify an Asexual

1   Archie. "Queer Flagging 101: How to Use the Hanky Code to Signal the Sex You Want to Have." Autostraddle, August 28, 2018, www.autostraddle.com/queer-flagging-101-how-to-use-the-hanky-code-to-signal-the-sex-you-want-to-have-430594.

2   Alix Genter. "Appearances Can Be Deceiving: Butch-Femme Fashion and Queer Legibility in New York City, 1945–1969." *Feminist Studies*, vol. 42, no. 3, 2016, pp.604–631. Project MUSE, doi:10.1353/fem.2016.0041.

3   Sarah Prager. "Four Flowering Plants That Have Been Decidedly Queered." *JSTOR Daily*, January 29, 2020, https://daily.jstor.org/four-flowering-plants-decidedly-queered.

4   Emma Rosenblum. "The Ellen Page Inception Look: Asexual Chic." Vulture, July 19, 2010, www.vulture.com/2010/07/ellen_pages_outfits_in_incepti.html.

5   Cora Harrington. "The Asexual Model Redefining What It Means to Wear Lingerie." The Lingerie Addict, September 28, 2020, www.thelingerieaddict.com/2020/09/asexual-lingerie-model.html.

6   Christina Cauterucci. "A Cultural History of Why Lesbians Love Rings of Keys." *Slate Magazine*, December 21, 2016, https://slate.com/human-interest/2016/12/the-lesbian-love-of-key-rings-and-carabiners-explained.html.

7   Jeanine Tesori and Lisa Kron. *Fun Home: A New Broadway Musical*, PS Classics, 2015.

8   Angela Chen. *Ace: What Asexuality Reveals about Desire, Society, and the Meaning of Sex.* Beacon, 2021, p.81.

9   José Criales-Unzueta. "What Is Queer Fashion, Anyway?" them, October 11,

2021, www.them.us/story/queer-fashion-chromat-aaron-potts-elliot-page-willy-chavarria.

10   A-spectacular Life. "Jessica Rabbit Is Literally a Sex Symbol Though She Can't Be Asexual?" tumblr, https://life-of-an asexual.tumblr.com/post/189372571686/jessica-rabbit-is-literally-a-sex-symbol-though.

Ode to a Black Ring

1   Jessica Kellgren-Fozard. "The History of Queer Coding [CC]." YouTube, June 19, 2020, www.youtube.com/watch?v=GsO4fZYHQic.
2   Adrienne Rich. "Compulsory Heterosexuality and Lesbian Existence." Signs: Journal of Women in Culture and Society, vol. 5, no. 4, 1980, pp.631–660, www.jstor.org/stable/3173834.

Asexuality and "Snowflake" Syndrome

1   David Fincher. Fight Club. Twentieth Century Fox, 1999.
2   "No, 'Snowflake' as a Slang Term Did Not Begin with 'Fight Club.'" Merriam-Webster, www.merriam-webster.com/words-at-play/the-less-lovely-side-of-snowflake.
3   Rhys McKay. "Snowflakes: What Is the Snowflake Generation?" New Idea, February 24, 2020, www.newidea.com.au/snowflake-generation.
4   Brad Bird. The Incredibles. Buena Vista Pictures, 2004.
5   Brennan Lee Mulligan and Molly Ostertag. Strong Female Protagonist. Top Shelf Productions, 2018.

On Neuroticism and Labels

1   Thomas A. Widiger and Joshua R. Oltmanns. "Neuroticism Is a Fundamental Domain of Personality with Enormous Public Health Implications." World Psychiatry, vol. 16, no. 2, 2017, pp.144–145.
2   Thomas A. Widiger and Joshua R. Oltmanns. "Neuroticism is a fundamental domain of personality with enormous health implications." World Psychiatry, vol. 16, no. 2, 2017, pp.144–145, www.ncbi.nlm.nih.gov/pmc/articles/PMC5428182
3   Rainer Maria Rilke. Letters to a Young Poet. First published 1929.

Asexuals Are Here, and They're Organizing

1   Lisa Orlando. "The Asexual Manifesto, Lisa Orlando." Scribd, 1972, www.scribd.com/document/414122159/The-Asexual-Manifesto-Lisa-Orlando
2   "Interview with Jeremy Atherton Lin." Geeks OUT, October 14, 2021, www.geeksout.org/2021/10/14/interview-with-jeremy-atherton-lin.
3   "Interview with Jeremy Atherton Lin." Geeks OUT, October 14, 2021, www.geeksout.org/2021/10/14/interview-with-jeremy-atherton-lin.
4   Stefania Sarrubba. "This asexual model is launching London's first asexual club for Pride." Gay Star News, June 22, 2019, www.gaystarnews.com/article/london-ace-of-clubs-asexual-pride.

Interview with Maia Kobabe

1   Maia Kobabe. *Gender Queer: A Memoir*. Lion Forge, 2019, p.179.

Interview with Shari B. Ellis

1   Geeks OUT. "Out of the Deck: A Conversation on Aro Ace Identity and Representation." *YouTube*, November 25, 2021, https://www.youtube.com/watch?v=wS1_XJLgPgU&t=1448s

Part III: Getting into the Nuances of Sexual and Romantic Attraction
Explaining the Different Types of Attraction

1   Amanda Chatel. "What Are the Different Types of Attraction?" Yahoo!Life, January 20, 2022, www.yahoo.com/lifestyle/different-types-attraction-213133455.html.

2   Secondlina's Panels, https://secondlina.tumblr.com/post/21955456091/a-comic-about-the-different-types-of-attraction.

3   "Sexual Attraction vs Sexual Arousal." Asexuality New Zealand Trust, February 25, 2018, https://asexualitytrust.org.nz/what-is-asexuality/attraction-vs-arousal.

4   Angela Chen. "The Rise of the 3-Parent Family." *The Atlantic*, September 22, 2020, www.theatlantic.com/family/archive/2020/09/how-build-three-parent-family-david-jay/616421.

5   Danielle Braff. "From Best Friends to Platonic Spouses." *The New York Times*, May 1, 2021, www.nytimes.com/2021/05/01/fashion/weddings/from-best-friends-to-platonic-spouses.html.

6   Fran Barona. "Romantic or Disgusting? Passionate Kissing Is Not a Human Universal." Human Relations Area Files, July 17, 2015, https://hraf.yale.edu/romantic-or-disgusting-passionate-kissing-is-not-a-human-universal.

7   Lisa Jenn Bigelow. "Girl's Best Friend." In Katherine Locke and Nicole Melleby, eds. *This Is Our Rainbow: 16 Stories of Her, Him, Them, and Us*. Alfred A. Knopf, 2021, pp.20–21.

8   Jaeyeon Yoo. "Korean American Stories about Kinship and Intimacy." Electric Lit, August 18, 2021, https://electricliterature.com/yoon-choi-stories-skinship-korean-american.

9   "Kangaroo Care." Cleveland Clinic, June 29, 2020, https://my.clevelandclinic.org/health/treatments/12578-kangaroo-care.

10   Nicole K. McNichols. "The Vital Importance of Human Touch." *Psychology Today*, August 3, 2021, www.psychologytoday.com/us/blog/everyone-top/202108/the-vital-importance-human-touch.

11   Sirin Kale. "Skin Hunger Helps Explain Your Desperate Longing for Human Touch." Wired UK, April 29, 2020, www.wired.co.uk/article/skin-hunger-coronavirus-human-touch.

12   "What Kind of Attraction? A History of the Split Attraction Model." Historicallyace, October 24, 2016, https://historicallyace.tumblr.com/post/152267147477/what-kind-of-attraction-a-history-of-the-split.

13   Dorothy Tennov. *Love and Limerence: The Experience of Being in Love*. Chelsea, Mi, Scarborough House, 1999, p.251.

The Flip Side of the Asexuality Coin: Aromanticism

1   Angela Chen. *Ace: What Asexuality Reveals about Desire, Society, and the Meaning of Sex*. Beacon, 2021, p.124.
2   Elizabeth Brake. "Amatonormativity." Elizabeth Brake, August 29, 2017, https://elizabethbrake.com/amatonormativity.
3   *Katherine Ryan: Glitter Room*. Directed by Linda Mendoza, Performance by Katherine Ryan, Irwin Entertainment, 2019, Netflix, www.netflix.com/title/80238020.
4   "No Love for the Wicked aka: Villainous Aromantic Asexual." TV Tropes, https://tvtropes.org/pmwiki/pmwiki.php/Main/VillainousAromanticAsexual
5   Leo Tolstoy. *Anna Karenina*. First published 1878.

On Marriage and Queerplatonic Relationships

1   Deidre Olson. "Why I Married My Platonic Best Friend." Shondaland, April 13, 2021, www.shondaland.com/live/family/a36098765/why-i-married-my-platonic-best-friend.
2   Danielle Braffe "From Best Friends to Platonic Spouses." *The New York Times*, May 1, 2021, www.nytimes.com/2021/05/01/fashion/weddings/from-best-friends-to-platonic-spouses.html.
3   Erin Blakemore. "Women Got 'Married' Long before Gay Marriage." History, June 22, 2020, www.history.com/news/women-got-married-long-before-gay-marriage.
4   The Week Staff. "How Marriage Has Changed over Centuries." *The Week*, January 10, 2015, https://theweek.com/articles/475141/how-marriage-changed-over-cent.
5   Anne Helen Petersen. "The Escalating Costs of Being Single in America." Vox, December 2, 2021, www.vox.com/the-goods/22788620/single-living-alone-cost.
6   David Elliot "'Til Death Do They Part?' Not for Some Americans with Disabilities." Coalition on Human Needs, February 18, 2022, www.chn.org/voices/til-death-do-they-part-not-for-some-americans-with-disabilities.

Models of Love

1   Jenna Birch. "7 Distinct Greek Words Describe Different Kinds of Love—Which Have You Experienced?" Well+Good, March 29, 2022, www.wellandgood.com/greek-words-for-love.

Interview with Julie Sondra Decker

1   Julie Sondra Decker. *The Invisible Orientation: An Introduction to Asexuality*. Skyhorse Publishing, 2014.
2   "(A)Sexual (Official Trailer)." *YouTube*, May 23, 2012, www.youtube.com/watch?v=AYMh9zkt6r4.

Part IV: On Sex and Intimacy
Sex-Positive, Sex-Neutral, Sex-Repulsed, Sex-Averse, Tomato, Tomahto, Etc.

1   Allena Gabosch. "A Sex-positive Renaissance," December 8, 2014, https://allenagabosch.wordpress.com/2014/12/08/a-sex-positive-renaissance.
2   "You Can Be Asexual and Sex-Positive—Here's Why It Matters." Healthline, August 30, 2021, www.healthline.com/health/healthy-sex/asexual-sex-positivity.
3   Ebony Purks. "What Sex-positivity Means to Me as an Asexual Person." Adolescent, July 28, 2021, www.adolescent.net/a/what-sex-positivity-means-to-me-as-an-asexual-person.
4   Erika Moen and Matthew Nolan. "Sex-positive." Oh Joy Sex Toy, March 15, 2016, www.ohjoysextoy.com/sex-positive.
5   Tab Kimpton. "Shades of a 118 – Discord Comics." www.discordcomics.com, March 24, 2014, www.discordcomics.com/comic/shades-of-a-118/. Accessed 5 Apr. 2022
6   Jeana Jorgensen. "Becoming an Alt-Ac Sex Educator, Part III." Inside Higher Ed, August 12, 2016, www.insidehighered.com/advice/2016/08/12/sex-negativity-mind-set-academe-essay.
7   Anastasia Hanonick. "What Is Purity Culture and Why It Is Extremely Damaging to Young Girls and Women." The University News, April 7, 2021, https://unewsonline.com/2021/04/what-is-purity-culture-and-why-it-is-extremely-damaging-to-young-girls-and-women.
8   Gabrielle Kassel. "What Does It Actually Mean to Be 'Sex-positive'?" Healthline, September 3, 2020, www.healthline.com/health/healthy-sex/sex-positive-meaning.
9   "Attitudes Towards Sex." Ace Week, https://asexualawarenessweek.tumblr.com/post/190576643684/attitudes-towards-sex-knowing-whether-or-not-a.
10 Cut. "Guess Who's Straight | Lineup | Cut." YouTube, March 4, 2021, www.youtube.com/watch?v=ZdMeDbJFnoM.

On Relationships and Consent

1   Isabella Rotman. A Quick & Easy Guide to Consent. Limerence Press, 2020.
2   Crystal Raypole. "How Do You Know If You Were Sexually Coerced?" Healthline, December 1, 2020, www.healthline.com/health/sexual-coercion.
3   Samantha Vincenty. "What to Know about Open Relationships." Oprah Daily, October 31, 2019, www.oprahdaily.com/life/relationships-love/a29643939/open-relationship-meaning
4   "Polyamory." Psychology Today, www.psychologytoday.com/us/basics/polyamory.
5   Elisabeth Sheff. "Fidelity in Polyamorous Relationships." Psychology Today, January 29, 2019, www.psychologytoday.com/us/blog/the-polyamorists-next-door/201901/fidelity-in-polyamorous-relationships
6   Angela Chen. "How to Negotiate Better Consent: An Asexual Perspective." Autostraddle, October 30, 2020, www.autostraddle.com/consent-asexuality-angela-chen

7   Emily Nagoski, quoted by Elizabeth. "Willing Consent." Prismatic Entan-glements, May 17, 2011, https://prismaticentanglements.com/2011/05/17/willing-consent. Reproduced with permission of Emily Nagoski.

8   Blue Seat Studios. "Tea Consent." YouTube, May 12, 2015, www.youtube.com/watch?v=oQbei5JGiT8.

Other Useful Things About Sex that You Might Want to Know

1   Kasandra Brabaw. "7 Health-Related Reasons to Look at Your Vulva with a Mirror." Well+Good, August 2, 2021, www.wellandgood.com/health-related-vaginal-mirror.

2   Cheryl Wischhover and Liv McConnell. "What is a Hymen? 9 Facts about Hy-mens and the Concept of Virginity." TeenVogue, July 10, 2019, www.teenvogue.com/story/facts-about-hymen-and-virginity

3   G.C. Houle. "Working out the Kinks by G.C. Houle." Oh Joy Sex Toy, March 27, 2018, www.ohjoysextoy.com/working-out-the-kinks.

4   TED. "The Truth about Unwanted Arousal | Emily Nagoski." YouTube, June 4, 2018, www.youtube.com/watch?v=L-q-tSHo9Ho.

5   Emily Nagoski. Come As You Are: The Surprising New Science That Will Trans-form Your Sex Life. Simon & Schuster, 2021, p.191.

6   Emily Nagoski. Come As You Are: The Surprising New Science That Will Trans-form Your Sex Life. Simon & Schuster, 2021, p.288.

On the Erotic and Intellectual Merits of Fanfiction

1   Yasmin Benoit. "Here Is What Asexual People Think about Porn." Lustzine, October 20, 2021, https://erikalust.com/lustzine/voices/asexuality.

2   Hannah Macauley-Gierhart. "The Complicated Reality of Gender Bias in Writing and Publishing." Writer's Edit, January 5, 2016, https://writersedit.com/news/complicated-reality-gender-bias-writing-publishing.

3   Jane Hu. "The Revolutionary Power of Fanfiction for Queer Youth." Medium, July 17, 2017, https://medium.com/the-establishment/the-importance-of-fanfiction-for-queer-youth-4ec3e85d7519.

4   Brenna Twohy. "Brenna Twohy—Fantastic Breasts and Where to Find Them." Button Poetry, YouTube, August 17, 2014, www.youtube.com/watch?v=bXey2_i7GOA&t=56s.

5   Lev Grossman. "The Boy Who Lived Forever." Time, July 7, 2011, http://content.time.com/time/arts/article/0,8599,2081784,00.html.

Part V: Delving Deeper
To Be "Queer" or Not to Be

1   "About the Q." PFLAG, https://pflag.org/blog/about-q.

2   Julie Sondra Decker. The Invisible Orientation: An Introduction to Asexuality. Skyhorse Publishing, 2015, p.80..

3   Alice Michelini. "Asexual Perspective: When Violence Is as Invisible as Ori-entation." LGL National LGBT Rights Organization, January 13, 2016, www.lgl.lt/en/?p=11900.

4 Julie Sondra Decker. *The Invisible Orientation: An Introduction to Asexuality.* Skyhorse Publishing, 2015, p.56.

5 Michelle Denton. *Rape Culture: How Can We End It?* Lucent Press, 2018, p.31

6 "Musings on the Law." Asexuality Archive, April 19, 2019, www.asexualityarchive.com/musings-on-the-law.

7 Michele Kirichanskaya. "Let's Talk Asexuality: Every Question You Ever Had about Asexuality Answered." Femestella, February 13, 2020, www.femestella.com/what-is-asexuality-david-jay-aven-interview.

8 Panumas King. "Michel Foucault on the Insane, the Criminals, and the Sexual Deviants." OUPblog, June 19, 2019, https://blog.oup.com/2019/06/michel-foucault-insane-criminal-sexual-deviants.

9 UN Women. "Intersectional Feminism: What It Means and Why It Matters Right Now." United Nations, July 1, 2020, www.unwomen.org/en/news/stories/2020/6/explainer-intersectional-feminism-what-it-means-and-why-it-matters.

10 "All the Ways to Be with Bryan Washington & Ocean Vuong." A24films.com, December 21, 2020, https://a24films.com/notes/2020/12/all-the-ways-to-be-with-bryan-washington-ocean-vuong.

11 The New School. "bell hooks—Are You Still a Slave? Liberating the Black Female Body | Eugene Lang College." *YouTube*, May 7, 2014, www.youtube.com/watch?v=rJkohNROvzs

On Gatekeeping and the "Gold Star Asexual"

1 Michele Kirichanskaya. "It's 2021. Why Are Doctors Still Trying to 'Cure' Asexuality?" Bitch Media, June 21, 2021, www.bitchmedia.org/article/doctors-still-mistreat-asexual-patients.

2 Louis Rabinowitz. "Yasmin Benoit Is on a Mission to Make Asexuality More Visible." Notion, December 13, 2021, https://notion.online/yasmin-benoit-is-on-a-mission-to-make-asexuality-more-visible.

3 Sciatrix, "The Construct of the 'Unassailable Asexual.'" Knights of the Shaded Triangle, October 23, 2010, https://shadedtriangle.proboards.com/thread/18.

4 Judith Heumann. "Defying Obstacles in 'Being Heumann' and 'Crip Camp' | The Daily Show." *The Daily Show with Trevor Noah*, March 10, 2020, www.youtube.com/watch?v=ybcQbpSVo3c&t=235s.

5 "Disability and Health." World Health Organization, December 1, 2020, www.who.int/news-room/fact-sheets/detail/disability-and-health.

6 "1.7% of Sexual Minority Adults Identify as Asexual." UCLA School of Law, Williams Institute, August 8, 2020, https://williamsinstitute.law.ucla.edu/press/sm-asexuals-press-release.

7 Angela Chen. *Ace: What Asexuality Reveals about Desire, Society, and the Meaning of Sex.* Beacon, 2021, p.98.

8 Andrew M. Seaman. "Change in LGBT Health Sparked 50 Years Ago in Philadelphia." *Reuters*, July 3, 2015, www.reuters.com/article/us-wellness-lgbt-history/change-in-lgbt-health-sparked-50-years-ago-in-philadelphia-idUSKCN0PD22W20150703.

9 Archie. "Grease Bats: Gold Star Slut." Autostraddle, 29 July 2017, www.autostraddle.com/grease-bats-gold-star-slut-388541

Tips for Coping with Acephobia and Other Garbage

1   Susan Forward and Craig Buck. *Toxic Parents Overcoming the Legacy of Parental Abuse.* Bantam, 2002.

2   Ashley Laderer. "How to Practice Mindful Breathing and the Proven Benefits That It Offers." Insider, April 15, 2020, www.insider.com/why-is-mindful-breathing-important.

3   Ashley Marcin. "9 Ways Crying May Benefit Your Health." Healthline Media, April 14, 2017, www.healthline.com/health/benefits-of-crying.

4   Louie Dexter, Karolina Brooke, and Elizabeth Frates. "The Laughter Prescription: A Tool for Lifestyle Medicine." *American Journal of Lifestyle Medicine,* vol. 10, no. 4, 2016, pp.262–267.

5   Kristin Neff. "Exercise 4: Supportive Touch." Self-Compassion, February 23, 2015, https://self-compassion.org/exercise-4-supportive-touch/#.

6   "Exercising to Relax." Harvard Health, July 7, 2020, www.health.harvard.edu/staying-healthy/exercising-to-relax.

Am I Repressed?

1   Robert Lopez and Jeff Marx. *Avenue Q: The Musical,* 2004.

2   Dino Felluga. "Modules on Foucault: On Panoptic and Carceral Society." Introductory Guide to Critical Theory, January 31, 2011, Purdue University, https://cla.purdue.edu/academic/english/theory/newhistoricism/modules/foucaultcarceral.html.

3   "Ethics Explainer: The Panopticon—What Is the Panopticon Effect?" The Ethics Centre, May 16, 2019, https://ethics.org.au/ethics-explainer-panopticon-what-is-the-panopticon-effect.

4   Meg-John Barker. *Queer: A Graphic History.* Icon Books, 2016, p.66.

5   Shiri Eisner. "Monosexism." In A. Goldberg (ed.) *The SAGE Encyclopedia of LGBTQ Studies,* vol. 1, pp.793–796. SAGE Publications, 2016, https://sk.sagepub.com/reference/the-sage-encyclopedia-of-lgbtq-studies/i8278.xml.

6   Adrienne Rich. "Compulsory Heterosexuality and Lesbian Existence." *Signs: Journal of Women in Culture and Society,* vol. 5, no. 4, 1980, pp.631–660, www.jstor.org/stable/3173834.

Sacks of Yellow Fat

1   Racheldoesstuff. "Heavy Boobs (feat. Rachel Bloom)." *YouTube,* March 28, 2016, www.youtube.com/watch?v=aZx5zfkG6oU&t=8s.

2   Vivian Kane. "Girls Respond to Their School's Sexist Dress Code." The Mary Sue, June 7, 2017, www.themarysue.com/war-on-bra-straps-dress-codes.

3   "Sara "Saartjie" Baartman." South African History Online, June 11, 2018, www.sahistory.org.za/people/sara-saartjie-baartman.

4   David Pilgrim. "The Jezebel Stereotype—Anti-Black Imagery—Jim Crow Museum—Ferris State University." Ferris.edu, 2012, www.ferris.edu/HTMLS/news/jimcrow/jezebel/index.htm.

5   M'Jean Mason. "The Antithesis of Malehood: Being Asexual as a Hypersexualized Being." AZE, vol. 4, no. 4, 2021, https://azejournal.com/article/2021/9/4/the-antithesis-of-malehood-being-asexual-as-a-hypersexualized-being.

It's 2023. Why Are Doctors Still Trying to "Cure" Asexuality?

1   "Better Half." *House*, created by David Shore, season 8, episode 9, NBCUniversal Television Distribution, 2012.

2   Thomas Coy. "The Professional Division over the Treatment of Homosexuality and How It Has Been Influenced by the Gay Political Movement." Master's thesis, May 7, 2012, https://deepblue.lib.umich.edu/handle/2027.42/117692.

3   F. Murray. "Asexuality Was Considered a Disorder?!" Ace Week, October 29, 2020, https://aceweek.org/stories/asexuality-in-the-dsm.

4   Sian Ferguson. "What Does It Mean to Be Allosexual?" Healthline, November 21, 2019, www.healthline.com/health/allosexual.

5   Shelby K. Flanagan and Heather J. Peters. "Asexual-Identified Adults: Interactions with Health-Care Practitioners." *Archives of Sexual Behavior*, vol. 49, no. 5, 2020, pp.1631–1643.

6   Sophia Mitrokostas. "7 Things You Should Know About Identifying as Aromantic—or Not Being Romantically Attracted to Others." Insider, July 25, 2018, www.insider.com/what-is-aromantic-2018-7.

7   "The Invisible Orientation: An Introduction to Asexuality." Julie Sondra Decker, https://juliesondradecker.com/?page_id=1767.

8   Angela Chen. *Ace: What Asexuality Reveals about Desire, Society, and the Meaning of Sex.* Beacon, 2021, p.88.

9   "Ban Conversion Therapy—Yasmin Benoit." Facebook, March 23, 2021, www.facebook.com/stonewalluk/videos/192988222630860.

10 Anna Goshua. "Asexual People Deserve Better from Our Medical Providers." *HuffPost*, October 22, 2018, www.huffpost.com/entry/opinion-asexual-people-doctors_n_5bcccfd6e4b0d38b58796672.

11 Shantanu Agrawal and Adaeze Enekwechi. "It's Time to Address the Role of Implicit Bias within Health Care Delivery: Health Affairs Forefront." Health Affairs, January 15, 2020, www.healthaffairs.org/do/10.1377/forefront.20200108.34515/full.

12 Rachel Charlene Lewis. "Heteronormative Healthcare Is a Huge Disservice to Queer Women." Bitch Media, September 23, 2020, www.bitchmedia.org/article/heternormative-healthcare-queer-women.

13 Priya Krishnakumar. "This Record-Breaking Year for Anti-Transgender Legislation Would Affect Minors the Most." CNN, April 15, 2021, www.cnn.com/2021/04/15/politics/anti-transgender-legislation-2021/index.html.

14 Ryan K. Sallans. "Lessons from a Transgender Patient for Health Care Professionals." AMA *Journal of Ethics*, vol. 18, no. 11, 2016, pp.1139–1146.

15 "Misgendering in Medicine: How to Improve Care of Transgender and Gender Non-Binary Patients." in-Training, September 19, 2020, https://in-training.org/misgendering-in-health-care-and-how-to-improve-20983.

16 Michael Waters. "Asexuality is often considered a recent invention of the internet. But a closer look at queer history proves 'aces' have long existed IRL." Slate, March 6, 2020, https://slate.com/human-interest/2020/03/asexuality-history-internet-identity-queer-archive.html.

Part VI: Religion and Identity
Thoughts from a Nice Jewish Ace

1   Michele Kirichanskaya. "Notes from an Asexual Jew." Hey Alma, November 23, 2020, www.heyalma.com/notes-from-an-asexual-jew.
2   Ayda. "Navigating Asexuality as a Muslim Woman." Beyond the Hijab, December 31, 2018, https://beyondhijab.sg/2018/12/31/navigating-asexuality-as-a-muslim-woman.
3   Rabbi Hanan Schlesinger. "One Jew, Two Opinions." My Jewish Learning, www.myjewishlearning.com/article/one-jew-two-opinions.

On "Kosher Sex" and Judaism's Thoughts on Sexual Relationships

1   Melanie Malka Landau. "Good Sex: A Jewish Feminist Perspective." In Danya Ruttenberg (ed.) *The Passionate Torah: Sex and Judaism*. New York University Press, 2009, p.97.
2   Melanie Malka Landau. "Good Sex: A Jewish Feminist Perspective." In Danya Ruttenberg (ed.) *The Passionate Torah: Sex and Judaism*. New York University Press, 2009, p.98.
3   Danya Ruttenberg (ed.) *The Passionate Torah: Sex and Judaism*. New York University Press, 2009, p.2.
4   Melanie Malka Landau. "Good Sex: A Jewish Feminist Perspective." In Danya Ruttenberg (ed.) *The Passionate Torah: Sex and Judaism*. New York University Press, 2009, p.100.
5   Elliot N. Dorff. "A Jewish Perspective on Birth Control and Procreation." In Danya Ruttenberg (ed.) *The Passionate Torah: Sex and Judaism*. New York University Press, 2009, p.157.

Owning Your Truth Is a Mitzvah

1   "The Basic Purim Story." Chabad.Org, www.chabad.org/holidays/purim/article_cdo/aid/645995/jewish/The-Basic-Purim-Story.htm.
2   Rebecca Cormack. "Carnival Contrast: What Makes Purim and Mardi Gras Distinctly Unique?" Jewish Federation of Great New Orleans, www.jewishnola.com/purim/contrastingcarnival.
3   Ariella Assouline. "Queen Esther's Story Means More to Me after Coming Out." Hey Alma, March 16, 2022, www.heyalma.com/queen-esthers-story-means-more-to-me-after-coming-out.
4   Nicole Neroulias. "Gay Jews Connect Their Experience to Story of Purim." *Washington Post*, February 24, 2007, www.washingtonpost.com/archive/local/2007/02/24/gay-jews-connect-their-experience-to-story-of-purim/9a8ef3fd-eb2f-4121-a600-82d00114d93f.
5   Lindsay Eanet. "Drag Performers Turn Purim into a Queer Joy Extravaganza." Hey Alma, March 9, 2020, www.heyalma.com/drag-performers-turn-purim-into-a-queer-joy-extravaganza.

Interview with Ellen Huang

1   Yefim Kogan. "Why Are Jews from the Former Soviet Union Often Called Russians?" Jewish Federation of the Berkshires, June 15, 2021, https://jewishberkshires.org/community-events/berkshire-jewish-voice/berkshire-jewish-voice-highlights/why-are-jews-from-the-former-soviet-union-often-called-russians.

2   Rabbi David J. Meyer. "What the Torah Teachers Us About Gender Fluidity and Transgender Justice." Religious Action Center of Reform Judaism, September 20, 2018, https://rac.org/blog/what-torah-teaches-us-about-gender-fluidity-and-transgender-justice.

3   Essie Shachar-Hill. "A Guide for the Gender Neutral B-Mitzvah." Keshet, June 19, 2019, www.keshetonline.org/resources/a-guide-for-the-gender-neutral-b-mitzvah.

Part VII: Conclusion
Queerness, Labels, and Ambiguity in the Search for Self

1   Tab Kimpton. "Shades After." Discord Comics, Southampton, 2015, p.33.

2   Rainer Maria Rilke. *Letters to a Young Poet.* Penguin Classics, 2016.

3   Zora Neale Hurston. *Their Eyes Were Watching God.* Virago Press, 2018.

Ace Symbols

1   Keena. "I Saw the Sign: LGBT Symbols Then and Now." Autostraddle, June 21, 2012, www.autostraddle.com/i-saw-the-sign-lgbt-symbols-then-and-now-140061.

2   Jill Brooke. "Six Flowers That Define LGBTQ+ Movement in History." Flower Power Daily, June 16, 2020, https://flowerpowerdaily.com/six-flowers-that-define-lgbtq-movement-in-history.

3   Matt Mullen. "The Pink Triangle: From Nazi Label to Symbol of Gay Pride." History, June 3, 2019, www.history.com/news/pink-triangle-nazi-concentration-camps.

4   Jill Brooke. "Six Flowers That Define LGBTQ+ Movement in History." Flower Power Daily, June 16, 2020, https://flowerpowerdaily.com/six-flowers-that-define-lgbtq-movement-in-history.

5   Gabrielle Bellot. "The Queer Literary Origins of Wonder Woman." Literary Hub, June 1, 2017, https://lithub.com/the-queer-literary-origins-of-wonder-woman.

6   Matthew Haag. "Gilbert Baker, Gay Activist Who Created the Rainbow Flag, Dies at 65." *The New York Times*, April 1, 2017, www.nytimes.com/2017/03/31/us/obituary-gilbert-baker-rainbow-flag.html.

7   "The Asexuality Flag." Asexuality Archive, February 20, 2012, www.asexualityarchive.com/the-asexuality-flag.

8   Tab Kimpton. "01 Sir-Fabulous." Discord Comics, www.discordcomics.com/minoritymonsters/01-sir-fabulous.

9   Cami Miceli. "13 Things That Are Ace Culture." OutWrite, December 9, 2019, https://outwritenewsmag.org/2019/12/13-things-that-are-ace-culture.

Index